OCCASIONAL PUBLICATIONS
OF THE
NAVY RECORDS SOCIETY
Vol. 2

THE ANTHONY ROLL

THE NAVY RECORDS SOCIETY was established in 1893 for the purpose of printing unpublished manuscripts and rare works of naval interest. The Society is open to all who are interested in naval history, and any person wishing to become a member should apply to the Hon. Secretary, Department of War Studies, King's College London, Strand, London WC2R 2LS. The annual subscription is £30, which entitles the member to receive one free copy of each work issued by the Society in that year, and to buy earlier issues at much reduced prices.

———————

SUBSCRIPTIONS and orders for back volumes should be sent to the Membership Secretary, 5 Goodwood Close, Midhurst, West Sussex GU29 9JG.

British Library Add. MS 22047, m. 1
(Anthony Anthony's second roll)
Open to show the second entry, the *Anne Gallant* (see below, pp. 64–5)

THE ANTHONY ROLL
of Henry VIII's Navy

Pepys Library 2991 and British Library Additional MS 22047
with related documents

Edited by
C.S. Knighton and D.M. Loades

PUBLISHED BY ASHGATE
FOR THE NAVY RECORDS SOCIETY
in association with
THE BRITISH LIBRARY and MAGDALENE COLLEGE, CAMBRIDGE
2000

The introductory text is copyright © the Navy Records Society, 2000

Published by
Ashgate Publishing Limited
Gower House
Croft Road
Aldershot
Hants GU11 3HR
England

Ashgate Publishing Company
131 Main Street
Burlington, Vermont 05401–5600 USA

Ashgate website: http://www.ashgate.com

British Library Cataloguing-in-Publication data

The Anthony roll of Henry VIII's navy: Pepys Library 2991 and British Library additional MS 22047 with related documents. – (Navy Records Society occasional series; no. 2)
1.Anthony, Anthony 2.Great Britain. Royal Navy – Lists of vessels – History – 16th century 3.Great Britain. Royal Navy – History – 16th century 4.Great Britain – History, Naval – Tudors, 1485–1603
I.Knighton, C.S. (Charles Stephen) II.Loades, D.M. (David Michael) III.Navy Records Society IV.British Library V.Magdalene College
359.8′32′0942′09031

Library of Congress Cataloging-in-Publication data

The Anthony roll of Henry VIII's navy: Pepys Library 2991 and British Library additional MS 22047 with related documents/edited by C.S. Knighton and D.M. Loades.
Includes bibliographical references and index.
1. Great Britain – History, Naval – Tudors, 1485–1603 – Sources. 2. Great Britain – History – Henry VIII, 1509–1547 – Sources. I. Title: Anthony roll of Henry the Eighth's navy. II. Knighton, C. S. III. Loades, D. M. IV. Pepys Library. Manuscript. 2991. V. British Library. Manuscript. Additional 22047. VI. Navy Records Society (Great Britain)

DA86.A78 2000
942.05′2—dc21   99-057955

ISBN 0 7546 0094 7

Typeset in Times New Roman by Bournemouth Colour Press and printed on acid-free paper and bound at the University Press, Cambridge.

Contents

Preface

This volume is offered as a Millennium celebration; not that 2000 marks any special anniversary in the history of the Royal Navy. The Kings's, and Queens's, ships have served these islands for rather more than half of the Christian era. At a relatively recent point in that time, just over 450 years ago, the fleet appears visibly and strikingly over the horizon. In the last year of the reign of Henry VIII an officer of the ordnance, Anthony Anthony, compiled a complete visual record of the royal ships; and because it was his professional concern, he appended an inventory of each vessel's munitions. His manuscript, the Anthony Roll (in fact originally three separate rolls, two of which were bound as a volume by their later owner Samuel Pepys) is a unique record of the navy at a crucial time in its history.[1] Individual illustrations from the Roll have been published many times before; Anthony's painting of the *Mary Rose*, the sole contemporary representation, is especially well known. But the complete Roll has never been printed before now.[2] The unusual and large format of the MS has discouraged previous publication; even now what is provided is not a complete facsimile. All 58 ship illustrations are reproduced from newly commissioned colour photographs, while the accompanying texts are printed adjacently, in the original spelling. In this way it is hoped that the visual and textual elements of the document are presented to best advantage, retaining their juxtaposition in a format suited to the pages of a book. A further illustration is printed as frontispiece showing the disposition of a ship and its underlay text, as revealed by unrolling the document in its original form.

By bringing together the parts of the Roll, separated for over 300 years, Anthony's original sequence of entries can now be enjoyed and studied in entirety for the first time. Just some of its many facets are discussed in the Introduction, for which (in addition to editorial contributions) essays were commissioned from experts in several particular fields.

To complement Anthony's document of 1546, in Part Two of this volume there is a transcript of one of the most important and complete inventories of the fleet as it was in 1514, in the early years of Henry's reign. This manuscript, like Anthony's, is in part already familiar but is here printed in full for the first time.[3] Unlike Anthony's specialist ordnance inventory, the 1514 lists also include rigging and miscellaneous equipment. In order to match the sectional layout of the Anthony MS in Part One, the 1514 inventory is printed page-by-page as the original, again in its 16th-century spelling. The Glossary (Appendix III) is designed to help with archaic spellings of familiar words, as well as explaining technical and obsolete terms. The Glossary also explains some terms used in the introductory essays.

A caution must be expressed, as more particularly discussed below, about the verisimilitude of the illustrations of the Anthony Roll. It is not to be expected that these were individual portraits, drawn from life. Even in relation to Anthony's chief interest, the ordnance, there are obvious distortions and discrepancies between illustrations and texts.

Ships, especially warships, are magnificent but perishable. Before Anthony had finished his manuscript, the second grandest of the ships he had drawn lay at the bottom of Portsmouth harbour. A few years later the grandest of all was ignominiously burnt at her moorings. The various destinies of the other ships in the Anthony Roll and the earlier inventory can be traced in the brief service lists given as Appendix II. But it is not his ships which give Henry VIII a claim to be the founder of the modern navy as much as the administrative – and indeed physical structures which he gave to the service. By this token the last entry in the 1514 inventory (the contents of the storehouse at Erith)[4] is arguably of more enduring significance than the fleet now re-assembled as Anthony drew it.

Notes

1. For the naval history of the period see generally D.M. Loades, *The Tudor Navy: An Administrative, Political and Military History* (Aldershot, 1992) and N.A.M. Rodger, *The Safeguard of the Sea: A Naval History of Great Britain*, I, *660–1649* (1997). The classic older history, M. Oppenheim, *A History of the Administration of the Royal Navy and of Merchant Shipping in relation to the Navy from 1509 to 1660* (1896, republ. Aldershot, 1988) remains a valuable compendium, though its detail is not always to be trusted. The most complete list of the fleet is in T. Glasgow jr, 'List of ships in the royal navy from 1539 to 1588 ...', *MM*, LVI (1970), pp. 299–307. Rodger (pp. 475–83) updates this for ships of 100 tons and above.

2. This was judged 'remarkable and deplorable' by Professor Rodger (*Safeguard of the Sea*, pp. 548–9 (n. 35)). We are glad to rectify this.

3. Oppenheim, *History*, pp. 372–81, printed the first section (for the *Henry Grace à Dieu*) of what was then known as 'Chapter House Book, vol. XIII'; the name derived from the Chapter House of Westminster Abbey, where exchequer records were housed from the 16th to the 19th century.

4. Cf. Rodger, *Safeguard of the Sea*, p. 222.

Acknowledgements

Crown copyright material is reproduced by permission of the Keeper of the Public Records. The text and illustrations of the Anthony Roll are the copyright of the Master and Fellows of Magdalene College, Cambridge, and the Board of the British Library, and are reproduced here by their kind permissions.

The Pepys Librarian, Dr Richard Luckett, has greatly encouraged this project, and has given assistance scholarly and practical. The Assistant Librarian, Aude Fitzsimons, and the Library Assistant, Bridget Alexander, have given much support; we also thank all at Magdalene who have helped with administration. Dr Knighton is particularly grateful to the Master and Fellows of Magdalene, and to the Principal of Westminster College, Cambridge, for hospitality during the making of this volume. We are grateful to David Way for co-operation in publishing. We owe a great deal to Ann Payne for help in arranging the photography at the British Library, and in many other ways in addition to her written contribution here. To her, and to John Bennell, Maria Hayward, Alexzandra Hildred, Stuart Vine, and Timothy Wilson, we are greatly obliged for their several expert essays in the Introduction. Gerry Bye and Laurence Pordes deserve special thanks for their original photographs of the Roll. We also thank Christopher Dobbs and Andrew Elkerton at the Mary Rose Trust for help with other illustrations and supporting material.

We are honoured that the Council of the Navy Records Society accepted and sponsored this special volume; we particularly thank Michael Simpson for his confidence in what we undertook. We are extremely grateful to Ellen Keeling and all at Ashgate who have brought our concept to life.

C.S.K.
D.M.L.

The Navy Records Society acknowledges with gratitude a generous subvention towards publication from the Worshipful Company of Shipwrights.

Notes on contributors

Editors

C.S. Knighton, M.A., Ph.D., D.Phil., is on the editorial staff of the Public Record Office, and has edited two volumes of state papers. He compiled the catalogue of *Modern Manuscripts* in the Pepys Library at Magdalene College, Cambridge (1981), and contributed to *Samuel Pepys and the Second Dutch War* (NRS 1995).

D.M. Loades, M.A., Ph.D., Litt.D., F.S.A., F.R.Hist.S., taught at the universities of St Andrews, Durham, and Wales (Bangor), and is now professor emeritus of the University of Wales and honorary research professor of the University of Sheffield. His publications include *The Tudor Navy. An Administrative, Political and Military History* (1992), and he contributed to *British Naval Documents 1204–1960* (NRS 1993).

Essayists

John E.G. Bennell, M.Litt., has been interested in ships, mainly of 1540–1600, for more than fifty years. Since editing a London port book of 1565 for his Oxford thesis, he has studied the social and economic history of the Elizabethan city and port of London. He has contributed to the *Mariner's Mirror* on the subject of English 16th-century oared vessels.

Maria Hayward, M.A., Ph.D., trained as a textile conservator, and completed a thesis titled 'The possessions of Henry VIII'. She is now a lecturer at the Textile Conservation Centre, University of Southampton.

Alexzandra Hildred, B.A., M.I.F.A., was educated at the University of Sheffield, and has extensive experience as a marine archaeologist. Her association with the *Mary Rose* began as an archaeological diver at the site in 1979. She has held several appointments at the Mary Rose Trust, and since 1998 she has been curator of ordnance. She has published numerous reports on her findings.

Ann Payne, B.A., F.S.A., F.R.Hist.S., is Head of the Department of Manuscripts at the British Library (formerly in the British Museum), which she joined as an Assistant Keeper in 1965. Her main fields of research are in medieval and early modern history, with a particular interest in heraldic, antiquarian and topographical manuscripts. She has contributed to numerous volumes of the quinquennial *Catalogue of Additions to the Manuscripts in the British Library* and has published books, articles and exhibition catalogues based on aspects of the manuscript collections.

Stuart Vine, B.Sc., was educated at The Queen's University, Belfast and the University of Wales (Cardiff). From 1981 to 2000 he held a number of appointments at the Mary Rose Trust, latterly that of curator. He now works for *FT* Knowledge.

Timothy Wilson, M.A., M.Phil., F.S.A., was research assistant in the Department of Weapons and Antiquities at the National Maritime Museum from 1978 to 1980. From 1980 to 1990 he was Assistant Keeper with responsibility for Renaissance applied art collections at the British Museum. Since 1990 he has been Keeper of the Department of Western Art at the Ashmolean Museum and fellow of Balliol College, Oxford. He is the author of *Flags at Sea* (1986. 2nd edn., 1999).

Photographers

G.D. Bye, M.A., A.B.I.P.P., is head of the photographic department at Cambridge University Library. His published work includes the facsimile of Pepys's MS catalogue in the new *Catalogue of the Pepys Library at Magdalene College, Cambridge* (1991).

Laurence H. Pordes is senior photographer at the British Library; he has contributed to numerous publications, including *Maps in Tudor England* (1993).

Illustrations

black and white

Other diagrams and archaeological drawings accompany the Glossary

colour

The images here printed are on average 65.6% actual size. For technical reasons the % reduction has been varied, notably with ship no. 1 (63%) and ship no. 30 (51.5%). Measurements for the 58 original drawings are given below, in inches, from bow to stern at the waterline (except for no. 30, in which the bow is not visible; here the measurement is from the point at which the leading port side oar cuts to waterline, to the stern)

1	$4^3/_4$	13	$3^1/_8$	25	$4^7/_8$	37	$3^1/_2$	49	$2^7/_8$
2	$4^1/_8$	14	$3^1/_8$	26	$4^7/_8$	38	$3^5/_8$	50	$2^7/_8$
3	$3^3/_4$	15	3	27	$5^7/_{16}$	39	$3^3/_4$	51	$2^3/_4$
4	$3^5/_8$	16	$3^1/_8$	28	$4^7/_8$	40	$3^3/_4$	52	$2^{15}/_{16}$
5	$3^1/_2$	17	$2^7/_8$	29	$4^7/_8$	41	$3^7/_8$	53	3
6	$3^5/_8$	18	3	30	$10^2/_{10}$	42	$3^3/_4$	54	$2^{13}/_{16}$
7	$3^1/_4$	19	$3^1/_8$	31	$4^1/_4$	43	$3^3/_4$	55	3
8	$3^3/_8$	20	$3^1/_4$	32	$4^7/_{16}$	44	$3^5/_8$	56	3
9	3	21	$5^3/_8$	33	$4^3/_{16}$	45	$3^3/_4$	57	3
10	$3^1/_4$	22	$5^5/_{16}$	34	$3^5/_8$	46	3	58	$2^{15}/_{16}$
11	$3^1/_4$	23	$5^1/_{18}$	35	$3^5/_8$	47	$2^7/_8$		
12	$3^1/_4$	24	$5^3/_{16}$	36	$3^7/_8$	48	$2^7/_8$		

Abbreviations

Adair, 'English galleys'	E.R. Adair, 'English galleys in the sixteenth century', *EHR*, XXXV (1920), pp. 498–504
APC	J.R. Dasent, ed., *Acts of the Privy Council of England*, new series, 32 vols. (1890–1907)
Ashley, 'Tudor office of ordnance'	R. Ashley, 'The organization and administration of the Tudor office of ordnance', B.Litt. dissertation, University of Oxford (1972)
Auerbach, *Tudor Artists*	E. Auerbach, *Tudor Artists* (1954)
Auerbach, 'Vincent Volpe'	E. Auerbach, 'Vincent Volpe, the King's painter', *Burlington Magazine*, XCII (1950), pp. 222–8
Barber, 'Henry VIII and map-making'	P.M. Barber, 'Henry VIII and map-making', in D.R. Starkey, ed., *Henry VIII: a European Court in England* (1991), pp. 145–51
Barber, 'Pageantry, defense, and government'	P.M. Barber, 'England I: Pageantry, defense, and government: maps at court to 1550', in D. Buisseret, ed., *Monarchs, Ministers and Maps* (Chicago and London, 1992), pp. 26–56
Beets, 'Cornelis Anthonisz.'	N. Beets, 'Cornelis Anthonisz.', *Oud-Holland*, LVI (1939), pp. 160–84
Bellew, '*Mary Rose*'	Sir G. Bellew, 'An examination of the flags and heraldry on the contemporary pictures of the *Mary Rose*', *The Coat of Arms*, new series, V, no. 122 (1982), pp. 47–53
Bennell, 'Oared vessels'	J.E.G. Bennell, 'English oared vessels of the sixteenth century', *MM*, LX (1974), pp. 9–26, 169–85
BL	British Library, London
Bodleian	Bodleian Library, Oxford
Byrne, *Lisle Letters*	M. St.C. Byrne, ed., *The Lisle Letters*, 6 vols. (Chicago, 1981)
Chappell, *Tangier Papers*	E. Chappell, ed., *The Tangier Papers of Samuel Pepys* (NRS LXXIII, 1935)
Colvin, *King's Works*	H.M. Colvin, *et al.*, eds., *The History of the King's Works*, 6 vols. (1951–82)
CPR	*Calendar of the Patent Rolls*
Croft-Murray & Hulton, *British Drawings*	E. Croft-Murray and P. Hulton, *Catalogue of British Drawings*, I (British Museum, 1960)
CSPD	*Calendar of State Papers, Domestic Series*
CSP Spanish	*Calendar of State Papers, Spain*
de Beer, *Evelyn*	E.S. de Beer, ed., *The Diary of John Evelyn*, 6 vols (Oxford, 1955)
Derrick, *Memoirs*	C. Derrick, *Memoirs of the Rise and Progress of the Royal Navy* (1806)
E	Exchequer (PRO) [in textual notes to Part Two, referring to E 101/57/2]
EHR	*The English Historical Review*
Glasgow, 'List of ships'	T. Glasgow jr, 'List of ships in the royal navy from 1539 to 1588 – the navy from its infancy to the defeat of the Spanish Armada', *MM*, LVI (1970), pp. 299–307 [further abbreviated as 'Glasgow' in Appendix II]
Harvey, *Maps in Tudor England*	P.D.A. Harvey, *Maps in Tudor England* (1993)
Howard, *Sailing Ships of War*	F. Howard, *Sailing Ships of War 1400–1860* (Greenwich, 1979)
Laughton, *Spanish Armada*	J.K. Laughton, ed., *State Papers relating to the Defeat of the Spanish Armada, anno 1588*, 2 vols. (NRS I, II, 1894)
Lloyd & Thurley, *Henry VIII*	C. Lloyd and S. Thurley, *Henry VIII: Images of a Tudor King* (1990)
Loades, *Tudor Navy*	D.M. Loades, *The Tudor Navy: An Administrative, Political and Military*

	History (Aldershot, 1992)
	[further abbreviated as 'Loades' in Appendix II]
LP	J.S. Brewer, J. Gairdner and R.H. Brodie, eds, *Letters and Papers, Foreign and Domestic, of the Reign of Henry VIII*, 21 vols. and Addenda (1862–1932).
MM	*The Mariner's Mirror*
Oppenheim, *Accounts and Inventories*	M. Oppenheim, ed., *Naval Accounts and Inventories of the Reign of Henry VII, 1485–8 and 1495–7* (NRS VIII, 1896)
Oppenheim, *History*	M. Oppenheim, *A History of the Administration of the Royal Navy and of Merchant Shipping in relation to the Navy from 1509 to 1660 with an Introduction treating of the preceding period* (1896, republ. Aldershot, 1988)
Perrin, *British Flags*	W.G. Perrin, *British Flags* (Cambridge, 1922)
PL	Pepys Library, Magdalene College, Cambridge
PRO	Public Record Office, London
Rodger, *Safeguard of the Sea*	N.A.M. Rodger, *The Safeguard of the Sea: A Naval History of Great Britain, I, 660–1649* (1997)
	[further abbreviated as 'Rodger' in Appendix II.]
Rodríguez-Salgado, *Armada*	M. Rodríguez-Salgado, *Armada 1588–1988* (1988)
Rose, *Navy of the Lancastrian Kings*	S.P. Rose, ed., *The Navy of the Lancastrian Kings: Accounts and Inventories of William Soper, Keeper of the King's Ships, 1422–1427* (NRS CXXIII, 1982)
Rule, *Mary Rose*	M.H. Rule, *The Mary Rose: The Excavation and Raising of Henry VIII's Flagship* (2nd edn., 1983)
Shelby, *John Rogers*	L.R. Shelby, *John Rogers: Tudor Military Engineer* (Oxford, 1967)
SP	State Papers (PRO)
	[in textual notes to Part Two, referring to entries in SP 1/230 as identified in key at p. 110 below]
Spont, *War with France*	A. Spont, ed., *Letters and Papers relating to the War with France, 1512–1513* (NRS, X, 1897)
State Papers ... Henry the Eighth	*State Papers during the Reign of Henry the Eighth*, 11 vols. (Record Commission, 1830–52)
Tanner, *Naval Minutes*	J.R. Tanner, ed., *Samuel Pepys's Naval Minutes* (NRS LX, 1926)
Tomlinson, *Guns and Government*	H.C. Tomlinson, *Guns and Government: The Ordnance Office under the Later Stuarts* (Royal Historical Society, Studies in History series, no. 15, 1979)
TRHS	*Transactions of the Royal Historical Society*
VCH	*Victoria County History*
Wilson, *Flags at Sea*	T. Wilson, *Flags at Sea* (2nd edn., 1999)
Wilson, 'Saint George'	T. Wilson, 'Saint George in Tudor and Stuart England', M.Phil. dissertation, The Warburg Institute, University of London (1976)

All works cited in this volume are published in London unless otherwise stated.

Editorial note

Texts are presented in their original spelling, following the normal conventions of transcription; the letters u/v and i/j are rendered according to modern usage, however they appear in the MS. The double ff is treated as a single letter except within a word. The ampersand is written in full. The abbreviation 'di' (half) is extended to 'demy' where it forms part of a word, but 'd'' is used in figures even if more fully written in the MS. The abbreviation for dozen is always given as 'doss'', however written. Figures are written as in the MS. The frequent multiplier by 20 given as '$\overset{XX}{iiij}$' (i.e. 20 x 4 = 80) is retained thus; it is also found within more complex numbers, as 'cc$\overset{XX}{iiij}$xiij' (= 293). The abbreviation for 1000 is 'm^{l}' or 'j m^{l}' as occurring. Incorrect singular/plural usage ('top pece ij') is retained. The flourished 'j' descender is retained for single or final minims. 'Xpoffer' is rendered 'Christoffer'.

Letters miswritten are corrected within the text and flagged to an explanatory textual note. Words supplying defects in the MS are placed within square brackets. Words supplying syntactical lacunae are placed within square brackets and flagged to textual notes. In Part Two, as more fully explained in the separate editorial note (p. 110), the symbols E and SP denote other documents collated with the main text. Figures superscribed are placed within round brackets. The symbol † indicates blank in MS where unspecified (rather than nil) quantity is meant. 'MS' always means the principal text being edited.

Punctuation and capitalization are editorial. Paragraphing is editorial, but reflects as far as possible the layout of the MSS. For the E 36/13 inventory the page structure of the MS is retained, including the running heads. For the Anthony Roll the shape of the MS requires a restructuring which nevertheless retains the relationship of each text entry to its illustration; for this see further the technical description of the MS on pp. 6–9 below.

Part One

The Anthony Roll

I   The Manuscript and its Compiler
C.S. Knighton

Anthony Anthony (d. 1563), who compiled the three rolls here printed and presented them to Henry VIII in 1546, served that king and his three successors as an official of the ordnance. His career shows that it was possible to retain a place of importance in successive Tudor regimes. Aside from his principal appointment, Anthony was a man with many interests: merchant, courtier and historian. He was not, however, quite all that has been claimed of him. A persistent but unsubstantiated suggestion has been made that he was the brother of the Dutch artist Cornelius Anthoniszoon. This is an attractive idea, because it might account for Anthony Anthony's own venture into maritime art.[1] Yet it cannot be. When this same Anthony Anthony, surveyor of the ordnance, died, he left an interest in the Ship brewhouse in East Smithfield. The same property had been bequeathed by William Anthony, brewer (d. 1535) to his only named son, Anthony.[2] It follows that Anthony Anthony, compiler of the MS, had no brother. His father was almost certainly the William Anthony of Middelburg in Zeeland who received a patent of denization on 26 January 1503.[3] Anthony Anthony himself was classified as an Englishman for tax purposes, though on occasion he was still referred to as a Fleming.[4] He had married, on 4 October 1517, Anne, the daughter of William Roy; their only child, a daughter, lived for just four months in 1519. Anthony's wife died in 1559, and he subsequently married Alice, widow of John Norton, who survived him.[5] Anthony's father had supplied Henry VIII's army with beer in partnership with a fellow Fleming, Henry Johnson *alias* Janssen. Johnson would in 1537 be named first surveyor of the ordnance, and no doubt introduced his partner's son into that service.[6] Anthony Anthony's life was a combination of guns and beer. His official duties can never have provided full-time employment, and he was able to become also a prominent member of the London brewers' company.[7]

In 1530 he was licensed to export 200 tuns of beer; in the following year he had similar licence for 60 tuns. His activities brought complaints from the London victuallers in 1536, who alleged that Anthony and 'other Flemings' brought Flemish and Holland goods into St Katharine's dock under cover of darkness, evading the customs. This does not seem to have troubled him; in 1538 he was permitted to buy and export 200 tuns of double beer and 200 weys of cheese annually for seven years. In 1545 he was licensed to employ more than the statutory number of four alien journeymen.[8] Among his business associates was Lord Lisle, the governor of Calais; Anthony is found entertaining Lisle's daughters in London, and sending a hogshead of wine to Lisle himself.[9]

Anthony wrote a chronicle of events from 1522 to 1558; the original does not survive, but it was known to the other 16th-century London historians Stow and Holinshed, and was referred to by Bishop Burnet in his *History of the Reformation*.[10] Extracts were made by the antiquary Elias Ashmole in 1659 (from which some of the biographical information given here is derived). The chronicle is of some independent interest, presenting the view of the world from the Tower of London: the coming and going of prisoners, and the ceremonial discharge of ordnance, feature prominently. An early entry, 26 May 1522, records Henry VIII and the Emperor Charles V embarking aboard the *Henry Grace à Dieu* and the *Mary Rose* at Dover. The hazards of Anthony's profession are dramatically evident in the account of an explosion at one of the gunpowder stores on Tower Hill on 30 April 1552; twelve men were killed and Anthony himself, standing close by, was slightly hurt.[11] Anthony also wrote an account of Elizabeth I's coronation.[12] There is no evidence of the education he must have received; but there was no shortage of high quality teaching available to the sons of the London merchant community in the early 16th century.

Anthony's first position in the crown's service was as a groom of the chamber; he is so described from September 1530. On 7 October 1533 he was appointed one of the gunners at the Tower of London, at a shilling a day, and so he remained notionally until his death – although the duties would have long been exercised by deputy.[13] At what stage he became a clerk of the ordnance office is uncertain. From the 28th year of Henry VIII [1536/7] he held the office of clerk of the deliveries, responsible for all issues from and returns to the stores; this brought him another daily shilling.[14] About the time he attained this post he is found deputising briefly for the head of his department.[15] There was, again c. 1537, an enlargement of the ordnance office with the creation of the post of surveyor or overseer. This officer took over work previously done by the master gunner, who was now exclusively concerned with weapons training.[16] An incident in February 1537 shows Anthony acting decisively to earn royal approval. A parade of ordnance was to take place in St

James's Park before the king. The principal exhibit, a double cannon, was said to be unavailable because its axle was not ready. Anthony over-ruled Henry Johnson and his other colleagues by insisting that the piece be brought to the park 'with all the speed possible', where it was duly seen and admired on 16 February by the king and his court.[17] It is perhaps not surprising that Anthony was at the time spoken of as surveyor, although this post in fact went first to Johnson. On 29 April 1537 Anthony was designated one of four founding 'masters and rulers' of the fraternity of St George for promotion of archery and shooting – the body which came to be called the Honourable Artillery Company.[18]

It was therefore as a clerk of the ordnance that Anthony was employed when he compiled his rolls. We cannot be sure if he had already drawn the *Mary Rose* when he heard of the disaster which occurred on 19 July 1545. He was at this time hard at work supplying the king's forces encamped at Portsmouth; on 21, 22 and 23 July the privy council wrote from there to Anthony with urgent orders for munitions.[19] It is probable that the hope that the *Mary Rose* could be salvaged is the reason why she appears in the MS which Anthony presented to the king in the following year.[20] The compilation can hardly have been intended as a working inventory. No doubt it was expected that the king would enjoy showing foreign ambassadors and other visitors the firepower which the royal navy could command. Like all gifts to royalty it must also have been offered with some expectation on the part of the donor. Henry VIII did not live long enough to confer any favours; but on 23 January 1549 his son appointed Anthony to be master surveyor of the ordnance in the Tower, Calais, Boulogne and elsewhere, for life, with a daily fee of 2s. (£36 10s. per year) backdated to Michaelmas 1547.[21]

One part of these responsibilities was soon redundant, for Edward VI's government returned Boulogne to France in 1550. Anthony supervised the evacuation of the English ordnance there to Calais or back to London.[22] During 1552 he was busy answering government enquiries into the financing of his department.[23] On 1 February 1560 he surrendered his patent of office, receiving on 15 February a new grant jointly in survivorship with Henry Iden. By this authority Iden succeeded to the post on Anthony's death, and served until his own death on 2 December 1568.[24] In the last months of his life Anthony was still active, supplying armament for the expedition against Le Havre.[25]

There is little evidence of Anthony's personality, save for a couple of quarrels. He had an argument with the lieutenant of the ordnance over the siting of a new staircase at the office, and a long-running row with his neighbour in the parish of St Botolph without Aldgate about a party fence. In the latter case he emerged victorious.[26] He made his will on 23 August 1563, and it was proved on 9 October following. His beneficiaries were mostly his personal servants and merchant colleagues; among them Harman Harrison, to whom he left his crossbow and fowling piece. He gave the brewers' company £4 for a feast at his funeral.[27] His final account as surveyor was presented in 1566 by his widow, in association with a handgun maker in the office, William Partridge, whom she had since married. In 1580 Partridge was licensed to alienate a 'Banquetinge House' built by Anthony Anthony in East Smithfield.[28]

Exactly a hundred years later the first and third of Anthony's rolls were given by Charles II to Samuel Pepys. Just this much is known from a note Pepys added to the volume into which he had the rolls bound.[29] Pepys was at this time out of office, having been obliged to surrender his secretaryship of the admiralty in May 1679 when accused (quite falsely) of popish treason. Having cleared his name, he went to see the king at Newmarket towards the end of September 1680, hoping to get 'something settled' by way of compensation for his loss of revenue.[30] Not only did he gain access to the king, but in the course of meetings on 3 and 5 October he took down by dictation Charles's account of his escape after the battle of Worcester. The story was already famous, and the king wanted Pepys to edit and publish the official version (which he never did).[31] It seems most probable that the gift of the Anthony MS was suggested at or was a result of this prolonged tête-à-tête between Pepys and the king. Pepys was currently much engaged in collecting material for a history of the navy – another unfulfilled scheme, which he must surely have mentioned to the king. Pepys must have known of the existence of Anthony's MS because it is referred to in a discourse on the cross of St George which Serjeant-Surgeon John Knight presented to him in January 1678.[32] It may even be that the rolls were among the 'pieces relating to the Navy' which John Evelyn had discovered while rummaging through the royal library at Whitehall in the previous month.[33] A present so embarrassingly generous that Pepys would be ashamed to ask for money as well would have been for Charles II an ideal and characteristic way of rewarding his servant without actual expense.

But only two of the three rolls were to be found in 1680. The second was not discovered in the royal library at St James's until 1690, when the keeper, Henry Thynne, alerted Pepys to its existence. With Thynne's permission Pepys was able to extract details from the second roll, and to have some of its illustrations copied.[34] There was no question now of the second roll joining the others in Pepys's collection. He had resigned office at the fall of James II, never acknowledging William and Mary as sovereigns, and suffering somewhat in consequence in the first years of their reigns. He would probably have refused a gift from William III even if it had been offered. It must, therefore, have been in 1690 or thereafter that Pepys took the decision to cut up the first and third rolls to make the present volume. References to the MS while in Pepys's custody are disappointingly meagre.[35] At Pepys's death in 1703 the whole of his library, at the time kept at William Hewer's house on Clapham Common, passed to his nephew and heir John Jackson. Following Jackson's death, in accordance with Pepys's bequest, the library passed to his old college at Cambridge, Magdalene, where it arrived in July 1724 and where it remains.[36]

The Anthony Roll (as the Pepysian codex has come to be known) was not among the first items in the library to attract attention following its coming to Magdalene.[37] In 1782 Thomas Kerrich, F.S.A., a fellow of the college, made copies of several of Anthony's illustrations.[38] In the same year an engraving by Isaac Basire of the *Henry Grace à Dieu* was published in the Society of Antiquaries' journal *Archaeologia*, accompanying an article by J. Topham, who first called public attention to 'this curious book, beautifully drawn'.[39] It was at this time concluded that the second roll had disappeared; or, at any rate, was not part of the royal library given by George II to the British Museum.[40] It must, however, have remained in the private keeping of the royal family, since William IV (when duke of Clarence) gave it to his daughter Mary, the fourth of his ten children by Dorothy Jordan. King William was, of course, a keen student of naval history (indeed, his reading of it aloud drove one of Mrs Jordan's predecessors from his house).[41] Mary FitzClarence (raised, like her brothers and sisters, to the status of the issue of a marquess in 1831) is not known to have had any nautical interest.[42] But in 1824 she had married Charles Robert Fox, illegitimate son (by a chronological mischance) of the 3rd Lord Holland and his wife. Fox had made an unhappy start to a naval career, his ship having been sunk on his first voyage; but turning to the army he rose to the rank of major-general. Most significantly he held, from 1832 to 1835, the office of surveyor of the ordnance, and was therefore Anthony's successor. Fox was also a bibliophile and a numismatist of international reputation. It is to be presumed that the second roll was displayed to visitors at Fox's house at Addison Road, Kensington.[43] But its presence there was unknown to scholars.

In January 1857 the keeper of manuscripts at the British Museum, Sir Frederic Madden, was astonished to find brought to him for expertise what he instantly recognised as the supposed missing part of the Anthony MS. He had seen the Pepys volume at Magdalene in 1831 and again in 1841; in the following year he had examined it in detail and made some drawings from it. It now transpired that Lady Mary Fox (as she now was) wanted to sell her roll to raise funds to build a church 'or something of that kind'. Madden guessed that she would want £100 for it, though he felt it should simply be handed over to the royal library (in effect, to his own keeping), from which he suspected Pepys of having purloined the other parts in the first place. He reported disparagingly that the Fox MS was an incomplete part of a series, and the least interesting, suggesting £15 as its true value. In fact the asking price was £50, which was declined. But on 5 May Fox learned that Lady Mary would now agree to £15, and the MS was duly purchased for this sum.[44] It was numbered Additional MS 22047, and remains in its original form as a roll. It should be recorded that while the present edition was being prepared, the second roll moved with the rest of the British Library's manuscript collection to the new premises at St Pancras (1999).

Technical description

(i) *General*

The MS originally consisted of three separate rolls, each composed of a sequence of vellum membranes. The second roll remains in that form in the British Library. The first and third rolls were converted into a codex, now in the Pepys Library at Magdalene College, Cambridge. Within each of these three parts each successive membrane is attached to its precursor by glue, apparently original and remaining fully effective. There is an overlap of approximately 3/4 inch where the head of each succeeding obverse is attached to the reverse of the preceding membrane. The MS is written throughout in a single hand (including rubrications and the gold lettering of the first three ship titles); there is every reason to suppose the writer was Anthony Anthony himself. The framed signature which appears at the foot of each roll (pp. 61, 79, 106, below) corresponds strikingly with his undoubted signature to a holograph letter in the State Papers.[45]

(ii) *British Library Additional MS 22047*

The second roll is here complete in its original form, comprising six membranes of vellum 27 1/2 ins [70 cm] wide, and of varying depths (m. 1: 34 3/4 ins [88 cm], mm. 2, 3 & 4: 37 ins [94 cm], m. 5: 35 ins [89 cm], m. 6: 17 ins [43 cm], in all 16 ft 5 3/4 ins [502 cm]). These measurements are taken from the head to the bottom of the obverse, and take no account of 3/4 inch overlaps where the sections are joined on the reverse. Membranes 3–6 are numbered in apparently the original hand in the top left-hand corners. The first membrane is endorsed 'Purchased of Lady Mary Fox 23d May 1857'. The roll is now held by, but not attached to, a wooden spindle. The heading has at some time been treated with a reagent to bring faded writing into temporary visibility. In consequence of this now deprecated archival practice, the affected area is rendered illegible thereafter. Fortunately its content can be reconstructed from the equivalent formulae of the other rolls.

(iii) *Magdalene College, Cambridge, Pepys Library 2991*

In order to create a bound volume for incorporation in his library, Pepys had the first and third rolls cut into unequal sections, so that the ship illustrations and their corresponding inventory texts would appear together, while occupying pages of optimum size. The first ship in the first roll, the *Henry Grace à Dieu*, required a double-spread. Most of the remaining ships in the first and third rolls occur in adjacent pairs, and therefore occupy left and right pages, with their texts across both pages (that for the left-hand ship above that for the right-hand ship). The pages are 13½ x 22 ins [34.5 x 56 cm], each section of the (27½ ins wide) original, extended vertically with new material as necessary, being folded to create a bifolium attached to the binding on a guard. The outer edges have been very slightly cropped. Where a section of the original roll could form a bifolium of uniform (22 ins) depth, it is incorporated directly into the gathering. Where a shorter section of the original was needed, it was pasted to sections of new vellum, fitted above and/or below so as to provide pages of the required size. The horizontal joins of the original MS therefore occur at irregular places in the volume.[46]

Once the two rolls had been cut and the new page structure had been created, cropped elements of the rubricated ornament were carefully re-copied. Pepys then introduced rubricated vinets framing the roll headings and each page; this was a regular adornment of his MSS and albums, and he appears to have engaged a woman with the sole duty of marking out these red lines. The original matter was then interleaved with title-pages and other apparatus drawn up by Pepys's clerks. For the most part the new leaves were also vellum, but two paper insertions were also made. One of these contains a tabular synopsis of the first roll, not part of Anthony's original, but also not the work of Pepys's clerks. It must have been compiled in the late 16th- or early 17th-century (and so is of interest as record of Anthony's MS being consulted at that period). There is no equivalent summary of the other two rolls.

It is the purpose of the present edition to represent, as far as possible, the sequence of Anthony's original MS. The Pepysian addenda are therefore omitted from the text printed below.[47] A summary is given here to illustrate the composition of Pepys 2991; entries in bold are the sections of Anthony's MS, occurring in the edited text at the pages indicated in square brackets to the right. Each of these entries also gives: in round brackets, the depth of the section of the original vellum (excluding overlap to the reverse where occurring); the measurement from the top of each such section to the point of any original join (as on the obverse where occurring); if the bifolium is formed from a complete section of the original MS it is marked 'unbacked'.

Synopsis of Pepys's volume

[frontispiece] Engraving of Henry VIII, 6⁹⁄₁₀ x 11⁶⁄₁₀ ins [17.5 x 29.5 cm]. By Gerrit Valck after Adriaan van der Werff [E. Chamberlain, comp., *Catalogue of the Pepys Library at Magdalene College, Cambridge*, III, ii, *Prints and Drawings: Portraits* (Woodbridge, 1994), p. 14. J. Charrington, *A Catalogue of the Engraved Portraits in the Library of Samuel Pepys, F.R.S.* (Cambridge, 1936), p. 78. Pepys had another copy of this engraving: PL 2978, p. 52b].

[p. i] 'A Declaration of the Royall Navy of England composed by Anthony Anthony, one of the Officers of the Ordnance, and by him presented to K. Hen. 8. año Reg^ni. 38°. Dñi 1546. in 3 Parchment-Rolls (here thus reduced) containing vizt.

Roll 1st. – Shyppes.
  2^d. – Galliasses.
  3^d – Pynásses & Roe=Bargys.
Whereof y^e 1st. & 3^d. were given me añ°. 1680 by my Roy^ll. Master K. Charles 2^d; and y^e other (since found,) is resting añ°. 1690, in y^e R^ll. Lib^ry. at St James's.' [Pepys's title-page, the original orthography here reproduced].

[pp. i–iii]	**Anthony's title to the three rolls.**	[p. 41]
	(10¾ ins [27 cm])	
[p. iv]	Pepys's normal book-plate (engraved portrait, from Kneller)	
p. 1	Half-title to the first roll, of ships, and to the first ship.	
pp. 2–3	**Anthony's title to the first roll.**	[p. 41]
	Henry Grace à Dieu.	[no. 1]
	(17 ins [43 cm])	
p. 4	*blank*	
p. 5	Half-title to next.	
pp. 6–7	**Mary Rose. Peter.**	[nos 2, 3]
	(22 ins [56 cm]; join at 19¾ ins [49.5 cm])	

p. 8	*blank*	
p. 9	Half-title to next.	
pp. 10–11	**Matthew. Great Bark.**	[nos **4, 5**]
	(22 ins [56 cm]; unbacked)	
p. 12	*blank*	
p. 13	Half-title to next.	
pp. 14–15	**Jesus of Lübeck. Pauncy.**	[nos. **6, 7**]
	(16 ins [40.5 cm]); join at 11½ ins [29 cm])	
p. 16	*blank*	
p. 17	Half-title to next.	
pp. 18–19	**Morian. Struse.**	[nos **8, 9**]
	(16 ins [40.5 cm])	
p. 20	*blank*	
p. 21	Half-title to next.	
pp. 22–3	**Mary of Hamburg. Christopher of Bremen.**	[nos **10, 11**]
	(16½ ins [41.5 cm]); join at 14¾ ins [37.5 cm])	
p. 24	*blank*	
p. 25	Half-title to next.	
pp. 26–7	**Trinity Harry. Small Bark.**	[nos **12, 13**]
	(16¾ ins [42.5 cm])	
p. 28	*blank*	
p. 29	Half-title to next.	
pp. 30–1	**Sweepstake. Minion.**	[nos **14, 15**]
	(17 ins [43 cm])	
p. 32	*blank*	
p. 33	Half-title to next.	
pp. 34–5	**Lartique. Mary Thomas**	[nos **16, 17**]
	(17 ins [43 cm])	
p. 36	*blank*	
p. 37	Half-title to next.	
pp. 38–9	**Hoy Bark. George.**	[nos **18, 19**]
	(16½ ins [41.5 cm])	
p. 40	*blank*	
p. 41	Half-title to next.	
pp. 42–3	**Mary James.**	[no. **20**]
	Anthony's summary of first roll.	
	(22 ins [56 cm]; join at 18 ins [45.5 cm])	
p. 44	*blank*	
pp. 45–8	(inserted on two thicknesses of paper to form pages 11½ x 21½ ins [21 x 54 cm])	
	General abstract of the first roll, showing tonnages, men, guns of brass, guns of iron, gunpowder, shot of iron, shot of stone and lead, bows, bills etc , munitions, habiliments for war. [The title, on p. 45, is Pepysian; the table itself, on pp. 47–8, is earlier but not Anthony's original.]	
p. 49	Title to the second roll, of galleasses.	
p. 50	*blank*	
p. 51	Abstract of the second roll, listing the ships, their tonnages and complements; with note that 'exemplifications' of 6 of these galleasses are found in Pepys's 'Abstract=Book' (PL 2219)	
p. 52	*blank*	
p. 53	Title to the third roll, of pinnaces and row barges, and to the first two vessels.	
pp. 54–5.	**Anthony's title to the third roll.**	
	Falcon. Saker.	[nos **36, 37**]
	(22 ins [56 cm]; join at 17¾ ins [44.5 cm]; unbacked)	
p. 56	*blank*	
p. 57	Half-title to next.	

pp. 58–9	**Hind. Roo.**	[nos **38, 39**]
	(15 ins [38 cm])	
p. 60	*blank*	
p. 61	Half-title to next.	
pp. 62–3	**Phoenix. Merlin.**	[nos **40, 41**]
	(15½ ins [39 cm])	
p. 64	*blank*	
p. 65	Half-title to next.	
pp. 66–7	**Less Pinnace. Brigandine.**	[nos **42, 43**]
	(15 ins [38 cm])	
p. 68	*blank*	
p. 69	Half-title to next.	
pp. 70–1	**Hare. Trego Renneger.**	[nos **44, 45**]
	(15 ins [38 cm])	
pp. 72	*blank*	
p. 73	Half-title to next.	
pp. 74–5.	**Double Rose.**	[no. **46**]
	(12½ ins [31.5 cm])	
p. 76	*blank*	
p. 77	Half-title to next.	
pp. 78–9	**Flower de Luce. Portcullis.**	[nos **47, 48**]
	(15 ins [38 cm])	
p. 80	*blank*	
p. 81	Half-title to next.	
pp. 82–3	**Harp. Cloud in the Sun.**	[nos **49, 50**]
	(15½ ins [39 cm])	
p. 84	*blank*	
p. 85	Half-title to next.	
pp. 86–7	**Rose in the Sun. Hawthorn.**	[nos **51, 52**]
	(14 ins [35.5 cm])	
p. 88	*blank*	
p. 89	Half-title to next.	
pp. 90–1	**Three Ostrich Feathers. Falcon in the Fetterlock.**	[nos **53, 54**]
	(14 ins [35.5 cm])	
p. 92	*blank*	
p. 93	Half-title to next.	
pp. 94–5	**Maiden Head. Rose Slip.**	[nos **55, 56**]
	(14½ ins [37 cm])	
p. 96	*blank*	
p. 97	Half-title to next.	
pp. 98–9	**Gillyflower. Sun.**	[nos **57, 58**]
	Anthony's summary of the third roll.	
	(22 ins [56 cm]; unbacked)	
p. 100	Alphabetical list of ships in all three rolls.	
	General abstract of tonnages and complements.	
pp. 101–2	(inserted on paper, 11½ x 9 ins [29 x 23 cm])	
p. 101	Written around Pepys's usual end-plate (his monogram with fouled anchors), note that the galleasses were taken from the original in the Kings's Library at St James's, 'lent me by my Friend M^r. Thynn Library=Keeper there', the other two being from the original rolls given to Pepys by Charles II.	
p. 102	*blank*	
p. 103	Engraving of Henry VIII, approx. 2½ x 4¾ ins [6.5 x 12 cm], cut to the outline of the standing figure. A version deriving from the lost Holbein fresco at Whitehall, with the king holding a sceptre in his right hand. Not mentioned in the library catalogues by Chamberlain or Charrington (cf. frontispiece).	

The volume is handsomely bound in red turkey ornamented with drawer-handle tooling; the case measures 15 x 22¼ ins [38.5 x 56.5 cm]. The front and rear covers each have three brass escutcheons for clasps, engraved respectively with Pepys's crest, shield, and device of his monogram with fouled anchors; the braces to these clasps have been lost. The spine is blocked: 'K.HEN.8 / NAVY / 1546 / PAR / ANTH. / ANTHONY.' The binding was the work of John Berresford, whom Pepys employed for many of his most valued items. Berresford was a neighbour of the Navy Office in Mark Lane; he would receive a ring at Pepys's funeral.[48]

The cutting and binding of the first and third rolls would now be regarded as an improper manner of preserving archival and artistic material of such importance. It is particularly unfortunate that the first three, and finest, illustrations in the first roll are split by the gathering, with some immediate loss of detail, and resultant wear. By chance the second roll (in which all but two of the illustrations appear centrally) did not suffer in the same way. Pepys did, however, create a bibliographic treasure in its own right. There is no possibility that the volume at Magdalene would now be disbound.

Pepys's books are arranged in his library by size, in ascending numerical order to 3000. No. 2991 is, as its number indicates, almost the largest. Its notional place is in one of the side cupboards of Pepys's desk, which came to Magdalene along with the books and the twelve glass-fronted presses in which most of them are housed. For many years no. 2991 has been displayed in a showcase, and the pages with the *Henry Grace à Dieu* and the *Mary Rose* were most often on view. Despite careful control of lighting, there has been some fading to these illustrations and discolouration of the vellum. The British Library's roll has aged in ways which reflect its different format and custody; the illustrations at the head of the roll, most frequently opened, have suffered the more in consequence. The weathering and wear to which the separate parts of the MS have been subject are necessarily evident in the photographs made for the present edition.

Notes

1. See further discussion by Ann Payne below, pp. 24–5.
2. PRO, PROB 11/25, f. 196v (will of William Anthony, 1535); PROB 11/46, f. 240v (will of Anthony Anthony, 1563).
3. *CPR, 1494–1509*, p. 314. No William (or Anthony) Anthony occurs in W. Page, ed., *Letters of Denization and Acts of Naturalization for Aliens in England, 1509–1603* (Huguenot Soc. of London Publications, VIII, 1893), pp. 6–7.
4. R.D. Lang, ed., *Two Tudor Subsidy Assessment Rolls for the City of London: 1541 and 1582* (London Record Soc. XXXIX, 1993 for 1992), pp. 96, 99.
5. Bodleian Library, Oxford, MS Ashmole 861, p. 330. PRO, PROB 11/46, f. 240v. It has been implied that William father of Anthony Anthony was a man born at Cologne, subsequently resident at St Katharine's by the Tower, London, and father of Derick Anthony, chief engraver of the mint: S.W. Rawlins, ed., *Visitation of London 1568* (Harleian Soc. Visitations, CIX–CX, 1963), pp. 71–2, employing annotations by J. Challenor Smith to the previous edition (by J.H. Howard and G.J. Armytage, Harleian Soc. Visitations, I, 1869, p. 43). However the original visitation material includes no Anthony Anthony, and the will evidence demonstrates that the surveyor of the ordnance was an only son. It must be concluded that there were two families of Anthony in St Katharine's – one of goldsmiths, the other of brewers. But they were probably related, which may explain how Anthony Anthony came to supply a clock to Henry VIII in 1531, and to present another as a New Year gift in 1534: *LP*, V, no. 1799 (p. 756). BL, Add. MS 38857, f. 30 (I owe this reference to Ann Payne).
6. *LP*, III, i, no. 919 (p. 333); III, ii, no. 3261. R. Ashley, 'The organization and administration of the Tudor office of ordnance', B.Litt. dissertation, University of Oxford (1972), pp. 222–3.
7. *CPR, 1560–3*, p. 254.
8. *LP*, IV, iii, no. 6654([21]); V, no. 627(16); XIII, ii, no. 249(9); XX, i, no. 465(97); Addenda, ii, no. 1053.
9. *LP*, XII, ii, no. 711; XIII, i, no. 997; XIV, i, no. 617. Printed in M. St. C. Byrne, ed., *The Lisle Letters* (Chicago, 1981), IV, p. 164; V, pp. 126, 420.
10. Bodleian, MS Ashmole 861, pp. 330–50. J. Stow, *The Annales of England* (1592), sig. a4. R. Holinshed, *The Third Volume of Chronicles* (1586), p. 1090 (follows Anthony's account of the duke of Northumberland's burial, without citation). These references are owed to Mr G. Hill (letter to Mr R.C. Latham, 2 August 1982: PL Office Papers). G. Burnet, *History of the Reformation*, ed. N. Pocock (Oxford, 1865), I, pp. 315, 537. One of Burnet's references, relating to the fall of Anne Boleyn, was known to Pepys: E. Chappell, ed., *The Tangier Papers of Samuel Pepys* (NRS LXXIII, 1935), p. 215. Pepys refers to [vol. I] p. 197 of the edition of 1679–1715 (PL 2383–4).
11. Bodleian, MS Ashmole 861, pp. 331, 334.
12. Bodleian, MS Ashmole 861, pp. 299–300 (order of making knights of the bath); MS 863, pp. 201–10 (general account of the coronation rite); MS 863, pp. 211–12 (ceremonial at Queen Elizabeth's coronation).

The last item is printed from another copy [PRO, SP 15/9, no. 9] in C.G. Bayne, 'The coronation of Queen Elizabeth', *EHR*, XXII (1907), pp. 666–71.

13. *LP*, IV, iii, no. 6654([21]); VI, no. 1383(4).

14. BL, Sloane MS 871, ff. 144v, 145v. Ashley, 'Tudor office of ordnance', p. 42, citing BL MS as here, but apparently misreading the regnal year as 18 [1526/7] for '28'. H.C. Tomlinson, *Guns and Government: The Ordnance Office under the Later Stuarts* (Royal Historical Soc. Studies in History series, no. 15, 1979), p. 4 n. 3 (follows Ashley and so perpetuates '1527' for '1537'). The date is in any case only a *terminus a quo*. Anthony's deputy and eventual successor as clerk of the deliveries, Brian Hogge, was the first to receive (on 28 November 1570) a patent of the office: BL, Sloane MS 871, f. 145. *CPR, 1569–72*, p. 209.

15. *LP*, XI, no. 851 (Wriothesley to Cromwell, [?24 October] 1536, directing him to commit the king's orders to the master of the ordnance to Anthony in the master's absence). Ashley, 'Tudor office of ordnance', p. 42, sees this as indication of Anthony's rising importance in advance of his appointment as clerk of the deliveries. But the chronology is uncertain; Anthony may have acted as deputy because he was already one of the (two) senior clerks.

16. Ashley, 'Tudor office of ordnance', pp. 38, 63. Tomlinson, *Guns and Government*, p. 3.

17. PRO, SP 3/6, no. 75 (*LP*, XII, ii, App. no. 7. Byrne, *Lisle Letters*, IV, pp. 265–6).

18. *LP*, XII, ii, nos 617(10), 711; XIII, i, nos 384(26), 997. The artillery company's patent, which did not pass the great seal until 25 August 1537, is printed in full in G.G. Walker, *The Honourable Artillery Company 1537–1947* (2nd edn, Aldershot, 1954), pp. 2–5; I am grateful to the HAC's archivist emeritus, Jean Tsushima, for this reference.

19. *LP*, XX, i, nos 1235, 1244, 1252 (*APC*, I, pp. 214, 215).

20. Cf. *LP*, XX, i, no. 1255; XX, ii, nos 2, 3.

21. *CPR, 1547–8*, p. 353.

22. Bodleian, MS Ashmole 861, p. 341.

23. *CSPD, Edward VI*, p. 246. Ashley, 'Tudor office of ordnance', p. 47.

24. *CPR, 1558–60*, p. 282; *1563–6*, p. 324; *1569–72*, p. 4. For Iden, of whom little else is known, see P.W. Hasler, ed., *The House of Commons 1558–1603* (1981), II, p. 367.

25. PRO, SP 12/29, no. 12 (*CSPD, 1547–80*, p. 226).

26. S. Brigden, ed., 'The letters of Richard Scudamore to Sir Philip Hoby, September 1549–March 1555', *Camden Miscellany XXX* (Royal Historical Soc. Camden 4th ser. XXXIX, 1990), p. 120. J.S. Loengard, ed., *London Viewers and their Certificates* (London Record Soc. XXVI, 1989), pp. 56, 62–3.

27. PRO, PROB 11/46, ff. 240v–241v. Harrison was a clerk and deputy paymaster in the ordnance office: BL, Sloane MS 871, f. 134v.

28. PRO, E 351/2614, cited Ashley, 'Tudor office of ordnance', pp. 48–9. *CPR, 1578–80*, p. 171.

29. Below, p. 6.

30. R.G. Howarth, ed., *Letters and the Second Diary of Samuel Pepys* (1933), p. 102.

31. PL 2141 contains Pepys's original shorthand version, and the longhand recension he made from it. Both texts printed in W. Matthews, ed., *Charles II's Escape from Worcester* (1967), pp. 34–84. Pepys's record of the Newmarket meetings occurs on p. 80 of Matthews's edition.

32. PL 2877, p. 410 ('In [Henry VIII's] reigne we first grew great in ships of war of our own: a list of which is extant in a long parchment roll in his Majesty's hands').

33. E.S. de Beer, ed., *The Diary of John Evelyn* (Oxford, 1955), IV, pp. 214–15. Evelyn and Pepys were at the time in correspondence about naval matters for Pepys's history: PL 2873, pp. 56–9, printed in G. de la Bédoyère, ed., *Particular Friends: The Correspondence of Samuel Pepys and John Evelyn* (Woodbridge, 1997), pp. 117–19.

34. J.R. Tanner, ed., *Samuel Pepys's Naval Minutes* (NRS LX, 1926), pp. 100–1. Pepys records (without date): 'Mr. Thynne tells me that he has one Roll of Henry the 8th's galleys, with which what I saw in the King's Closet and the other in my own hand do (I believe) make up the whole Navy Royal at that time'. The volume he had made with illustrations from the 2nd roll is now PL 2219. Henry Frederick Thynne (d. 1705) was with his brother James joint-keeper of the king's library from 1677–89: de Beer, *Evelyn*, IV, p. 178 n.4. He was among the 'indefinite' friends invited to Pepys's funeral: J.R. Tanner, ed., *Private Correspondence and Miscellaneous Papers of Samuel Pepys, 1679–1703* (1926), II, p. 318.

35. In addition to the entry quoted in the preceding note, there is in Tanner, *Naval Minutes*, p. 193: 'Observe that there is no bow-line in Holben's pictures of ships, and two mizen-masts, in the Whitehall Gallery. And *quaere* whether they be so in my long Roll of Ships of that age'. This evidently pre-dates the cutting of the MS. In Chappell, *Tangier Papers*, p. 239: 'From Henry VIII's list observe the arms then allowed his ships'.

36. The disposition of the library since it came to Magdalene is described by F. Sidgwick in *Bibliotheca*

Pepysiana: A Descriptive Catalogue of the Library of Samuel Pepys, (1914–40), II, pp. xi–xiii.

37. Cf. R.C. Latham and W. Matthews, eds, *The Diary of Samuel Pepys* (1970–83), I, pp. lxxiii–lxxiv.

38. Kerrich's MS (which included transcription of parts of PL 2219) was printed with annotations in F.P. Barnard, 'Henry the Eighth's navy', in *A Miscellany: Presented to John Macdonald Mackay, LL.D. July 1914*, [ed. O. Elton], (Liverpool, 1914), pp. 132–41.

39. J. Topham, 'A description of an antient picture in Windsor Castle, representing the embarkation of King Henry VIII. at Dover, May 31, 1520, preparatory to his interview with the French King Francis I', *Archaeologia*, VI (1782), pp. 179–220; engraving facing p. 208; quotation from p. 207 note ‡; pp. 216–17 prints the ordnance inventory of the *Henry Grace à Dieu*, and is therefore the first publication of a part of Anthony's text.

40. This conclusion by Topham was followed by C. Derrick, *Memoirs of the Rise and Progress of the Royal Navy* (1806), p. 307, who nevertheless printed (pp. 303–6) a summary of the contents of all three rolls from a copy formerly in the possession of Vice-Admiral Sir Hugh Palliser (controller of the navy 1770–5 and subsequently commissioner of the Admiralty). Palliser's copy must have been, or derived from, one made when all three rolls remained in the royal library, and so perhaps related to the abstract of the first roll extant in PL 2991, pp. 45–8.

41. P. Ziegler, *King William IV* (1971), p. 75.

42. C. Tomalin, *Mrs Jordan's Profession* (1994), p. 310. I am grateful to Claire Tomalin for additional information about Lady Mary Fox.

43. F. Boase, ed., *Modern English Biography* (1892–1901), I, p. 1094. *Illustrated London News*, LXII (1873), p. 393 (obituary notice of General Fox). S. Keppel, *The Sovereign Lady: A Life of Elizabeth Vassall, third Lady Holland, with her Family* (1974), pp. 182, 231, 309, 311.

44. Bodleian, MS Eng. hist. c. 170 [Madden's diary], pp. 10, 11, 52, 157, 158. T.D. Rogers, ed., *Sir Frederic Madden at Cambridge* (Cambridge Bibliographical Soc. monograph no. 9, 1980), pp. 5, 17, 22–4. BL, Department of MSS, bound volume (unclassified), 'Acquisitions 1855–1857', recorded under 23 May 1857: purchase of vellum roll from Lady Mary Fox for £15 sanctioned (although three times the normal limit for a single acquisition). I am grateful to Ann Payne for locating this reference and giving me access to departmental records.

45. PRO, SP 12/29, no. 12.

46. For further discussion of the format of the MS see Ann Payne, below, pp. 23–4.

47. A fuller description of the Pepys volume is given in C.S. Knighton, comp., *Catalogue of the Pepys Library at Magdalene College, Cambridge*, V, ii, *Modern Manuscripts* (Woodbridge, 1981), pp. 174–6.

48. H.M. Nixon, comp., *Catalogue of the Pepys Library at Magdalene College, Cambridge*, VI, *Bindings* (Woodbridge, 1984), pp. xxiii–xxiv, 44; black and white plate 22 (showing front cover). R.J. Trise, '"For the love of the binding"', *Bookbinder*, XI (1997), p. 47 and colour plates 5 and 6 on p. 48 (showing rear cover and the endpapers, themselves dazzling displays of the paper-maker's craft, though here poorly reproduced).

II   The Ordnance
D.M. Loades

Anthony's ordnance list of 1546 presents an interesting comparison with the equivalent sections of the 1514 document printed in Part Two. There is a rich variety of terminology used to describe the guns listed in these two sets of inventories. Unfortunately it is all somewhat unstable, and usage changed considerably in the thirty-odd years between them.[1] It cannot be assumed that two guns called demi-culverins, even when they were mounted in the same ship at the same time, were necessarily of identical bore, or fired shot of the same weight. Nevertheless the names do give an approximate indication of size, and of whether they were made of 'brass' – an alloy which we would now call bronze – or iron. By the time that the Anthony Roll was written, iron guns might be either wrought or cast. English cast iron guns were a brand new phenomenon, but cast guns had been imported from Mechlin for some time, although probably not as early as 1514. Wrought guns were built up from strips of metal bound together by having rings of the same metal shrunk over them in the same manner that a wooden barrel was cooped. Such guns were usually breech-loading, having a separate chamber which was locked and wedged in place behind the barrel, and which contained the charge. It was normal to have two or more chambers for each such gun, in order to improve the rate of fire. Wrought guns were almost invariably made of iron. Cast guns were made in moulds, and were therefore somewhat easier to standardise. Clay moulds themselves had to be broken to extract the guns, but by making the moulds over a wooden core a measure of uniformity could be obtained. However there could be no standardisation between makers or over a period of time. Cast guns were almost invariably muzzle-loaders. Being made in one piece, the breech was gastight, thus increasing the force of the explosion and giving the shot more power. Muzzle-loaders were at first more dangerous to use, because of the risk that the gun itself would shatter. Bronze guns gave a minimal warning because they distorted before shattering. Iron not only gave no warning, but was more likely to shatter because of the greater risk of flaws occurring in the process of casting. The technology of iron casting improved considerably between 1514 and 1546, leading to an increased use of cast iron guns. However the risk remained, and although iron guns were cheaper, bronze continued to be used throughout the century.

Guns were mounted in a variety of ways, according to size and purpose. Small-calibre weapons, which resembled handguns, might be mounted on swivel holders to give greater flexibility in use, or they might be fastened directly to the woodwork of the ship as the power of their recoil was not sufficient to cause serious damage. Large guns, however, which could cause considerable strain and distortion, especially if several were fired simultaneously, were more commonly mounted either on solid blocks of timber, on wheeled carriages, or on sleds. In each case the recoil was contained within predetermined limits by ropes passed behind the mounting and secured to the ship's timbers on either side. The large guns mounted in the prows of contemporary galleys appear to have been secured directly to the frames of the ships,[2] but this was not usual with the port firing weapons mounted by English vessels. The earliest large serpentines were normally block mounted, but wheeled carriages were in use by about 1510, and were normal by 1545. Some have been recovered from the *Mary Rose*, and resemble in design those known to have been used, and recorded in drawings, later in the century. In 1514 there may have been more than one type, because the difference between 'shod wheles' and 'trothill wheles' suggests more than a distinction of size. It is possible that larger spoked wheels were used for carriages or sleds more akin to those used ashore. Wheels shod with iron could well have damaged the deck of a ship, and they went out of use in the later 16th century.

The original gunpowder, later called 'serpentine powder', was made by grinding saltpetre, sulphur and charcoal to a fine powder and mixing them together. It was unreliable because its ingredients were likely to separate out in storage. Cornpowder, which came into general use between the two inventories, was hydrated and sieved to produce granules of a standard size. It was more thoroughly mixed, and had also been through an additional process whereby the powder was formed into corns which were then glazed to resist damp and decomposition. For these reasons it was both more powerful and more reliable than serpentine powder, although the composition was the same. Generally a coarse-grain variety was used for large guns, and a finer for small guns and handguns. Shot came in innumerable different sizes, to fit the bore of the guns being used. It might be made of iron, stone or lead. Stone shot having relatively low mass could be fired from large-calibre guns using low-powered charges. It was much valued for its 'smashing quality' at short range, and was mainly fired from old-fashioned serpentines, often called 'stone guns', and cannon petros. One of the advantages of stone shot was that the supply was easily renewed, and most ships carried stone picks so that the crew could quarry and fashion a fresh stock when the opportunity presented itself. Lead pellets were used only in the smallest mounted guns, as well as in handguns. Lead was much more expensive than stone, but also had the advantage that it could be made on the spot. Several ships are mentioned as carrying supplies of lead, and shot moulds. The commonest shot used in big guns was iron, and was roughly spherical in shape – 'cannon balls'. At short range such shot could inflict severe damage, even on heavy timbers, but could not be easily manufactured if supplies ran out. The chain shot which was common by the end of the century does not seem to have been used at this early date, and the only variants noted in the inventories are '[cross] bar shot' (which was spiked), and 'dyce'. Dice were iron small shot which were roughly cube shaped, and served the same purpose as shrapnel. 'Darts' were like crossbow bolts, and could also be fired from small guns. In themselves they were simply anti-personnel weapons, but they could be loaded with 'wildfire', an adhesive combustible substance, with the intention of setting fire to the timber in which they became imbedded.

Reloading a chamber gun was a straightforward operation. The spent chamber was simply knocked out with a wooden mallet, and a replacement, ready primed, put in its place. The gun did not need to be cooled or moved, and there was no danger of premature ignition. Reloading a muzzle-loader was more tricky. In some cases it seems to have been done from outside the ship, by sending a man (or more probably a boy) to climb down and insert the charge. Not only was this difficult, it was extremely dangerous, and in battle potentially lethal. However, if the gun was fixed, there was presumably no alternative. Much more satisfactory was to haul the gun inboard, or allow it to come inboard on the recoil, and then to chock the carriage and reload inboard. This was certainly the method which later became universal, and was probably the normal method in these ships, given that most of the large guns were on carriages. The guns still had to be cooled and swabbed to remove burning detritus, and the appropriate powder charges were measured out in advance into canvas or paper cartridges. A correct charge was important for each particular gun; too little and the shot would fail to reach its target; too much and the gun might explode.

Using a big gun at sea was a highly skilled business. Quite apart from the hazards of securing and reloading the piece on a moving deck, it also had to be aimed. Such records as we have of the tactics employed in battle suggest that even as late as 1545 it was normal to sail straight towards an enemy, assuming the wind to be favourable, and to cant the side mounted guns as far as possible to enable them to fire ahead.[3] This is turn would mean that the guns were fired individually. There are some suggestions that whole broadsides of the later kind may have been conceived as early as 1545, but they were certainly not in general use. By the end of Henry VIII's reign specialised gunners were carried on every armed ship, but never enough for one to have been in charge of every gun, and we do not know exactly how they were deployed. Probably the biggest pieces had a specialist gunner in charge, and elsewhere one gunner would look after several weapons. The gun crews were seamen, and although many of them may have been experienced they were not, as far as we know, specially trained. In was the gunner's responsibility to 'lay' his piece, in accordance with the range and weather conditions, and the effectiveness of gunfire at anything more than point blank must have depended greatly on his skill. Every royal ship of more than about 60 tons also carried a master gunner who was not only responsible for deploying his gunners in battle stations, but also for the maintenance and storage of the guns when they were not in use. The English method of handling guns owed a lot to the influence of armed merchantmen and privateers, where it was normal for the gun crews to be composed of seamen, because soldiers were not available. At the time of the Armada campaign forty years later, Spanish gun crews were comprised of soldiers, whose relations with the seamen left a lot to be desired, and who had no experience of using their weapons at sea. English warships normally carried soldiers throughout the century, but they did not crew the guns.

Some of the 1514 inventories also include the locations of the guns, and this is unusual information. The ships had recently been on active service, so it is reasonable to suppose that these locations correspond to battle stations rather than to where the weapons happen to have been stowed for convenience. After the inventories had been taken, the bulk of these 'habillaments of war' were left in the custody of the masters and pursers of the ships. This should not be taken to mean that they remained in the ships, but that it was the responsibility of these officers to return them to the appropriate store; the Tower armoury for the big guns and Deptford or Woolwich for the rest. A small amount seems to have been left on board to provide for the security of the skeleton crew during the period of decommissioning.

The Anthony Roll reflects its compiler's professional concern with ordnance. The text beneath each illustration (printed adjacently in this edition) is exclusively concerned with guns, shot and ancillary equipment. However, the illustrations themselves appear to be of dubious reliability. We may assume that Anthony took care to represent the ships' guns as accurately as he could; but anyone who attempts to match the text descriptions with the illustrations will soon find that there are many discrepancies. Most obviously, guns are represented as firing aft from the forecastles in the first eleven ships shown. There is no clear explanation for this, although some ships including the *Mary Rose* did carry guns firing forward from the sterncastle.[4] Both these mountings would have required the guns to be canted outboard, unless they were intended to be anti-personnel weapons for use against boarders. It is possible that Anthony was concerned to illustrate every possible deployment, rather than restrict himself to what was actually used. It also has to be remembered that he showed the ships stern on, as all marine artists did. This had the advantage of showing the great guns mounted in the stern, but concealed any firing forward from the sterncastle. Perhaps he was merely compensating for this omission. He seems to have been prepared to defy the rules of perspective, as well as the realities of naval usage, in order to ensure that his particular discipline was displayed to maximum effect.

Notes

1. For a discussion of changing terminology and other aspects of the naval ordnance of this period, see R.A. Konstam, 'Naval artillery to 1550: its design, evolution and employment', M.Litt. dissertation, University of St Andrews (1987).
2. Sliding recoil carriages appear to have been adopted in some Mediterranean galleys as early as 1530. I am indebted to Professor Nicholas Rodger for this information, and for many other helpful suggestions.
3. N.A.M. Rodger, 'The development of broadside gunnery, 1540–1650', *MM*, LXXXII (1996), pp. 301–24. The 'whole' broadside was an initial discharge, because after that the rate of fire varied slightly from one gun to another.
4. See Alexzandra Hildred below, p. 17.

III   The Evidence of the *Mary Rose* Excavation

One ship drawn and inventoried by Anthony Anthony has been in large measure preserved. The *Mary Rose*, built in 1510–11 alongside the *Peter Pomegranate* (her companion in the Roll), sank on 19 July 1545 while defending Portsmouth from French invasion. Immediate attempts were made to lift her, and for some time afterwards items were recovered. A further salvage operation took place between 1836 and 1840. Modern search for the wreck began under Alexander McKee in 1965. In 1971 the first timbers were sighted. From 1979, Margaret Rule carried out a major excavation, culminating in the recovery of the hull on 11 October 1982. The hull and many of the thousands of recovered artefacts are displayed at the Mary Rose Trust museum at Portsmouth.[1] The Anthony illustration and inventory are the final record of the ship in service; the archaeological evidence from the continuing work of the Trust is therefore of greatest importance in assessing the reliability of the Anthony Roll in the case of this particular ship, and by extension for the rest.[2]

(i) The ship   *Stuart Vine*

Just under half the hull survives, the majority of the starboard side from the end of the forecastle to the rudder. The greater part of the after- or sterncastle also survives.[3] The bow and forecastle were not retrieved; the Tudor salvors removed the masts and yards during their otherwise unsuccessful salvage attempt.

Comparison of the surviving section of the hull with the illustration is a fascinating exercise. Some details of the illustration are extremely accurate, but when examined as a whole it is hard to believe that Anthony drew the ship from life. It would appear that the illustration is meant to depict the power and splendour of the ship rather than attempting an accurate depiction.

One is immediately struck by the strange, staggered arrangement of gunports at main deck level on the illustration. Two rows of gunports are shown, one immediately above the lower wale and one above the next wale, totalling nine gunports in all. The upper row of gunports have no lids. In reality, there was only one row of ports at main-deck level in the hull of the *Mary Rose*. Four of the ports were in the waist of the ship and three below the sterncastle. All the ports were lidded and situated between the second and third wales. Since we believe that the water level was approximately at the height of the lowest wale, a ship with ports in the position shown on the Anthony Roll would hardly have been practical or seaworthy.[4]

Turning our attention to the waist of the ship in the illustration, we find that the depiction and the evidence from the archaeological remains are very similar indeed. We have evidence for three semi-circular ports in the waist, with a series of vertical blinds (often called 'bulwarks' in contemporary accounts) above them. We have no evidence for the decorative shields shown in the illustration, but it would seem unlikely that these would have been in place during battle.[5]

Depicted above these shields is what appears to be anti-boarding netting. This ties in precisely with the recovered remains. A number of the joists that supported the netting were recovered from the wreck, as well as some small samples of what may have been the netting itself. The rebates in the rail that supported these joists above the blinds indicate that the netting was horizontal, not angled as shown in the Anthony Roll, although this may just be artistic licence to allow the netting to be seen.

Moving towards the stern, the depiction of four gunports at upper-deck level below the sterncastle is inaccurate. There is only evidence for two gunports in this area in the hull of the ship. Above the gunports there appears to be a continuous row of small ports in the drawing. There is no evidence whatsoever for these in the ship itself. It may be of some interest to note that these may have existed in the ship prior to rebuilding in either 1528 or 1536. There is an internal rail at waist level on the upper deck in this area that had closely spaced holes for swivel-gun stirrups. These swivel guns may have required a set of ports similar to those depicted. However, as shown these ports would have been set too high.

We are reasonably sure that there was only a single deck in the sterncastle of the *Mary Rose*. The castle was clad in external clinker planking up to waist level on the castle deck. Above this was a series of removable panels with ogival cut-outs, somewhat similar to those shown in the illustration of the sterncastle. These panels were removed during action to allow the swivel guns on the castle deck a clear field of fire and were found stored on the upper deck. Directly above these panels was a longitudinal beam with rebates cut in it for what appear to be small netting joists similar to those in the waist. On the available evidence it would appear that the actual sterncastle of the *Mary Rose* was considerably lower than that depicted in the illustration.

The depiction of the stern in the Anthony Roll picture almost certainly contains some gross inaccuracies. Of particular concern are the low-level ports apparently containing heavy sternchasers. As depicted, these are set lower in the hull than the main deck. This configuration is simply impossible. There is no orlop deck in the sternmost section of the hull, and even if there was, it would be close to, if not below, the waterline. We have also found no evidence to support the existence of gunports on the main deck in the stern. Both the extreme sheer of the deck and the lack of space in this area would seem to indicate that there were no guns mounted in this position. Above the main deck the hull has been eroded, so we cannot comment on the relative accuracy of this area of the illustration.

The design of the bow and forecastle area of the *Mary Rose* is proving extremely contentious. Because this area has broken away from the hull and has not so far been recovered, a number of different design theories have been aired. These range from the belief that the castle was constructed in the manner depicted on the Anthony Roll, to the much lower and perhaps more galleon-like castle depicted on the Basset Lowke model of the *Mary Rose* that can be seen in the *Mary Rose* museum. The Mary Rose Trust's interpretation of the forecastle relies on a mixture of archaeological observation and documentary evidence. The details of the construction were based on the evidence provided by the aftercastle. Some idea of the sheer of the castle was provided by the survival of the decorative panelling (identical to that of the aftercastle) that was found in storage on the orlop deck. Although some of the construction details of the forecastle are unavailable, it would seem possible that the castle was not as tall and did not extend forward as far as that depicted in the illustration.

At the very top of the mainmast a very small 'fighting' top is depicted. We were very fortunate to recover a spare top identical in observable detail to that shown. This top has a basal diameter of $2^2/_5$ ft. [0.72m] with a rim diameter of $4^7/_{10}$ ft. [1.45m]. It has an overall height of 2 ft. [0.6m]. The patterning on the depicted top is matched by angled 'figure of eight' decorations of dark pitch on the light coloured wooden staves of the real top.

Margaret Rule condemned Anthony's treatment of the standing rigging as no more than 'a confusing assemblage of shrouds, ratline and stays'. The excavation revealed in 1981 that the *Mary Rose* was not (as some had assumed from the picture) without the conventional rigging for securing the masts athwartships.[6]

In general the physical evidence suggests that the Anthony Roll illustrations should not be treated as totally accurate representations.

(ii) The munitions   *Alexzandra Hildred*

By 1546 the *Mary Rose* had been upgraded from 500 to 700 tons, with a complement of 185 soldiers, 200 mariners and 30 gunners. She was designed to carry 91 guns deployed over three decks, with the 14 heaviest on the main deck.[7] She is the second largest and second most heavily armed of the 58 vessels in the Anthony Roll. She is listed there as having 15 carriage-mounted 'brass' guns in addition to a substantial number of wrought iron guns: 24 carriage-mounted, and 52 ship-supported anti-personnel guns, 32 of which were wrought iron. In addition she carried 50 handguns, 250 longbows, 300 staff weapons, and 480 darts to be thrown from the fighting tops. Anthony's illustration distinguishes between the bronze and iron guns. Seven bronze are shown on the starboard side at the main and upper deck levels, with a total of 16 large guns over these decks making 32 of the 39 listed large carriage-mounted guns. The location of guns and shot revealed by the excavation complements the documentary evidence of the Roll in evaluating the fighting capacity of the ship.

Guns are listed as of 'brass' and iron, in descending order of size. The 'brass' guns were cast bronze muzzle-loaders, situated alongside the wrought iron breech-loaders previously thought to be obsolete by this time. Of three guns analysed, one is 77% copper alloyed with zinc, tin and lead; one 92% copper alloyed with tin, antimony and lead; one 93% copper primarily alloyed with tin but with small amounts of antimony, arsenic and nickel. The number and types vary slightly from those listed by Anthony. Most are inscribed with all or some details as to type, weight, and name of founder. All but two are dated, the earliest 1536, the latest 1543. This suggests that the ship was at least partially re-equipped after her 1536 refit, possibly for the 1544 campaign. Calibre and weight vary within the prescribed Tudor doctrines.

Bronze guns	inventoried	recovered (with dates)
cannons	2	2 (1535; undated)
demi-cannons	2	3 (1535; 1542; 1542)
culverins	2	3 (1535; 1542; 1543)
demi-culverins	6	2 (1537; undated)
sakers	2	0
falcons	1	0

The bronze guns included two of the only four cannons in the entire fleet. The six main-deck bronze guns (three per side: bow, midships, stern) included a mix of cannons (two, amidships), demi-cannons (two, stern) and culverins (two, bow). Ten of the 15 bronze guns have been recovered; four during the 19th-century salvage, the other six by the Mary Rose Trust. Five of the six were excavated from gun positions and were still on their carriages. The sixth had rolled from the port side and was separated from its carriage. In addition two carriages for main-deck bronze guns previously recovered were excavated, suggesting the original locations for these guns.

Only one of the six listed demi-culverins was found on site. It was on the castle deck in the stern, positioned to fire forward from a port in the sterncastle.[8] No such gun or port is shown in any of the Anthony Roll illustrations. The 19th-century salvors recovered one demi-culverin, but we cannot be certain of its location. The listed but unaccounted-for demi-culverins may have been located in two of the four vacant gunports in the upper deck at the stern; others could have been accommodated in the forecastle. All these locations would have been accessible to the Tudor salvors (paid to recover the guns).[9]

Several isolated portions of carriages for small bronze guns suggest the presence of sakers and falcons. These may have been in the forecastle, and could therefore remain in the seabed if not recovered by the Tudor salvors. The original presence of these guns is confirmed by finds of cast-iron shot, rammers, and powder ladles of suitable sizes.

In general, there is no reason to question the validity of the inventory for the 'brass' guns.

Twelve large wrought iron port pieces are listed. Eight can be accounted for on the main deck; two more could have been situated on the upper deck in the stern. Not enough of the structure survives to say whether the last two listed port pieces could have been placed in the bow or the stern, but there is enough stone shot to service two more.[10] Parts of eight port pieces were recovered, four in the 19th century and four by the Mary Rose Trust. Six of these were mounted on sledges hollowed out of single pieces of elm which retained the barrel, breech chamber, and breech-chamber wedge (forelock). Similar carriages supported the slings positioned on the upper deck, which has the space to accommodate six slings in the waist (three on each side) through the unlidded semi-circular ports shown in the Roll as three square ports.

It is likely that the largest wrought iron gun recovered from the upper deck in the waist is a sling, and that smaller-bore barrel fragments represent demi- and quarter-slings. Precise identification of these types is not possible. In total four slings were recovered, with broken elements of others. These guns were only positively identified by having been found loaded with cast iron, as specified ('shote of yron … for slyng[es]') in Anthony's inventory,[11] and by their position relative to size. The listed fowlers have not been identified.

There is no evidence for the positioning of large guns on the main deck as sternchasers. There is not a great deal of room for them, although they are clearly shown at what looks like main-deck level in a number of Anthony's illustrations. The only evidence of a gun firing out of the stern is a swivel gun (one of the 30 bases listed) found at upper-deck level. Remains of 13 bases (wrought iron guns held on miches or swivel yolks) in or under the forecastle suggest that these were positioned on the upper and castle decks. No 'toppe pecys' have been identified; illustrations suggest that these were akin to bases, but located in the fighting tops.

The only known examples of hailshot pieces are from the *Mary Rose*. Four (of 20 listed) have been identified by their size within the listings of iron ordnance, and from their being loaded with the 'dyce of yron for hayle shotte'. Those recovered were cast iron muzzle-loaders, having a rectangular bore which scatters the shot like 'hail', and a fin-like hook for supporting over a rail. All were found under the sterncastle or on the upper and castle decks. They represent 25% of the iron gun assemblage in the fleet, and are the second most prevalent iron gun in Anthony's inventory Their identification, along with confirmation of previous ascriptions to names to wrought iron guns in general, is a direct result of the excavation of the *Mary Rose*.

The inventory lists 50 handguns; remains of five have been identified.[12] These guns were too fragile to have survived in the quantity Anthony suggested.

Gunpowder is listed as serpentine and corned; most of the guns used the former.[13] Although certain constituents of the powder have survived in the bores and breech-chambers, the potassium nitrate has dissolved, impeding identification of the original composition.

Shot is listed as iron, and stone and lead; then in descending order of size for named guns. This has enabled identification of a number of named guns. The apparently large tolerance for windage (between $1/4$ and 1 inch has been observed) within the barrels of excavated guns makes matching shot to gun difficult, especially when some of the wrought iron guns accepted cast iron shot. What is clear is that there is more than the quoted number of shot. Nearly twice the listed number of iron shot were recovered, and 392 stone shot against 370 listed. The lead shot listed for bases is in reality composite shot of lead containing iron dice. The full 400 listed have not been recovered, but this type of object is still being found. The 1,000 lead shot for handguns are represented by less than 100. But these are very small, and could have been scattered off site.

The longbow and arrow assemblage is close enough to the Roll, with 179 of the 250 yew longbows accounted for. Although less than half the arrows are present, seven empty or partially filled chests could hold 8,400 of the 9,600 arrows listed (assuming documentary claim of 50 sheaves to a chest). We have no bowstrings, but plenty of barrels where they could have been kept. It is not to be expected that these would have survived.

The staff weapons were primarily located on the upper deck in the stern. Although remains of 121 bills survive, we have only 21 of the thinner pikes with much smaller heads. These could easily have floated away. None of the 40 dozen darts has been identified; but had these been in the tops, their absence would be unsurprising. It is possible that the three large incendiary darts recovered may be related to them.

Pick hammers, sledge hammers and commanders have been retrieved, though not in the large numbers quoted. The crowbars (for working the guns) may be represented by some of the amorphous iron concretions yet to be excavated.

4,000 tampions are listed; only 168 loose have been recovered, but 55 further reels have been identified. Made of poplar and stored in barrels, these would have been positively buoyant, and the low level of recovery is not unexpected. Canvas and paper royal for cartridges has predictably not been found. Recovery of a cartridge-former suggests that cartridges themselves were made on board.

Elements of most of the 'habillimentes for warre' survive. It is hard to distinguish which ropes were used solely for retaining the guns; but spare rope was certainly carried, as were nails (evidenced by two recovered). These would mostly have corroded away. More than the eight listed leather bags were recovered, but not all were necessarily for ammunition. No barrels with leather purses have yet been identified; they are presumed to be forerunners of the modern budge barrel. There is no evidence for the 6 dozen lime pots; nor for the sheep skins, though spare hides have been found. The trucks, spoked wheels and axle roughouts (not completely finished, so that they could be fashioned to fit either the bronze or wrought-iron gun carriages) found in the ordnance store on the orlop deck exactly match in number the spares listed. Spare elm is present, but doubtless not solely for the ordnance.

The excavation therefore confirms in many respects the listing of objects in the Anthony Roll. It should be remembered that the assemblage is incomplete, the site has suffered from interference, and much of the forecastle remains to be investigated.

Notes

1. M.H. Rule, *The Mary Rose: The Excavation and Raising of Henry VIII's Flagship* (2nd edn., 1983) has the most comprehensive account of the excavation and salvage. See also A. McKee, *How we found the Mary Rose* (1982), and E. Bradford, *The Story of the Mary Rose* (1982).
2. The other principal inventory of the *Mary Rose*, that of 1514, is printed below, pp. 139–42. Cf. the briefer ordnance list calendared in *LP*, XV, no. 196.
3. For details on construction see M.H. Rule and C.T.C. Dobbs, 'The Tudor warship *Mary Rose*: aspects of recent research', in M. Bound, ed., *The Archaeology of Ships of War* (International Maritime Archaeology Series, I, Oswestry, 1995), pp. 26–9. S.M. Vine, 'Some aspects of deck construction in the *Mary Rose*', *Proceedings of the Third Annual Conference for New Researchers in Maritime History* (Portsmouth, 1995), pp. 1–18.
4. On the gunports cf. F. Howard, 'Puzzle from the past', *Model Shipwright*, XXXVII (September 1981), pp. 42–3.
5. See Timothy Wilson below, p. 30 n. 17.
6. Rule, *Mary Rose*, pp. 136–40.
7. See A. Hildred and M.H. Rule, 'Armaments from the *Mary Rose*', *Antique Arms and Militaria*, IV, no. 2 (May 1984), pp. 17–24.
8. See reconstruction drawing by Debbie Fulford, reproduced in Rule, *Mary Rose*, p. 104. Cf. also David Loades, above, p. 14.
9. Cf. *CSPD, Edward VI*, p. 261.
10. See R.D. Smith, 'Port pieces: the use of wrought iron ordnance in the sixteenth century', *Journal of the Ordnance*

Society, V (1993), pp. 1–8. N. Hall, 'Building and firing a replica *Mary Rose* port piece', *Royal Armouries Yearbook*, 3 (1998), pp. 57–66.

11.   Most of the wrought iron guns raised from the *Mary Rose* have been radiographed, revealing that the carriage-mounted guns are formed of a stave-built inner tube, open-ended and covered by a single layer of alternating wide bands and narrow hoops, without any attempts to weld the barrel or include lead between the seams. The chambers are made similarly, but may have differing widths of staves, and more than one layer. Cf. R.D. Smith, 'Towards a new typology for wrought iron ordnance', *International Journal of Nautical Archaeology and Underwater Exploration*, XVII (1988), pp. 5–16.

12.   One is identical to a group from Gardone in northern Italy, recently purchased by the Royal Armouries.

13.   See David Loades, above, p. 12.

IV   An Artistic Survey
Ann Payne

At the end of each of the three sections of the Roll are the words 'Par me Anthony Anthony'; there seems little reason to doubt that this inscription covers both pictures and text. The illustrations are striking and boldly executed, but despite their appeal have few claims to be fine works of art. Their naive draughtsmanship and conformity to a pattern appear perfectly consistent with the abilities of a government official with a decent amateur grasp of form and colour.

Though the Roll might be intended as a serious inventory of Henry VIII's fighting fleet in 1546, the accompanying pictures were much more than ancillary decoration. The space allotted to them and the fact that they were done first indicate their importance to the project. It was to be a presentation set of rolls for the king. Each of the three rolls was approximately 5½ yards in length. Side by side they could be opened up for symmetrical exhibition – and royal examination – across a floor, on a table or indeed on a palace wall.[1] Anthony's design places the king's personal favourite, the untypical *Galley Subtle* – given rather more space than any other ship except the pre-eminent *Henry Grace à Dieu* – 7 ft. from the foot of the middle roll, where logically it may appear out of place but where it becomes a focal point of the overall display.

Anthony's determination to produce three rolls of closely similar length is demonstrated by the siting of the *Mary James*. His original design must have had the *Falcon*, the *Saker* and the *Mary James* as the three pinnaces occupying the first vellum membrane of his third roll. He had already completed the painting of this trio when, in a move evidently prompted by considerations of display, he cut off the *Mary James* and added it to the bottom of the first roll. Given the number of ships he had to accommodate on the third roll, it was going to extend, without this transfer, to six membranes and rather more than 17½ ft., compared with the five membranes and 14¾ ft., of the first roll, and the five and a half membranes and 16½ ft. of the second. In order to achieve aesthetic balance he was ready to attach a three-masted pinnace to a group of four-masted 'shyppes'.[2]

Anthony must have felt confident of a favourable reception for his Roll. The work was celebrating a period of naval expansion and success. King Henry was known to interest himself in the design and performance of ships. He seems also to have taken delight in pictures of them. For a monarch eager to flaunt the symbols and tokens of his royal power, there could be few more telling vehicles for dynastic display than warships – at sea or in reproduction – bristling with guns and decked out with rich arrays of Tudor devices and colours. At about this time Henry was presented with the painting, now at Hampton Court, of the *Embarkation of Henry VIII at Dover*, possibly in time for it to be a source of inspiration to Anthony Anthony in compiling his own painted fleet.[3] Although the King himself is present in the picture as the principal character – in regal pose, but at a distance – it is less a picture of King Henry than of Tudor might. That it is not a realistic picture of the 1520 occasion or accurate in the depiction of Tudor ships is immaterial compared with the main symbolism contained in the assembly of many well-armed ships, fully dressed in heraldic colour and royal emblems. It is a power picture of the fleet and as such must have pleased and flattered a proud king.

Henry received pictures of ships frequently. They came as features in the maps and bird's eye views which were the blueprints of military construction and increasingly the stuff of intelligence gathering. Maps or 'plats' were needed to review and redesign home defences, especially when foreign invasion threatened, to pin-point weaknesses and hazards, to plot the deployment of enemies and to chronicle the action of battles and sieges. They were becoming instruments and records of war. Those which divulged no sensitive material, but rather paraded his own jurisdiction and achievements, Henry would hang on his walls to impress his subjects and the representatives of rival courts.[4]

Where there was water drawn on maps, cartographers were wont to add ships, not just as ornament but to identify the areas of river and sea. Some of the most accomplished of the cartographic ships drawn for Henry were to be found in 'plats' of Dover and Calais. The view of Dover presented in 1538 to the king by the surveyor of works there, John Thompson, is dominated by its ships, two of which have been inset into the vellum from other sheets to add extra naval presence.[5] These three-masted vessels of the smaller kind, with crews active on board, are drawn in well-observed detail, possibly by the military engineer Richard Lee.[6]

In two versions of Calais harbour dating from the 1540s and usually associated with Lee or with a later surveyor of

1   BL, Cotton MS Augustus I.i.18. The French raid on Brighton, 1545, drawn by Anthony Anthony

works in Calais, Thomas Pettyt, the flotillas are equally splendid, though rather less prominent, and done with informed precision of line and the occasional flourish of heraldry and flag.[7]

It is illuminating that when men at court re-worked for Henry a plat drawn on site by John Rogers of the defence modifications proposed in Ambleteuse, near Boulogne, the plain functional ships of the forthright Rogers were, it seems, transformed for the king into exuberant (if clumsily drawn) craft overloaded with the detailing of figureheads, crosses of St George, ships' ladders, anchors and ropes.[8]

It is to ships such as these that the drawings of Anthony are most closely analogous. Surveyors and military engineers were required to make, or to have made, presentation drawings to please their king in which it might prove expedient to make ships as eye-catching as possible. Anthony was part of this milieu. He would, for example, have been familiar with Rogers, who was made a clerk of the ordnance in February 1544, before being ordered away a few months later to be surveyor of works in Boulogne,[9] and with Lee, who was redeveloping the fortifications of Calais when Anthony was supplying its ordnance.[10] Another leading map-maker, Richard Cavendish, had been a master gunner and may well have been known to Anthony.[11] It now seems clear, moreover, that Anthony was himself a maker of plats. Three surviving coloured drawings in the nature of picture-maps may be confidently attributed to him.

In July 1545, not long probably before he embarked on the 'declaration of the Kynges Majesties owne nave', Anthony drew and painted his version of an attack by a French fleet on Brighton (fig. 1).[12] A comparison of various features which appear in the Anthony Roll and the Brighton drawing identifies the hand as Anthony's, in particular the shape and shading of the ships, the drawing of rigging, streamers and oars, the representation of sea in heightened strips of colour below the hulls streaked with arcs of black waves, the arrangement and number of flags, and the hang of the spars on the four-masted Brighton ship which corresponds exactly to the standard pattern chosen by Anthony for his Roll.

The picture of Brighton bears the date 'Julye 1545' and inscriptions suggest an actual event. In the summer of 1514 Admiral Prégent brought a French force ashore at Brighton to pillage and burn before being beaten back to sea by local musters. Whether, as reported by some chroniclers, a similar assault on Brighton occurred in 1545 is not certain,

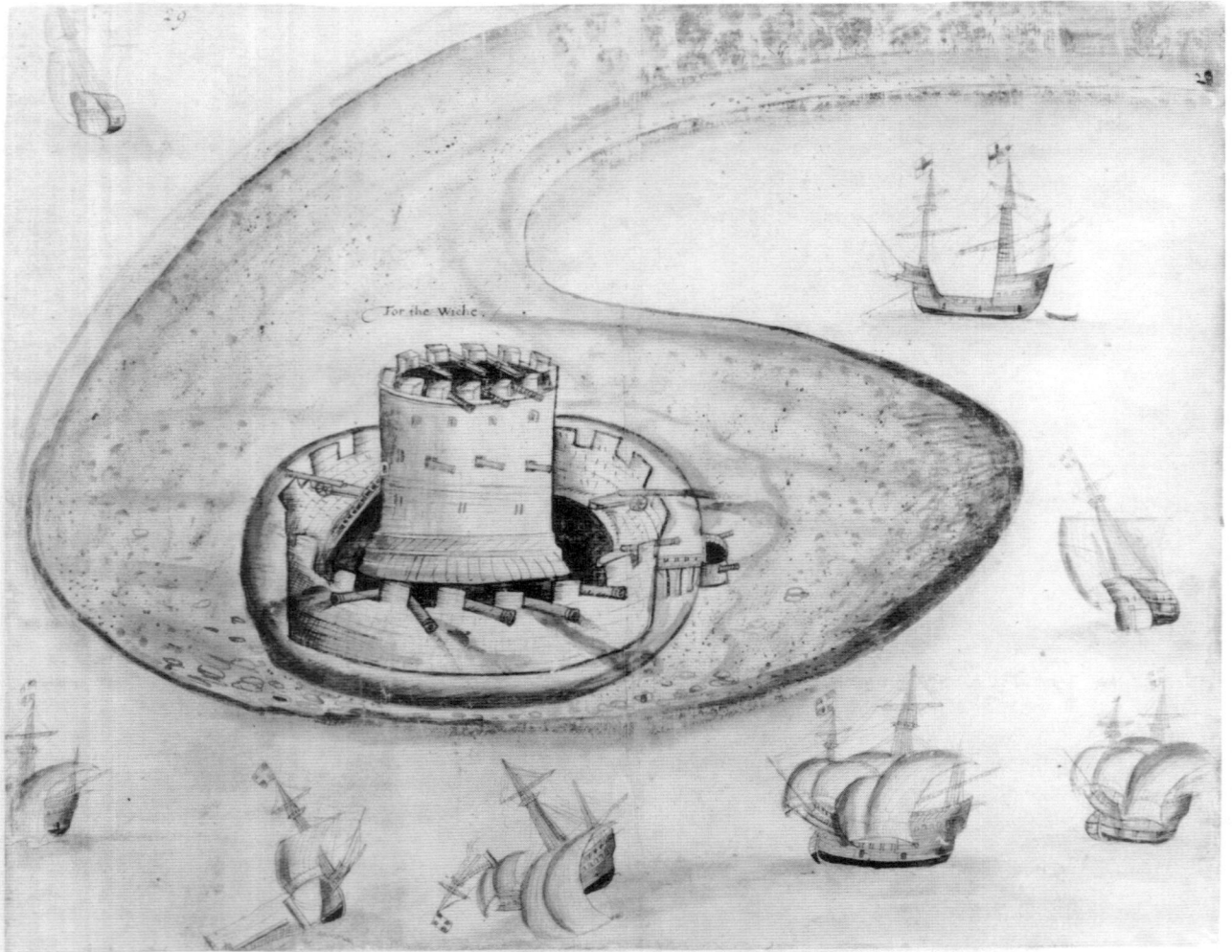

2   Bl, Cotton MS Augustus I.i.29. Coloured drawing of a fortification, believed to be by Anthony Anthony. The added inscription 'For the Wiche' suggests a connection with the Wych Channel in Poole Harbour, Dorset

although an attack was made on neighbouring Seaford. Opinion is divided on whether Anthony's drawing depicts the historical event of 1514 or a supposed one in 1545.[13] His writing of a chronicle marks him as a man with a sense of history, but the 1514 incursion must have been an incident of his childhood, and there appears no reason why he would illustrate it in 1545 except possibly in celebration of one of the king's earlier successes over the French fleet at a time when Henry had just driven off the French from Portsmouth. It seems more credible that Anthony believed he was depicting a recent 1545 occurrence, even if there was some confusion with events at Seaford, and that his purpose was to direct attention to weaknesses in coastal defences.

An illustration of another French naval attack, this time on a small, multi-gunned coastal fort, possibly designed for the Wych Channel in Poole Harbour, also appears to be in Anthony's hand (fig. 2).[14] His third plat, made in early October 1539, is a pictorial account of a proposed route out of the Low Countries for Henry's bride-to-be, Anne of Cleves (fig. 3).[15] Worked up from other maps (especially a rough sketch of the Zuiderzee itinerary made by the shipmasters John a Borough and Richard Couche),[16] it was a 'show' drawing for Henry and Cromwell in their dealings with the ambassadors from Cleves. Anthony took pains, therefore, with tidy geography and a reassuring display of English ships.[17]

Much of Anthony's life was spent close to ships. From his place of work at the Tower and from his residence in the neighbouring parish of St Botolph without Aldgate, he was well placed to observe at close quarters the diverse and abundant traffic of the Thames. As a brewer, with a brewhouse in the London docks (called pertinently the Ship) he provisioned ships with beer, staple beverage of sailors, and exported it by ship. As an officer of the king's ordnance he supplied ships with their munitions and arranged the transport of arms and equipment by ship. He was serving at a time when improvements in artillery were in large part determining changes to the design of ships: the positioning of gun ports, the siting of guns to avoid instability and to achieve forward fire, the re-thinking of beam width, castle height and rigging

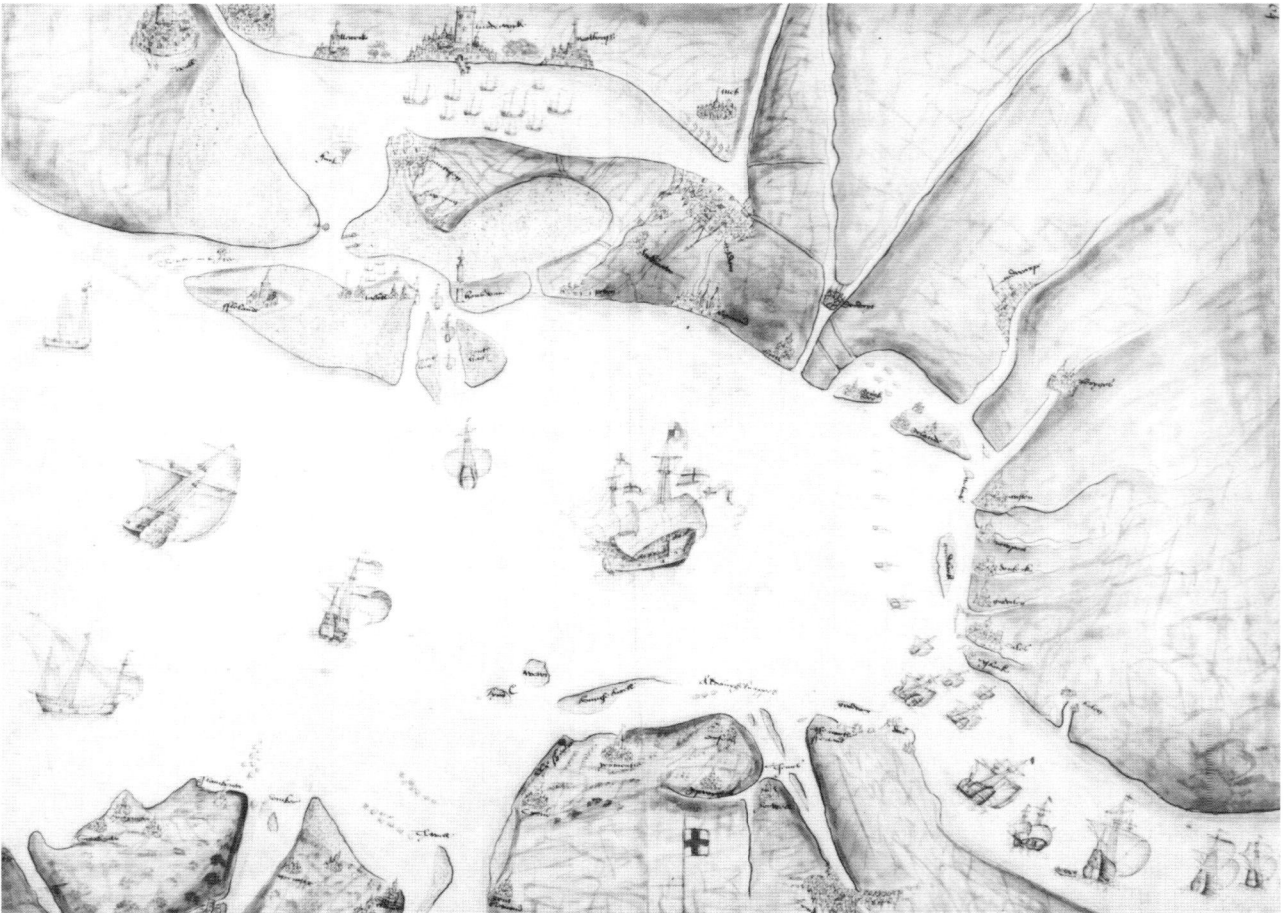

3   BL, Cotton MS Augustus I.ii.64. Projected route for Anne of Cleves's passage from the Low Countries, 1539, drawn by Anthony Anthony

to make ships with better firepower more manoeuvrable. The appearance of ships must have been often in his mind.

Anthony's Roll was completed and delivered to the king sometime in 1546. When it was started and how long it took him can only be guessed. It must surely have been the work of many weeks for a self-trained artist who was taking commendable care, until flagging over the lesser row barges of the third part. Sudden changes in the tone of his colours or in details of design may be detected here and there, which probably mark enforced, perhaps lengthy, stoppages. At the end of the third main membrane of the first roll, between the *Christopher of Bremen* and the *Trinity Harry*, the changes in style and palette are most marked.[18] After one set view of each boat belonging to the eleven ships up to this point, a different view is used for thirty-four ships thereafter. The sea becomes bluer but loses white highlights. On flags the *HR* monogram becomes for a while a regular feature, and three small fleurs-de-lis are mostly replaced by a single large one. The presence of the *Mary Rose* does not compel a starting date before 19 July 1545 when she went down off Portsmouth; until the middle of 1549 there seemed a realistic prospect of raising her and restoring her to a principal position in the fleet. We are given portraits of the *Antelope*, the *Tiger*, the *Bull* and the *Hart*, still being built at Deptford in March 1546 (the *Hart* was at sea by October), but not of the *Galley Blanchard*, captured from the French on 18 May 1546.[19] There seem to be no other visual hints as to dating.

Anthony's sheets of vellum were cropped to a standard width of 27½ ins [70 cm]. Since the finished work was to be in roll form, uniformity in the height of sheets was not an essential and measurements range from 34¼ to 37¾ ins [87 to 96 cm], with one sheet exceptionally shallow at 31 ins [79 cm], a half sheet (17¾ ins [45 cm]) to conclude the second roll, and small, make-up strips at the foot of the first roll and to provide his overall introduction which was probably done when everything else had been completed. Virtually nothing was wasted from a total of seventeen membranes, suggesting careful planning on Anthony's part.

While the sheets were still separate he marked on them his lay-out guide, with pricked holes fixing the intersections of the rulings which would contain his pictures and his text. Most of these prickings subsequently became the location for decorative florets and fleurs-de-lis. He sketched out his ships with plummet, painted them and added the pen-and-ink strapwork, rubrics and supplementary ornament. That all this was done before the sheets were stuck together is confirmed by, for example, the disappearance of the pencilled tip of the *Bull*'s masthead beneath an affixing overlap,[20] and the rather clumsy removal of a corner of the *Saker*'s allotted space to avoid the loss of a marginal rubric under the join.[21] The text was entered after the glueing of the sheets; the lists detailing the *Peter*'s complement are written across the seam between two membranes.[22] Elsewhere words have been written over paint.

Rubrics, titles and incidental decorations are in red or black except for the *Henry Grace à Dieu*, the *Mary Rose* and the *Peter*, which are dignified with unburnished gold.[23] A surprising amount of such gold is used on the ships themselves, where it appears not only on heraldic devices but for the highlighting of ships' timbers and anchors, and as basic cross-hatching. Silver has been applied to strengthen the whites of banners and streamers, and on the cannon, but it has oxidized to black. Anthony's colours, which include azurite, sap green, vermilion, indigo, ochre and white lead (which has not oxidized), are painted mostly in washes over sketched outlines of plummet. Ships' timber is in general light brown, deepened into shading at stem and stern to give a satisfactory three-dimensional effect, though masts and oars may be dark brown, red or orange. Red is used to pick out some ship decoration and for most of the anchors; black for bilges and to outline other features, especially the cannons, with strong contours. There is yellow on the reverse of streamers, white lead on the furled sails, green in the barrels of guns. Anthony's seas, bands of colour sometimes undulating, sometimes flat across the sheet, are in certain sections of the Roll a greyish green, and in others a richer blue. Above his horizontal guideline to fix the meeting of ship's hull and water he has generally topped up his sea to a more distant horizon with another band of, mostly, pale green which rarely matches the rest and by which he has managed to invent his own very pleasing distancing effect.

For the first two ships, the *Henry Grace à Dieu* and the *Mary Rose*, Anthony appears to have had independent drawings to copy. Both are marked up with a rectangular grid of the kind familiar in picture transfer. He seems to have found the system unmanageable or unsatisfactory because after these two ships he was content with free copying from the ships above, each new one adapted to accord with the particulars he had. Thus, the French-built *Salamander* and *Unicorn*, taken as prizes at Leith in 1544, have been given their handsome eponymous figureheads, and the prominent stern and quarter galleries of the *Greyhound*, the *Jennet*, the *Lion* and the *Dragon* have been drawn in with rather an exaggerated emphasis.

The result of Anthony's method is that the ships give the impression of a formulaic pattern. As in the *Embarkation*, the vessels sail persistently from left to right before the observer's oblique view. The spars all hang to a set, unchanging arrangement. Banks of oars all incline alike, rather forward, in mid-stroke. Boats are towed obediently behind.

With the *Galley Subtle*, so substantially different from the rest of the king's ships, something special was needed and Anthony achieved probably the most competent picture of the collection. The artist faced here a new challenge of untypical lines, oars and a visible crew. Perhaps he was well-acquainted with the craft, or he may have been copying from some good model drawing.

At the end of the 17th century the first and third rolls entered the collection of Samuel Pepys.[24] A comparison between these two, converted at that time into book form, and the second roll, still in its original form, demonstrates that Pepys was more interventionist than has been previously assumed. After cutting up the rolls and pasting the segments on to guards, adding new vellum borders above and below where these were needed to achieve a standard page size, Pepys and his assistants extended on to this new vellum those of Anthony's red and gold florets which had been truncated by their scissors. Furthermore, they introduced their own double red lines to frame the space for each ship and, with fleurs-de-lis added at the corners, to box inscriptions with imposing cartouches; and they had no compunction in applying these embellishments to both new and original vellum alike.

Anthony Anthony's name has been linked with three professional artists, but of these connections only one is certain. Anthony was close enough to Vincent Volpe, one of Henry VIII's principal painters, to be appointed an executor of his will when Volpe died in 1536.[25] Volpe had carried out decorative painting for the king's ships, but in the only surviving drawing firmly attributed to him, a picture-map of harbour works proposed for Dover in 1532, his portrayal of ships – sketchy, characterless vessels – suggests scant artistic interest in them.[26]

When Holbein's will of 1543 was discovered 1860, its reference to a 'Mr Anthony, the Kynges Servaunte, of Grenwiche' ('that he shalbe contented for all other thynges betwene hym and me') was construed by W.H. Black probably to indicate Anthony Anthony of the ordnance.[27] But 'Anthony' as forename or surname was not uncommon in Tudor London and Anthony Anthony is not known to have had any specific connection with Greenwich. An alternative claim has been made for Anthony Toto, another of the king's painters.[28]

It is not clear who invented the sibling relationship between Anthony Anthony and the Flemish artist and cartographer Cornelis Anthonisz. or Anthoniszoon. Anthony Anthony's father was William Anthony, whose will named no other son.[29] Cornelis was probably the son of Anthonis Egbertson and Annetje, daughter of the Amsterdam artist Jacob Corneliszoon van Oostzanen.[30] Kinship of some kind between Anthony and Cornelis is not, presumably, impossible, but there is little evidence that they were connected at all.

In 1939 Dr Nicholas Beets put forward claims that Cornelis Anthonisz. was responsible for various major Tudor paintings, including the Hampton Court *Embarkation*. In a footnote to his article Beets wrote: 'In that year [1546], the King received from one of his Officers of the ordnance – whose name, curiously, might indicate a brother of Cornelis Anthonisz. – Anthony Anthony, a beautiful book decorated with miniatures.'[31] Sir Geoffrey Callender, reporting the conclusions of Beets to a British audience, took up the conjectural relationship and consolidated it: 'Cornelis Anthoniszoon had a brother Anthonis Anthoniszoon. In this collocation of syllables, to an English tongue so unacceptable, students of naval history and nautical research will hardly recognize their old friend Anthony Anthony.'[32] Subsequent authorities have accepted the relationship.[33]

Beets saw persuasive similarities between the acknowledged works of Cornelis Anthonisz. and features of four paintings now at Hampton Court: the *Meeting of Henry VIII and the Emperor Maximilian*, the *Battle of the Spurs*, the *Embarkation of Henry VIII at Dover*, and the *Field of the Cloth of Gold*. His attribution of these paintings to Cornelis has not, however, been generally accepted.[34] In the background of the painting of the *Battle of the Spurs* there is a detailed prospect of the walled town of Thérouanne, labelled in the Dutch form 'Terwaen'. Beets pointed out that this prospect is virtually identical to a view of that town which occurs in a woodcut made by Cornelis Anthonisz., and bearing his monogram, portraying the siege of Thérouanne by Emperor Charles V in 1553. From this Beets concluded that painting and woodcut must be in the same hand, that is, the hand of Cornelis, ignoring the possibility that both might be copied from a common source.[35]

If Cornelis was painting in England in the 1540s, making some contribution to the Hampton Court pictures – conceivably, his view of 'Terwaen' to the *Battle of the Spurs* – and if there was a connection with Anthony Anthony, he might be in a position to assist the artistic efforts of the latter. But no echo of Cornelis is apparent in the Roll, unless it be in the relative fluency of the *Galley Subtle* and its crew. With some ingenuity a number of parallels, made intriguing by the coincidence of name, can be discovered between Anthony's 1545 painting of Brighton and a 1542 woodcut by Cornelis Anthonisz. illustrating an attack by Emperor Charles V on Algiers in October 1541, making it just possible that a sight of Algiers influenced Anthony in painting Brighton. But any such link remains tenuous and uncertain.

Pictures of ships in Henry's England ranged from the single unnamed vessel, such as the five-foot-high stylized carrack painted onto the wall of the church of St Dunstan, Snargate in Kent, to sizeable squadrons, as in the *Embarkation* or the lost Cowdray Park painting (known from Basire's engraving) of the 1545 action off Portsmouth in which some of the craft may be identified. Among these pictures the ships of the Anthony Roll are extraordinary in giving us an unprecedented, fully identified, fully illustrated list of the king's whole fleet. Anthony's standing as a draughtsman does not rest on the Roll alone. He was also a 'plat' maker, and more of his work in this field may be awaiting discovery in future examinations of Tudor maps. To the occupations of ordnance officer and brewer must be added for Anthony a role as one of the established makers of show drawings for the king.

Notes

1. P.M. Barber, 'England I: Pageantry, defense, and government: maps at court to 1550', in D. Buisseret, ed., *Monarchs, Ministers and Maps* (Chicago and London, 1992), pp. 42–5. I am grateful to my colleague Peter Barber of the BL Map Library for many useful points and suggestions made in discussion.

2. It is clear from the sea colours, the finish of the ships, and the artist's selection of flags that the *Mary James* does not belong in the same group as the *Lartique*, the *Mary Thomas*, the *Hoy Bark*, and the *George*, but with the *Falcon* and the *Saker*. Since Anthony had mapped out the first membrane of the third roll to include at the top his introductory statement, it was much easier for him to remove the *Mary James* from the bottom of the sheet than the *Falcon* or the *Saker*. He made his detaching cut along the baseline of the *Saker* drawing so that the area intended by the original plan for the *Saker* text could be used as the 'underlap' to stick the *Mary James* to the bottom of the membrane whose last ships were the *Hoy Bark* and the *George*. See also below n. 21.

3. For the dating of the picture to c.1545 see C. Lloyd and S. Thurley, *Henry VIII: Images of a Tudor King* (1990), p. 120, no. 22 and frontispiece (colour plate).

4. P.M. Barber, 'Henry VIII and mapmaking', in D.R. Starkey, ed., *Henry VIII: A European Court in England* (1991), pp. 145–51; and his 'Pageantry, defense, and government', pp. 32–7, 42–4.

5. BL, Cotton MS Augustus I.i.22,23 (*LP*, XXI, ii, App. no. 40).

6. The identity of the artist of the Dover picture-map (as with many of the 'plats' in the Cotton collection) has long been the subject of discussion. See A. Macdonald, 'Plans of Dover harbour in the sixteenth century', *Archaeologia*

Cantiana, XLIX (1937), pp. 111–14, plate 1. E. Croft-Murray and P. Hulton, *Catalogue of British Drawings*, I (British Museum, 1960), p. xxiv, where a case for a Flemish hand is put. L.R. Shelby, *John Rogers: Tudor Military Engineer* (Oxford, 1967), p. 21 n. 1. H.M. Colvin *et al.*, eds, *The History of the King's Works* (1963–82), III, pp. 13–14; IV, pp. 410–11, 744–5. Barber, 'Henry VIII and mapmaking', pp. 147–8, and his 'Pageantry, defense, and government', p. 49 n. 60. P.D.A. Harvey, *Maps in Tudor England* (1993), pp. 31–5, fig. 18 (colour).

7.   BL, Cotton MS Augustus I.ii.57A and Augustus I.ii.70 (*LP*, XX, ii, App. no. 36; XXI, ii, App. no. 30). Croft-Murray & Hulton, *British Drawings*, I, p. xxiii. P. Cowburn, *The Warship in History* (New York, 1965; London, 1966), p. 61. Colvin, *King's Works*, III, pp. 345–55, 358 n. 3, 401–4. F. Howard, *Sailing Ships of War 1400–1860* (Greenwich, 1979), pp. 46–7, figs. 55–9. Barber, 'Pageantry, defense, and government', pp. 41, 49 n. 60, 54 n. 124. The eccentricity in both the Dover and the Calais maps of having pink seas has sometimes prompted a conclusion that they were drawn by the same hand. But the styles of ship drawing do not match. It may be that the pigments of different artists have simply aged in the same way to pale pink, especially if these maps were chosen for wall display by the king. It seems unlikely that an artist who made his Dover ships so prominent and revelled in peopling them with sailors would be happy with the less conspicuous and totally un-manned Calais ships.

8.   BL, Cotton MS Augustus I.ii.73 (*LP*, XXI, i, no. 508(4)); the re-worked map is BL, Cotton MS Augustus I.ii.8 (*LP*, XXI, i, no. 508(3)). See Shelby, *John Rogers*, pp. 78–9, plates 17 and 18. Shelby conjectures that the hand of Henry himself may possibly be seen in the ships of the later map.

9.   *LP*, XIX, i, no. 141 (72). Shelby, *John Rogers*, pp. 50–2, 55.

10. *LP*, XVII, no. 880 (286).

11. Colvin, *King's Works*, IV, pp. 380, 689, 743–7. E.G.R. Taylor, *The Mathematical Practitioners of Tudor and Stuart England* (Cambridge, 1954), p. 169.

12. BL, Cotton MS Augustus I.i.18 (*LP*, XXI, ii, App. no. 6).

13. *VCH Sussex*, I (1905), p. 518 and facing illustr.; VII (1940), p. 245. J. Gairdner 'On a contemporary drawing of the burning of Brighton in the time of Henry VIII', *TRHS*, 3rd ser. I (1907), pp. 19–31. A. Anscombe, 'Prégent de Bidoux's raid in Sussex in 1514 and the Cotton MS. *Augustus I (i)*, 18' *TRHS*, 3rd ser. VIII (1914), pp. 103–11. L.G. Carr-Laughton, 'The burning of Brighton by the French', *TRHS*, 3rd ser. X (1916), pp. 167–73. Loades, *Tudor Navy*, p. 134. Harvey, *Maps in Tudor England*, p. 47, fig 27 (colour plate). Rodger, *Safeguard of the Sea*, pp. 183, 545 n. 21.

14. BL, Cotton MS Augustus I.i.29 (*LP*, XXI, ii, App. no. 53(2)). The inscription 'For the Wiche' has been plausibly linked to the area of Poole Harbour, Dorset, crossed by the Wych Channel: see the *Catalogue of the Manuscript Maps, Charts and Plans and of the Topographical Drawings in the British Museum*, I (1844), p. 75. During the late 1530s and early 1540s various forts were proposed at different points along the south coast, few of which were actually built. Anthony's design may have been one of those considered for Poole Harbour before the construction of the blockhouse on Brownsea Island, c. 1545–1547. But cf. Colvin, *King's Works*, IV, p. 527 n. 10.

15. BL, Cotton MS Augustus I.ii.64 (*LP*, XXI, ii, App. no. 23).

16. BL, Cotton MS Augustus I.ii.29 (*LP*, XXI, ii, App. no. 1). John a Borough and Richard Couche were sent in September 1539 on a secret mission to the Zuiderzee to survey the route: *LP*, XIV, ii, nos 309, 799.

17. For a discussion of the Anne of Cleves maps, BL Cotton MSS Augustus I.ii.29 and I.ii.64, see Barber, 'Henry VIII and map-making', p. 149, with plate; and his 'Pageantry, defense, and government', pp. 39, 52 n. 102 (where the attribution to Anthony is first proposed). Among the features that seem to characterize the drawing of Anthony are ports which have the visible 'jamb' on the wrong side; distinctive arched windows; the scrawl of waves below hulls; the shading of the ships, especially in the stern; the stippling of beaches; the rough outlining of 'fields' by zigzagging brush-strokes; the diagonal red (or sometimes gold) decorative bars along the sides of ships' castles.

18. PL 2991, between sheets at pp. 22–3 and 26–7.

19. *LP*, XXI, i, no. 498, referring to 'the 4 new ships a making at Depforde, 1,000 t.'; identified by Oppenheim (*History*, p. 51) as the *Antelope*, *Tiger*, *Bull* and *Hart*. *LP*, XXI, ii, nos 123, 134. Loades, *Tudor Navy* p. 137. See also John Bennell below, p. 35.

20. BL, Add. MS 22047, between mm. 2 and 3.

21. PL 2991, pp. 54–5. Because of the transfer of the *Mary James*, the second sheet of the third roll had to begin with the lists for the *Saker*. Faced with this new arrangement Anthony evidently miscalculated and began too high on the page, with enough space above for a glueing overlap only if a section of the *Saker*'s sea was cut away. See also above n. 2.

22. PL 2991, pp. 6–7.

23. I am grateful to Dr Michelle Brown for helpful advice concerning pigments.

24. See technical description above pp. 6–9.

25. E. Auerbach, 'Vincent Volpe, the King's painter', *Burlington Magazine*, XCII (1950), pp. 222–7; the text of Volpe's will is given on p. 226.

26. BL, Cotton MS Augustus I.i.19. Cf. *LP*, V, no. 1548.

27. W.H. Black, 'On the date and other circumstances of the death of the painter Hans Holbein as disclosed by the discovery of his will', *Archaeologia*, XXXIX (1863), pp. 272–6; the text of Holbein's will is given by A.W. Franks, *ibid.*, p. 2. Black's case for Anthony Anthony is supported by Auerbach, 'Vincent Volpe', p. 227.

28. J.G. Nichols, 'Notices of the contemporaries and successors of Holbein', *Archaeologia*, XXXIX (1863), p. 36.

29. For biographical details see C.S. Knighton above, p. 3.

30. F.J. Dubiez, *Cornelis Anthoniszoon van Amsterdam: zijn leven en werken ca. 1507–1553* (Amsterdam, 1969) pp. 9–13. Robert W. Karrow jr, *Mapmakers of the Sixteenth Century and their Maps* (Winnetka, Illinois, 1993), p. 42.

31. N. Beets, 'Cornelis Anthonisz.', *Oud-Holland*, LVI (1939), p. 183 n. 1. I am grateful to my colleague Rachel Stockdale for help with translation from the Dutch.

32. G.A.R. Callender, 'Cornelis Anthoniszoon', *MM*, XXV (1939), p. 444.

33. E.g. Sir Oliver Millar in *The Tudor, Stuart and Early Georgian Pictures in the Collection of Her Majesty The Queen* (1963), I, p. 55. S. Anglo in 'The Hampton Court painting of the Field of the Cloth of Gold considered as an historical document', *The Antiquaries Journal*, XLVI (1966), p. 305 n. 2. M. Russell, *Visions of the Sea: Hendrick C. Vroom and the origins of Dutch Marine Painting* (Leiden, 1983), pp. 42–3, followed by P. Kirsch, *The Galleon* (1990), p. 14, and in turn by Rodger, *Safeguard of the Sea*, p. 548 n. 35.

34. For a discussion of these paintings and their dating see Millar, *Tudor, Stuart and Early Georgian Pictures*, pp. 54–5, nos 22–25. Lloyd & Thurley, *Henry VIII*, p. 120, nos 20–3. Millar concedes that some of the figures come 'stylistically close to Anthonisz'.

35. Beets, 'Cornelis Anthonisz.', pp. 163–6, 184.

V   The Flags

(i) Function and heraldry
Timothy Wilson

The flags on the Anthony Roll are an amazing display. They are the most elaborate source we have for the flags flown on the ships of King Henry VIII, being richer in visual detail than all other sources put together. They are, however, when compared with the fragments of knowledge we have from other sources, in some aspects surprising.

The most spectacular flags in Anthony's drawings are the streamers that fly from one or more of the mastheads of every ship. These were as enormous as they look, like the streamer 51 yards long which had been supplied by the king's painter John Brown for the main mast of the *Henry Grace à Dieu* in 1514.[1] They all have St George's cross at the hoist, with the fly divided horizontally green and white. The cross of St George was by this time the principal national emblem of England, used in various combinations in innumerable flags and standards on land and sea;[2] on merchant ships, plain flags of St George's cross were often flown on mastheads. The use of the Tudor livery colours green and white[3] marks the ships out as in the king's service and in general these very large streamers seem to have been distinctive of royal ships.[4] They can hardly have been practicable at sea and were presumably flown when dressing ship for display or celebration.

Many of the streamers and some of the other flags have dark marks on the white ground, which at first sight appear to be heraldic charges. These are in silver paint, which has oxidized and turned a disfiguring black. The artist appears to have applied, particularly on the large ships in the first roll, highlighting in silver and gold; these marks may not have been intended to represent anything beyond the brilliant fluttering effect of flags, some of which would have contained metallic thread or paint.[5]

Unlike the ubiquitous streamers, the rectangular masthead flags seem to indicate a rudimentary system of command. In Henry VIII's reign, the foundations were being laid of what was in the following century to become an elaborate system of squadronal distinction by masthead flags and ensigns.[6] In 1545, the lord admiral, Viscount Lisle, had issued sailing orders for a fleet: the lord admiral was to carry a banner of the king's arms in his main top, and a flag of St George in his foretop; every ship in his division was to fly a flag of St George at the main. The admiral of the van squadron was to fly St George's cross at main and fore, and ships under his command at the fore only; the admiral of the wing squadron was to fly the same flag at mizzen and bonaventure mizzen, and the ships under his command the same flag at the mizzen.[7] The selection of masthead flags in the Roll seems to be loosely, and not coherently, based on a similar system. The *Henry Grace à Dieu* has flags of St George's cross[8] on three mastheads and, at the main, a flag with the royal arms[9] at the hoist and St George's cross in the fly. I have not found any other representation of such a flag, but an exchequer account of 7–10 Henry V (1420–2) mentions for the *Trinity Royal* 'baner de consilio de armis regis [et] Sancti Georgii' (a banner of council of the king's arms and of St George), which could perhaps have been of similar design.[10] Heraldic standards of the nobility had long had St George's cross at the hoist and various heraldic devices in the fly, so the combination might not have seemed as heraldically outlandish as it does in retrospect. The overall pattern of flags on this ship, the largest in the fleet, is sufficiently close to the 1545 instructions to suggest that this masthead flag was intended as a flag both royal and national, denoting the presence or command of the lord admiral.

The *Henry Grace à Dieu* is also distinguished from the other ships by having at the bowsprit a small pennant of St George's cross. In general the Roll does not give the special status to flags on ensign staff and jackstaff that they were to acquire in 17th-century and subsequent naval usage. However, this pennant may be seen as a sort of predecessor of the union jack (invented in 1606), which was to become the prime characteristic of royal ships.

The flag of St George's cross and the royal arms is also flown, at the fore, by the *Mary Rose*, the second-largest ship in the fleet, and presumably thought of as the vice-admiral's ship. She has the mainmast bare of flags.[11] At mizzen and bonaventure mizzen are flags with St George's cross at the hoist and the fly of one of the livery colours, green; this is a combination described by a 20th-century herald Sir George Bellew as 'unlikely',[12] but Anthony has clearly and deliberately drawn a number of variants of such vertically divided flags and, even if he had never seen flags exactly of this pattern, he must have thought them plausible.

The third ship listed, the *Peter*, flies at the fore a cross of St George; the mainmast is bare, and on her other two masts she flies flags of St George impaling green. The next eight ships in the first roll have the mainmast bare, and flags of St

George's cross on the other three masts. The eight following have a single St George's flag at the fore.[13] The vessels in the second roll all (except for the *Galley Subtle*, which is single-masted) have a single flag of St George's cross at the fore. In the third roll only the *Falcon*, the first of the pinnaces, and the *Double Rose*, the first of the row barges, have masthead flags, in each case St George's cross at the main.

There is clearly some vestige of system in these masthead flags and they cannot be interpreted as merely decorative. However, no ship in the Roll has a masthead at the mizzen or bonaventure mizzen alone, as is stipulated in Lisle's instructions; and whatever system underlies the arrangement seems incoherently carried through.

The most numerous flags in the Roll are those set on low flagstaffs along the decks. The first three ships are shown with rectangular flags, approximately twice as long as they are broad. The remainder are all approximately square, which accords with usage on land and with other evidence for deck-level flags on Tudor ships.[14] It is unclear whether the largest ships really had different-shaped deck flags, or whether Anthony corrected his practice after drawing the first three.

In the reign of Elizabeth I striped ensigns were to come to be widely used at an ensign staff at the stern, and representational flags were to fall out of fashion. In the Roll, although the early impact of the English Reformation[15] has eliminated the banners with pictures of saints which were so frequent in the bills and inventories of the early years of Henry VIII's reign, the decks of the grander ships are still lined with gorgeous displays of royal cyphers and badges[16] on expensively-made flags. In some cases, most spectacularly on the *Galley Subtle*, these deck banners are supplemented with painted shields.[17]

Not all the deck banners can be easily made out, but they include the following: St George's cross, alone, or impaling variations of the Tudor livery colours; the Tudor livery colours, usually striped, but sometimes combined in other ways; yellow and white stripes, the significance of which is unexplained;[18] the English royal arms, alone or combined with the livery colours;[19] the arms of France (three fleurs-de-lis), or a single fleur-de-lis;[20] banners apparently with a rose; and banners with Henry's *HR* cypher.

Anthony Anthony's expertise was in ordnance, rather than in flags and heraldry; and it does not seem likely that all the ships in his Roll were drawn from life. There is clearly a degree to which the purpose of the flags in the drawings – as it was in real life – is ornamental. It is therefore possible that some of the flags which seem heraldically odd, or difficult to make sense of, are mistakes. However, it does not seem likely that Anthony would have drawn flags that were manifestly implausible to a contemporary eye experienced in looking at ships, and we may regard the flags so lavishly painted as essentially reliable depictions of what could have been flown on Henry VIII's ships.

Acknowledgement

I am grateful to Peter Barber, John Cherry, John Goodall, David Loades, Richard Luckett, Lisa Monnas, Bruce Nicolls, Ann Payne, Michael Siddons, Barbara Tomlinson; and above all to Charles Knighton, for much erudite advice tirelessly and cheerfully given.

Notes

1   BL, Stowe MS 146, f. 142. T. Wilson, *Flags at Sea* (2nd edn., 1999), pp. 12, 93. See E. Auerbach, *Tudor Artists* (1954), p. 144. A. Payne, 'Sir Thomas Wriothesley and his heraldic artists', in M.P. Brown and S. McKendrick, eds., *Illuminating the Book: Makers and Interpreters. Essays in Honour of Janet Backhouse* (London and Toronto, 1998), pp. 148–53. See also below, p. 117.

2.   W.G. Perrin, *British Flags* (Cambridge, 1922), pp. 35–41 T. Wilson, 'Saint George in Tudor and Stuart England', M.Phil. dissertation, The Warburg Institute, University of London (1976), pp. 18–26. Note also the 'Discourse on the history of the cross of Saint George', written for Pepys by John Knight and presented in 1678: PL 2877, pp. 402–36.

3.   Livery colours were the colours in which a lord clothed his retainers; they were often the principal metal and colour in a shield of arms, but this was not always the case. Green and white were much used in the pageantry of the Tudor kings and queens. See S. Friar, *A New Dictionary of Heraldry* (1987), pp. 218–19.

4.   In other ship portrayals of the period, streamers are sometimes shown with St George's cross throughout, and often split into tails at the fly. There are split streamers of St George's cross throughout on two ships in the plan of Calais by Thomas Pettyt (*c*. 1545–50) in BL, Cotton MS Augustus I.ii.57a, reproduced by Howard, *Sailing Ships of Flags at Sea*, pp. 12–13.

5. Sir George Bellew, 'An examination of the flags and heraldry on the contemporary picture of the *Mary Rose*', *The Coat of Arms*, new series, 5, no. 122 (1982), pp. 47–53, supposed that these dark markings are subsequent defacements of the manuscript, but this does not seem probable. I am indebted to Ann Payne for advice on this issue. Some of the gold highlightings over the centre of crosses of St George, for example on the *Swallow*, might have been intended as roses or other heraldic charges.

6. Perrin, *British Flags*, pp. 74–124, and Wilson, *Flags at Sea*, pp. 12–26.

7. Instructions of 10 August 1545, printed in full below, p. 159.

8. The flag at the fore looks as if it contains two St George's crosses alongside each other, but this was probably not intended. Several of the flags in the Roll are similarly difficult to 'read' in the fly beyond a fold, rendering the artist's intention uncertain.

9. In this and all the other flags in the Roll, the royal arms are strictly speaking back to front, with the three lions in the first and fourth quarterings, and the fleurs-de-lis in the second and third. Instances of this arrangement, giving precedence to England over France, are not unknown, but the explanation is probably that, the flags all being drawn blowing to the left, the artist has not, as he should have by heraldic convention done, reversed the quarterings.

10. PRO, E 101/49/29, m. 15. Perrin, *British Flags*, p. 44 gives an abstract of the references to flags in this account.

11. Streamers do not, for this purpose, count as flags. The Pepys manuscripts contain several references showing that, at least by Pepys's time, a 'naked flagstaff' was seen as having definite significance; see Perrin, *British Flags*, p. 95, for a case where King Charles II is shown to have taken a personal interest in this abstruse-sounding issue.

12. Bellew, '*Mary Rose*', pp. 50, 52.

13. The *Mary James*, the last ship in the first roll is unique in its group in having no masthead flags; but as Ann Payne shows (above, p. 20) this illustration was a late adjustment to this position.

14. More elongated proportions for naval flags came into use from the end of the 16th century: Wilson, *Flags at Sea*, p. 86. For the flags associated with Sir Francis Drake preserved at Buckland Abbey, which are the only surviving 16th-century examples in England, see C. Gaskell Brown, *The Battle's Sound. Drake's Drum and the Drake Flags* (Tiverton, 1996).

15. See, for example, J. Phillips, *The Reformation of Images: Destruction of Art in England, 1535–1660* (Berkeley and Los Angeles, 1973); and on St George, Wilson, 'Saint George', pp. 58–9. However, traditional banners with saints, including St George, were used at Henry's funeral: J. Loach, 'The function of ceremonial in the reign of Henry VIII', *Past and Present*, 142 (February 1994), pp. 43–68 (a reference I owe to Charles Knighton). The Reformation does not, however, explain the apparent disuse of the wonderful-sounding streamers with heraldic beasts described in the 1514 inventories: below, pp. 29, 145.

16. It is mildly disappointing to find no examples of flags with badges referring to the name of the ship. The 1514 inventory for the *Peter Pomegranate* includes a banner of St Peter: below, p. 145. But Anthony's *Greyhound*, for example, does not show anything like the 'streamer with a greyhound' supplied to the *Henry Grace à Dieu* in 1514: Wilson, *Flags at Sea*, p. 94. Even figureheads referring to a ship's name seem infrequent, though they can be seen on the *Mary Rose*, *Salamander* and *Unicorn*.

17. The painted shields (pavises) on the *Galley Subtle* show: the royal arms; St George's cross on a field divided diagonally white and green; blue with a golden *H*; and blue with a fleur-de-lis.

18. It does not seem possible to connect this with the personal heraldry of the lord admiral, Viscount Lisle. In the standard attributed to him illustrated in College of Arms MS I 2, p. 136, the primary charge is a lion argent crowned or, which might prompt the supposition that he used white/silver and yellow/gold as his livery colours; but the standard has a fringe marked as or and azure. Since the fringe of a standard is normally an indication of the livery colours, the hypothesis that gold and silver were ever used as Lisle's livery colours looks improbable. See Lord Howard de Walden, *Banners, Standards and Badges from a Tudor Manuscript in the College of Arms* (De Walden Library, 1904), p. 288. I am indebted to John Goodall and Michael Siddons for learned advice on this point.

19. I cannot explain the flag on the *Peter* with the royal arms at the hoist green over blue at the fly.

20. The emblems from the arms of Spain (castles, red lions, pomegranates) which are described in the 1514 inventories (below, pp. 121, 125, 145) have disappeared. Royal heraldry was adjusted as necessary to reflect Henry VIII's matrimonial circumstances.

(ii) Fabric   *Maria Hayward*

On 13 December 1539 the earl of Southampton and Nicholas Wotton wrote to Henry VIII from Calais describing the preparation for Anne of Cleves's passage to England:

> [We] showed my lady the ship prepared for her passage and the other ships trimmed with streamers, banners and flags, and men on the tops, shrouds and yard arms. Ordnance was shot off, and she and all the strangers commended the sight.[1]

Flags were integral to royal pageantry at sea, just as they were on land and with the exception of streamers, the various types of flag were interchangeable between maritime and terrestrial use. The effect they created relied upon a combination of bright colours, striking heraldic designs and the quantity used. The illustrations in the Anthony Roll demonstrate this point admirably. The flags' basic construction was equally simple. Most were double sided and they could be made from either a single or double sheet, the latter sometimes having an interlining. Effects such as quartering and the cross of St George would be created by piecing different coloured fabrics. The Roll illustrates numerous St George's banners and green and white striped flags which would have been pieced. The banners were hand stitched, using either running or back stitch, with various types of seam and simple turned hems.[2] Embroidered flags would tend towards a double-sheet construction to support the motifs' weight while painted banners were often only a single sheet, possibly to compensate for the stiffening effect of the paint layer on the drape of the ground fabric. The pole sleeve, probably with an interlining for added rigidity, was used to hoist the banner or fit it on a flag pole. If a pole was not used, a length of rope could be inserted into the pole sleeve, secured at the top with a toggle.[3]

A range of fibres and weights of fabrics appear in the warrants ordering flags from the Tudor great wardrobe:[4] linen fabric included buckram and Normandy or Vitry canvas, woollen cloths were usually worsteds and silk fabrics ranged from damask to sarsenet.[5] Whichever fibre was chosen, generally the fabric would be tightly woven and lightweight, making it flexible yet durable. However, heavier cloths with less drape would suit small pennants where rigidity was acceptable. Cloth could be white or coloured with mordant or vat dyes. While the great wardrobe, the main fabric repository for the royal household, held large stocks of silk, this was used primarily for clothing and furnishings. Most of the linen was of high quality and intended for use as napery and bed linen and no woollen cloth was stocked. The accounts suggest that fabric was usually purchased for each commission rather than drawing on supplies within the great wardrobe. William Botrye, a London mercer, supplied tuke, buckram, Brussels cloth and camlet worth over £50 for one order of streamers and banners.[6] This reliance on external suppliers could cause problems. On 23 September 1539 William Gonson, keeper of the storehouses at Erith and Deptford, wrote to Thomas Cromwell about the flags for the reception of Anne of Cleves. Although Andrew Wright could supply fourteen streamers in fifteen days, the 180 flags and the 600 pennants were to be made from tuke and 'there is scarcely any to be bought here and it must be procured from Flanders. They cannot be done in less than 80 days after the King's pleasure is known'.[7] It is likely that the banners would have been made of the more expensive silks and wools, with the tuke reserved for the streamers and pennants.

There were two main methods of surface decoration: painting and embroidery. Painting was used most frequently because it was quick and relatively cheap, both important considerations when bulk orders were produced at short notice. However, it was also ephemeral, especially in the maritime environment which combined damp, salty conditions with wind which would repeatedly flex the thin paint layer.[8] Flags with painted designs were usually referred to as being either 'in colours' or 'in metal', such as two banners with crowned portcullises in metal belonging to the *Trinity Sovereign* in 1514.[9] The pigments would have been predominantly mineral in origin as organic pigments would have faded very quickly.[10] The binding media could have been either aqueous, such as glue and egg if protected with a wax coating, or oil based. Metallic effects on banners were created using coloured foils, probably combining tin foil with oil/resin varnishes tinted with verdigris for green or saffron for gold. Many of the flags and streamers decorated with coats of arms and badges that are depicted on the Anthony Roll would have been painted, as it was a very effective means of representing heraldry.

It is quite possible that a thin coating of wax, or wax in combination with a resin, was applied to painted areas or the complete surface to make them more resistant to sea water and rain and this would make the pigments appear brighter.

There are precedents for this. In 1295 the banners and streamer supplied for a privately owned galley built at Newcastle by Master William of Wayneflete were waxed.[11] While there is not direct evidence of this happening to Henry VIII's maritime flags, other objects were waxed, including a protective cover for the litter used by Catherine of Aragon at her coronation.[12] Designs generally consisted of small motifs, such as the painted and gilt motif in the top left corner of the Drake colours, so leaving the flag relatively flexible.

The painters who produced many of these flags worked on a wide variety of items for their royal patrons. In June 1514 Vincent Volpe, a Neapolitan painter in Henry VIII's service, submitted a bill for six streamers, 100 penselles and 50 banners for the *Henry Grace à Dieu* at a cost of £112 19s. 8d.[13] In addition, he produced plats of Rye and Hastings and helped to prepare for the revels held at Greenwich in 1527.[14] The painters also worked on the ships themselves. John Brown received payments of £31 16s. 8d. and £47 9s. 'for painting divers of our ships.'[15] While this instance probably refers to the sides of the ship, other work was possible. The illustrations of the *Unicorn* and the *Salamander* in the Anthony Roll include painted wooden figureheads.

Embroidered decoration tended to be restricted to use on silk and woollen flags. It was a more expensive and slower technique than painting and used expensive materials. Trumpeters accompanied the king in the *Embarkation* picture and their instruments were decorated with banners which were very likely to have been embroidered.[16] A red silk damask standard made for Don John of Austria for the battle of Lepanto in 1571 depicts the Crucifixion on the obverse and the Virgin on the reverse. It is worked with gold and silver metal wrapped thread and coloured silks.[17] The embroidery could be worked directly on to the ground fabric of the flag or as separate motifs. These motifs could be applied to many objects and examples appear in the 1547 inventory of Henry VIII's possessions: 'twoo crownes embrawderid vppon crimesen vellut', 'a flowre deluce embrawderid vppon crimesen vellut' and 'iij skutchions embrodrid with tharmes of Inglonde & Castell'.[18] The accounts are brief and rarely provide specific details of the stitches used. However, in 1514 the *Great Barbara* had ten banners of Spanish work which may refer to Spanish stitch or may reflect Henry's Spanish marriage.[19] Appliqué can be classified as an embroidery technique and it is likely that some of the cheaper, smaller flags were ornamented in this manner.

Evidence for staining as a decorative technique is more limited.[20] The exact definition of staining, as used in the 16th century, is hard to distinguish. Jo Kirby suggests that the colours were applied in an aqueous medium producing a stain on the ground fabric without forming a pigment layer on the surface.[21] The *Trinity Sovereign* had three streamers 'of lynen cloth steyned', which may record the type of decoration but could denote their condition.[22] More positive evidence comes from the payment of £142 4s. 6d. made to John Brown for painting and staining banners and streamers for the *Mary Rose* and the *Peter Pomegranate*.[23] A late 16th-century section of a Spanish linen pennant made for the *San Marco* bears an image of the Crucifixion which may well have been created using a staining technique.[24]

While the design was the key element, flags were often trimmed with expensive silk or metal thread fringes and some had decorative cords and tassels. In February 1510 Elizabeth Worssop, a London silkwoman, provided 'laces with buttons and tassels of silk and gold' for fifteen banners costing £11 0s. 9d. However, such passementarie was not suited to conditions at sea: the silk would tangle and metal threads with a high silver content would tarnish. The 'Cadow fringe' used to edge a large streamer made for the *Henry Grace à Dieu* in 1514 might have been a more robust woollen fringe.[25]

In July 1514 when thirteen of Henry VIII's ships were laid up, their streamers and banners, along with the sails and rigging were delivered to John Hopton, keeper of the navy storehouses at Erith and Deptford. However, when in use the flags and streamers were put in specific places. Streamers were flown from the mast tops while banners were placed on poles along the edge of the deck. The Anthony Roll depicts banners placed along the deck while the *Embarkation to Dover* shows them placed just in the bows in the forecastle. A number of these poles were listed amongst the stores on board, including fifteen 'standard stavers' for flags on the *Mary Rose* and eighteen on the *Peter Pomegranate*.[26] William Hayward, the king's joiner, supplied sixty poles costing 16d. each for the *Henry Grace à Dieu* in 1514, which were painted with oil paint 'in the kinges colours' for a further 6d. each.[27]

Ships heavily decked with flags and streamers, as they are in the Anthony Roll, were seen only on special occasions, in harbour. When at sea they probably only flew one or two flags, denoting their name and allegiance – certainly the long streamers were highly impractical. Flags used on ships were susceptible to physical damage from the wind, fading, water damage, discolouration and mould growth if they were stored wet. This may explain why new banners were ordered for each campaign. Those intended to provide long service would have been made from robust fabrics with pieced or embroidered designs – painted banners were too ephemeral for prolonged use at sea. The Roll undoubtedly represents flags and streamers made from the full range of silk, wool and canvas and which were embroidered, pieced or painted. The banners on or near deck level were likely to have been made of the best materials and decorated with the most expensive techniques and by the more skilled craftsmen. These flags were the most visible, they could have been used on land or sea and were relatively small, so keeping the cost within bounds. In contrast, the streamers were intended to be effective when viewed at a distance and were made from cheaper fabrics, with simpler designs.[28] Ultimately, the flags and streamers depicted on the Roll were intended primarily for show, with their appearance in the short term being more important than durability. Pageantry won out over practicality.

Acknowledgement

I should like to acknowledge the help and advice of Jo Kirby, Lisa Monnas, Timothy Wilson and Charles Knighton.

Notes

1. *LP*, XIV, ii, no. 677. The Calais–Dover crossing had been used in preference to the direct sea route from the Low Countries envisaged in Anthony's chart: cf. Ann Payne above, p. 22 and fig. 3.
2. See N. Tarrant, *The Development of Costume* (Edinburgh, 1994), pp. 14–16.
3. For further details see Wilson, *Flags at Sea*, p. 88; D. Hobbs, 'Royal ships and their flags in the late fifteenth and early sixteenth centuries', *MM*, LXXX (1994), pp. 388–94.
4. For a good introduction to the subject see K. Staniland, 'Court style, painters and the Great Wardrobe', in W.M. Ormrod, ed., *England in the Fourteenth Century: Proceedings of the 1988 Harlaxton Symposium* (Woodbridge, 1986), pp. 236–46.
5. For the range of linen available see H. Cobb, 'Textile imports in the fifteenth century: the evidence of the customs' accounts', *Costume*, XXIX (1995), pp. 1–11.
6. PRO, E36/1, f. 31v (*LP*, I, ii, no. 3608 (p. 1498)).
7. *LP*, XIV, ii, no. 213.
8. Some flags were painted all over, e.g. a small flag made by Agnes van den Bossche for Ghent: C. Harbison, *The Art of the Northern Renaissance* (1995), p. 65.
9. Below, p. 121.
10. I am very grateful to Jo Kirby of the National Gallery for her advice on pigments and painting techniques.
11. J.T. Tinniswood, 'English galleys 1272–1377', *MM*, XXXV (1949), p. 234.
12. PRO, LC 9/50, f. 181v.
13. BL, Stowe MS 146, f. 124 (*LP*, I, ii, no. 2967). A month later the ship had two more streamers, 60 large flags, twenty dozen targets and seven top armours: below, p. 117.
14. Auerbach, 'Vincent Volpe', pp. 222–7, and her *Tudor Artists*, p. 190.
15. PRO, E 36/1, ff. 35v (*LP*, I, ii, no. 3608 (p. 1500 *bis*)).
16. Cf. *LP*, I, i, no. 1778.
17. M. Rodríguez-Salgado, *Armada 1588–1988* (1988), p. 65. The standard measures 19'8" x 16'2" (600 x 560 cm) and is in the collection of the Patrimonio Nacional, Real Armería de Madrid.
18. An example is provided by a dragon biting its own tail made for the Order of the Dragon founded by King Sigismund of Hungary (d. 1437): D.R. Starkey, ed., *The Inventory of King Henry VIII* (1998–), I, nos 14548–50.
19. Below, p. 131.
20. N. Mander, 'Painted cloths: history, craftsmen and techniques', *Textile History*, XXVIII, ii (1997), pp 137–40.
21. Personal communication.
22. Below, p. 121.
23. PRO, E 36/1, f. 31v (*LP*, I, ii, no. 3608 (p. 1498)).
24. Rodríguez-Salgado, *Armada*, p. 225. It measures 12' 9½" x 9' 8" (390 x 294 cm) and belongs to the Stedelijk Museum De Lakenhal, Leiden.
25. PRO, E 101/417/4. *LP*, I, ii, no. 2799. The silkwoman Elizabeth, wife of John Worssop, scrivener of London, also supplied material for the trousseau of Henry VIII's sister Mary on her marriage to Louis XII of France: *LP*, I, ii, no. 3343. The definition of 'cadow' is uncertain, although it may possibly be related to a 'cadow' fringe which was made of worsted (personal communication by Natalie Rothstein to Timothy Wilson).
26. Below, pp. 142, 145.
27. PRO, E 101/417/4. *LP*, I, ii, no. 2799.
28. The swallow-tailed pennons bearing a knight's coat of arms and badges were most probably painted as the technique would provide the detail without the weight inherent in embroidered motifs. However, these pennons served a very different purpose to the streamers used at sea.

VI   The Oared Vessels
John Bennell

An intriguing aspect of the Anthony Roll is the inclusion of a number of ships shown being propelled with oars; unless one is familiar with this narrow aspect of Tudor naval history, the presence of these fourteen 'un-English' vessels calls for some explanation. Moreover, their positions within the Roll invite comment, since the *Galley Subtle* appears among the galleasses in part 2, while the other thirteen, the rowbarges, form the final portion of part 3, following the pinnaces. Accordingly, certain questions suggest themselves. Since rowing ships were not a customary feature of the English navy, why were these vessels built? Why do they appear in the Roll where they do? In answering these questions, we shall see both Henry VIII and his warships in a new light.

Galleys in the English service

Rowed craft of some kind have, of course, been a valuable part of the English navy, and many others, for centuries. Ships' boats were in daily use for transporting personnel, provisions and munitions, and carrying despatches; and for manoeuvring and propelling the parent vessel, by short-term towage, when circumstances required. On expeditions, the ship's tender would be sent away for taking soundings in shallow waters, and exploring confined places in a coastline or on a river. In time of war, other employments could include boarding or landing parties, and cutting-out operations. However, without denying the great value and convenience of such services, one would hesitate to class a rowing-boat as a warship.

Further back in time, there were, indeed, oared fighting ships. The large rowing-boats used as war vessels by the Romans, Saxons, Vikings and their successors were all very well in their times but the continued development of the sailing-ship, improved navigational skills, and widespread use of naval ordnance combined to make the galley an anachronism. Such was not the case with some foreign navies, where local conditions kept the galley in favour, notably, in the Mediterranean, and off the Low Countries; indeed, galleys and similar ships were used in the Baltic throughout the 18th century.[1] English interest in galleys in the 16th century came through chance contact with foreign nations, though such craft were not entirely strange to English waters.

One English port had long been visited by Mediterranean galleys, albeit in a commercial connection, as the so-called 'Flanders galleys', which linked Venice with England and the Netherlands. For over two centuries, galleys from Italy and Spain came regularly to Southampton, for cargoes of wool, bringing spices, wines and exotic fabrics; one of the last of them returned from that port in 1534.[2] Understandably, the merchant galley was broader in the beam, and heavier, than the war galley, and was unusual in having three masts[3] instead of the customary one or two.

As it happened, Henry VIII's navy had itself contained a few oared vessels earlier, though details are sparse and rather contradictory. Thus, in 1517, there were ships named the *Rose*, *Katherine* and *Great* galleys which, though rowed, were not galleys, and two rowbarges (60 tons each; names not known but perhaps were the *Sweepstake* and *Mary Fortune*).[4] In fact, rowed craft came in a wide variety of types and sizes (e.g. galleass, galley, galliot, frigate),[5] being often sailing ships which carried oars for propulsion as required, but confusion is caused by the loose terminology then employed.

During 1539–40, when a Franco–Imperial alliance threatened to invade his schismatic kingdom, Henry VIII constructed a chain of coast-defence 'castles' from Milford Haven, around southern England, to Hull, and then turned his attention to the navy, sending to Italy for three shipwrights experienced in building galleys.[6]

In late 1542 the English captured Pierre de Bidoux, sieur de l'Artigue. He had constructed galleys, both as lieutenant to his uncle Prégent (commander of the French galleys), and as vice-admiral of Brittany, so offered his services to Henry VIII in time for the Anglo-French war, 1543–46. The king granted him an annual fee of £50, from 8 July 1543,[7] increased to £75, from 25 March 1545.[8] These were considerable sums, and, since Henry built no more galleys than the *Subtle*, we may suspect that l'Artigue worked on other types. In addition to three earlier vessels, Henry built further galleasses in 1544 (two), 1545 (three) and 1546 (four), and thirteen rowbarges, in the latter year. Two galleasses were captured from the Scots (1544), and four galleys from the French: the *Galley Blanchard* (1546), *Mermaid* (1549),

Speedwell and *Tryright* (both 1560). The *Blanchard* appears to have been returned in 1547; the others are gradually lost sight of.[9] The *Galley Eleanor* was loaned to the English by the Prince de Condé (1562) but subsequently retained and renamed the *Bonavolia*.[10]

The Anglo–Spanish war, 1585–1604, saw a renewed English interest in galleys. In 1588, the *Bonavolia* was used merely for patrol work, in the Thames estuary,[11] but five galleys were built on the Thames: the *Mercury* (1592), and the *Advantagia*, *Gallerita* (both 1601), *Superlativa* and *Volatilia* (both 1602).[12]

In all, the Roll describes 58 warships, and its three parts define these as ships (part 1), galleasses (part 2), and pinnaces and rowbarges (part 3). As mentioned earlier, 14 ships (the *Galley Subtle* with 13 rowbarges) are shown under oars but this is illusory, since the Roll includes many more craft which could be, and often were, rowed. Examination of the Roll reveals that the total of 58 vessels is made up of 20 examples of ships being great-ships, ships and barks; 15 galleasses, comprising one galley, ten actual galleasses, and four 'ships'; ten pinnaces and 13 rowbarges. Here, then, is the explanation of the apparently haphazard layout of the Roll: whereas the 20 ships were sailing vessels (on occasion, the small barks could be rowed, but this was less usual), all the others (in parts 2 and 3) could be handled under oars. Hence, the 14 oared vessels (the galley and 13 rowbarges) have now become 38 rowing craft. In theory, a distinction could be drawn between those ship types which were essentially oared (i.e. galleass, galley and rowbarge) and the pinnaces often so employed, but the Roll itself presents difficulties in this respect.

References in the following descriptions to artillery pieces or gun- or oar-ports *on the broadside* represent what is visible in the illustrations, so comprise only half the actual state.

The galley

The galley had three methods of attack: first, was its main armament, trained by manoeuvring the vessel. This was mounted on fixed beds in the bows, for firing forward, and comprised a large piece, known as the *corsia*, 'courser', on the centre-line, flanked by two or four of smaller calibre. Otherwise, there were darts and small guns in the fighting-tops; and a few swivel-guns on deck. Second, was ramming, by means of a 'beak' extended from the bows. Third, because the galley lay so low in the water, it had an elevated platform forward, called an *arrumbada* in Spanish,[13] from which soldiers could fire their hackbuts.[14] However, an earlier name *apostis* (cf. 'apostle' from Greek ἀπόστολος 'one sent forth'), shows that its original purpose was to allow soldiers, from either beam, to board an enemy vessel.

Foreign galleys were constructed in various sizes, including the commander's *capitana*, the slightly smaller whole galley, and the half-galley. The *Galley Subtle*'s name was, in fact, a generic term (Old French *galere subtile*, 'narrow galley') for a standard size, and she was smaller than her Mediterranean counterparts.

The oarsmen in English galleys were either convicted felons or paid seamen, but difficulty of supply restricted their use. Captured galleys were retained in English service but later returned, with their oarsmen. Even France experienced manning problems, sometimes having convicts but no galleys (as in 1592 and 1594), and vice versa (from 1600).[15] John Knox was fortunate to survive, for nineteen months of 1547–9, rowing in a French galley.[16]

As shown in the Roll, the *Galley Subtle* was of 200 tons, and her complement numbered 242 mariners and eight gunners. She was probably smaller than a two-masted French (commander's) galley of 1622, which, measured from her drawings, had a keel of 116 ft., and length overall of 172 ft., with a beam of 19 ft., 27 ft. over the rowing-frame, for a depth in hold of 10 ft.: by the English rule, this gave a tonnage of (116 x 19 ÷ 10 =) 220 tons. No armament is shown but there were benches (and oars) for 260 rowers.[17]

Anthony's drawing shows the *Galley Subtle*'s flush deck, with the rowing-benches flanked by pavisades on each beam, to protect the crew from enemy arrows. The overseer, dressed in a bonnet, full-skirted armorial doublet and baggy breeches, seems to be beating time to regulate the strokes of the oars, about 24 on each side. The single mast, with its fighting-top, carried the lateen sail's incredibly-long yard, of typical galley construction: instead of a single, weak spar, two long spars were fished together, without a scarf but bound together with several wooldings.

The bow had a spiked, iron-shod balk for a ram, and the *apostis* forward can just be made out. Astern was the usual tilt, with the bails supporting a decorative awning, here made from cloth of gold.[18] The awning bears a large roundel of the royal arms, between four smaller ones with the cross of St George; and a green dragon figure-head facing aft.

The *Galley Subtle* was one of the 'wafters' (escorts) attached to the fleet's vanguard for Henry VIII's invasion of Scotland (1544); on 5 May her captain, Richard Broke, captured the island fort of Inchgarvie in the Firth of Forth.[19]

Pinnaces

The third part of the Roll contains twenty-three ships, comprising ten pinnaces and thirteen rowbarges. Of very modest size, pinnaces were predominantly sailing ships, though mostly adapted for operation under oars, when the need arose. They could be employed on any kind of action where ships' boats were too small, and would often serve as tenders to larger vessels. It was usual, on a voyage of discovery, for one or more of the smallest size to be carried on board: these were specially made, in prefabricated sections, for ease of stowage, ready to be assembled ashore for use as required.

The ten pinnaces in the Roll have burthens of 80, 40, 20 and (the *Hare*) 15 tons, so that the larger ones would resemble the lesser sailing barks, while the rest were the smallest craft to accompany a naval force at sea. It is noticeable that all ten were built in 1545 (two perhaps a little before) or 1546.

Curiously, in March 1546, ships assigned for reinforcing the Channel fleet included 'the 10 shalloppes of ye West countrye', totalling 450 tons and 400 men,[20] showing that *these* ten were also pinnaces (though the term 'shallops' was sometimes used for the later rowbarges). Despite the success of the 1546 rowbarges, they were replaced by pinnaces, once the war was over.

Rowbarges

Ordinarily, the term 'rowbarge' might suggest no more than a small, undecked boat, little more than the captain's gig. A new, generic definition was introduced in 1546, when the thirteen rowbarges described in the Roll were constructed. On 29 April 1546, his ambassador in London told Charles V that:

> during the last three days 18 pinnaces, newly built in the form of foysts, have sailed from here [London]. They have on each side fifteen or sixteen oars, and are all well and similarly equipped both with regard to the size of their artillery and to their crews.[21]

The new, 20-ton craft, named for royal badges, were built long and low, with a small forecastle; short, open waist, with anti-boarding nets rigged; and a very long half-deck: they were greatly-reduced copies of the new galleasses. Each of the three masts had a single yard and sail, presumably with a lateen mizzen.

Each rowbarge had a complement of from 33 to 41 seamen and four gunners. The main armament of these 'light vessels' was intended to have been a demi-culverin in the bows[22] but the Roll shows that only five had received this. Hence, the standard armament was a demi-culverin and/or a saker, with six bases. The individual rowbarges differed slightly in detail, as modifications were introduced: indeed, their order in the Roll (as nos 46–58) suggests that this reflected the sequence of their building. Thus, only the *Double Rose* (no. 46) had a fighting-top, on its mainmast, and nos 46–54 carried two gunports on the broadside; from the *Maiden Head* on (nos 55–58), only one gunport was fitted, but these four mounted a pair of guns in stern ports.

Having served their intended purpose, ten rowbarges were sold out of the service in 1548–9, and one in 1555, while the other two were dropped from the active list.[23] In the longer term, pinnaces would be more serviceable, and six of the replacements, of 30–50 tons, were named *Double Rose, Flower de Luce, Maiden Head, Portcullis, Rose in the Sun* and *Rose Slip*.[24]

Galleasses

The galleass concept was a compromise, intended to produce a major warship which had greater manoeuvrability than the conventional sailing vessel but with greater armament than that carried by the galley. To that end, all lower-deck guns were supplanted by rowing-benches.

In its preamble, Anthony's second roll purports to describe the fifteen galleasses depicted therein but there are only 14 such vessels, since one is the *Galley Subtile*; the headings for the last four (i.e. the *Greyhound, Jennet, Lion* and *Dragon*) style these 'ships', though these differ only in being three-masted and having stern-galleries. Of the 14, three were built in or before 1539 (*New Bark, Lion, Jennet*), and the rest were constructed in 1544 (*Swallow, Dragon*; plus two prizes, taken from the Scots, *Salamander* and *Unicorn*), 1545 (three: *Grand Mistress, Anne Gallant, Greyhound*) and 1546 (four: *Antelope, Bull, Hart* and *Tiger*).

The typical (pre-1546) galleass was four-masted, with main- and top-sails on fore- and main-masts, and single lateen sails on main- and bonaventure-mizzens; and three fighting-tops. The forecastle was quite short, with a gun in the eyes, and a long, sharply-steeved bowsprit. The waist had an open rail, sometimes concealed behind pavises, with nettings rigged above. The half-deck was unusually long, with two or three gunports on the side, and two stern-chase guns; while the main deck had three or four gunports. The bow was fitted with an iron-tipped, above-water ram, with an artillery piece mounted behind it. The four galleasses of 1546 differed in having flush decks, with slight rises forward and aft; a single row of gun-ports on the broadside, being either six (*Bull*), eight (*Tiger*) or nine (*Antelope* and *Hart*); and smaller complements. Most armaments comprised culverins, demi-culverins and sakers; the 1546 galleasses should have mounted six or eight cannons each[25] but only two carried so much as a demi-cannon. (In 1589, new warships could be armed only by taking ordnance from castles and forts.)[26]

Plainly, Anthony's fourteen galleasses – with their reduced upperworks or flush deck, low profile and ram bow – were intended for rowing, yet not one is depicted with its oars. The only galleasses shown with oar-ports seem to be the *Grand Mistress*, where they are placed between the lower-deck guns, and the 1546 ships, where the ports vary in number, from 19 (*Antelope*) to 28 (*Bull*) a side. Comparison with one of the Neapolitan galleasses of the 1588 armada[27] is instructive:

	total complement
Girona	589 (i.e. 289 + 300 rowers)
Grand Mistress	250
Bull	120

While building, the four 1546 galleasses were allocated crews totalling 720 men but they were to receive only the 640 shown herein[28] though this shortfall, of twenty men per ship, may have been recognition of the fact that their ordnance was going to be incomplete. The galleasses were termed 'fast wingers'[29] when they acted as 'wafters' (escorts) to the fleet's 'wing',[30] and they worked very effectively when employed with pinnaces or rowbarges.

Conclusion

The Anthony Roll records a race against time which Henry VIII won. He began construction of the *Galley Subtle* and, in December 1544, attempted to obtain ten galleys from Emperor Charles V, unsuccessfully.[31] Thereafter, Henry turned his attention to new, more-powerful types of ships. Thus, to answer a question posed earlier, the galleasses and rowbarges were built for warding-off French attacks, using oared vessels, on the English coast, as comparable forces in an offensive–defensive role (what the Tudors called 'prevention').

Ironically, this English achievement came by way of French expertise: the able assistance of the sieur de l'Artigue and the capture of the Scottish galleass *Salamander* (1544), which, built in France,[32] provided a pattern. Despite their seemingly weak construction, the rowbarges were fast and very manoeuvrable, and – particularly when carrying their intended armament – quite capable of attacking a galley on the quarter with impunity; and they worked well with the galleasses.

During April and May 1546, four 'shallops', i.e. rowbarges, were off Ambleteuse, near Boulogne, ready to intercept French victuallers; two hoys captured by a French foist were retaken by four rowbarges; and four galleasses (the *Grand Mistress, Anne Gallant, Salamander* and *Greyhound*) with six or seven rowbarges headed-off eighteen French galleys.[33] However, in this matter, the last word is due to the lord admiral. On 15 May 1546, Lord Lisle wrote telling Sir William Petre how, walking with his counterpart, the admiral of France, he had told him that England was now well equipped, 'having made 8 or 10 new gallyasses … besides sundry light vessels, as swift with oars as their galleys', whereupon d'Annebault hurriedly turned the conversation to sport.[34] On 7 June 1546, the war was ended.

The lesson of the improved sailing qualities of the oar-less galleass was not forgotten, and, soon, 'brought to the form of a galleass'[35] became a synonym for a ship's improvement by reduction of its upperworks and lower profile. Henry's short-term expedient was to influence the design of countless English major warships for the following half-century.

Notes

1. R.C. Anderson, *Oared Fighting Ships from Classical Times to the coming of Steam* (2nd edn., King's Langley, 1976), pp. 90–9.
2. A.A. Ruddock, 'Merchants and shipping in medieval Southampton', in *Collected Essays on Southampton*, ed. J.B. Morgan and P. Peberdy (1968), pp. 48–56, at pp. 51–5.
3. A.A. Ruddock, *Italian Merchants and Shipping in Southampton, 1270–1600* (1951), pp. 19, 20.

4.   Derrick, *Memoirs*, pp. 6, 7. Oppenheim, *History*, pp. 41, 58. J.E.G. Bennell, 'English oared vessels of the sixteenth century', *MM*, LX (1974), pp. 9–26, 169–85, at p. 15.

5.   Some notes on these appear in Bennell, 'Oared vessels', *passim*.

6.   Oppenheim, *History*, p. 59.

7.   *LP*, XVIII, ii, nos 107(11), App. no. 15 (p. 384).

8.   *LP*, XX, ii, no. 707(5).

9.   Glasgow, 'List of ships', pp. 304, 305 (Edward VI, no. 11, Eliz. I, nos 7, 8). E.R. Adair, 'English galleys in the sixteenth century', *EHR*, XXXV (1920), pp. 500–2.

10. Glasgow, 'List of ships', p. 305 (Eliz. I, no. 18).

11. J.K. Laughton, ed., *State Papers relating to the Defeat of the Spanish Armada, anno 1588* (NRS I, II, 1894), I, pp. 336–8.

12. For further details see Bennell, 'Oared vessels', pp. 22–3.

13. Rodger, *Safeguard of the Sea*, p. 212.

14. As shown in Hendrik Cornelisz. Vroom's painting of the battle of Haarlem Lake, 1573 in the Rijksmuseum, Amsterdam.

15. D.J. Buisseret, 'The French Mediterranean fleet under Henri IV', *MM*, L (1964), pp. 297, 303.

16. J.G. Ridley, *John Knox* (Oxford, 1968), pp. 66–83.

17. Buisseret, 'French Mediterranean fleet', plate 9, facing p. 304.

18. Presumably the covering from the galley's poop that was given to the lord admiral in 1551: *APC*, III, p. 257.

19. *LP*, XIX, i, nos 416, 472, 534; cf. nos 518(3), 533.

20. *LP*, XXI, i, no. 498.

21. *CSP Spanish*, VIII, pp. 389–90 (*LP*, XXI, i, no. 700).

22. *LP*, XXI, i, no. 837.

23. Glasgow, 'List of ships', p. 303 (Henry VIII, nos 47–59). Oppenheim, *History*, p. 101.

24. T. Glasgow jr, 'The navy in Philip and Mary's war, 1557–1558', *MM*, LIII (1967), p. 321 n. 3. Glasgow, 'List of ships', pp. 303, 304.

25. *LP*, XXI, i, no. 837.

26. *CSPD, Addenda 1580–1625*, p. 436.

27. Laughton, *Spanish Armada*, II, p. 380.

28. *LP*, XXI, i, no. 498. Oppenheim, *History*, p. 51 n. 78.

29. Rodger, *Safeguard of the Sea*, p. 212.

30. *State Papers ... Henry the Eighth*, I, ii, p. 812.

31. *LP*, XIX, ii, nos 752, 783.

32. Oppenheim, *History*, p. 50 n. 51.

33. *LP*, XXI, i, nos 706, 874.

34. *LP*, XXI, i, no. 837.

35. Oppenheim, *History*, pp. 128–9.

The Anthony Roll

The First Roll

Pepys 2991

1

[pp. ii–iii]   Anno Domini 1546.

Here After insuyth a declaration of the Kynges Majesties owne nave of sundere kyndes of shyppes belongyng unto hys grace, that ys to say shyppes, galliasses, pynnasses and roo baergys, with every shyppe and shyppys naem, with evere galliasse and galliasse naem, with evere pynnasse and pynnasse naem, and with evere roo baerges naem; as also the ordenaunce, artillary, munitions and habillmentes for the warre for the armyng of evry of them and for theyr deffence agaynst theyr ennymys apon the see: anno regni regis Henrici octavi xxxviij.

[pp. 2–3] In thys the fyrst rolle declaryng the nombre of the Kynges Majesties owne shyppes, with evre shyppe and shyppes naem with theyr tunage and nombre of men; as also the ordenaunce, artillary, munitions and habillimentes for warre for the armyng and deffence of every of the sayd shippes agynst theyr ennemys uppon the see. That ys to saye:

The Harry Grace a Dieu

Tunage – m.

Men {souldiours – cccxlix; marryna[r]s – cccj; gonnars – l}: vij^c.

For the Harry Grace a Dieu. Ordenaunce, artillary, munitions, habillimentes for the warre, for the armyng and in the deffence of the sayd shyppe to the see.

Gonnes of brasse. Cannons – iiij. Demy cannons – ij. Culveryns – iiij. Demy culveryns – ij. Sakers – iiij. Cannon perers – ij. Fawcons – ij.

Gonnes of yron. Porte pecys – xiiij. Slynges – iiij. Demy slynges – ij. Fowlers – viij. Baessys – lx. Toppe pece – ij. Hayle shotte pecys – xl. Handgonnes complete – c.

Gonnepowder. Serpentyn powder in barrelles – ij lastes. Corne powder in barrelles – vj.

Shotte of yron. For cannons – c. For demy cannons – lx. For culveryns – cxx. For demy culveryns – lxx. For sakers – cxx. For fawcons – c. For slynges – c. For demy slynges – l. Crosse barre shotte – c. Dyce of yron for hayle shotte – iiij^{ml}.

Shotte of stoen and leade. For cannon perer – lx. For porte pecys – ccc. For fowlers – c. For toppe peces – xl. For baessys, shotte of leade – ij^{ml}. For handgonnes, shotte of leade – ij^{ml}.

Bowes, bowestrynges, arrowes, morrys pyckes, byllys, daertes for toppys. Bowes of yough – v^c. Bowestrynges – x groce. Lyvere arrowes in shevys – vij^{c}l. Morrys pykes – cc. Byllys – cc. Daertes for toppis in doussens – c.

Munitions. Pyckhamers – xx^{ti}. Sledgys of yron – xij. Crowes of yron – xij. Comaunders – xij. Tampions – v^{ml}. Canvas for cartowches – xx^{ti} ellys. Paper ryall for cartowche – j qwayer. Fourmes for cartowches – vj.

Habillimentes for warre. Ropis of hempe for wolyng and brechyng – x coylles. Naylis of sundere sortes – j^{ml}. Bagges of ledder – xij. Fyrkyns with pursys – vj. Lyme pottes – xx doussen. Spaer whelys – iiij paier. Spaer truckelles – iiij paier. Spaier extrys – xij. Shepe skynnys – xxiiij. Tymber for forlockes and koynnys – c foete.

2

3

[pp. 6–7]

The Mary Rose

Tunage – vij^c.

Men {souldiours – clxxxv; marrynars – cc; gonnars – xxx^{ti}}: iiij^{c}xv.

For the Mary Rose. Ordenaunce, artillary, munitions, habillimentes for the warre, for the armyng and in the deffence of the sayd shyppe to the see.

Gonnes of brasse. Cannons – ij. Demy cannons – ij. Culveryns – ij. Demy culveryns – vj. Sakers – ij. Fawcons – j. Somma – xv.

Gonnes of yron. Porte pecys – xij. Slynges – ij. Demy slynges – iij. Quarter slyng – j. Fowlers – vj. Baessys – xxx. Toppe pecys – ij. Hayle shotte pecys – xx^{ti}. Handgonnes complete – 1.

Gonnepowder. Serpentyn powder in barrelles – ij last. Corne powder in barrelles – iij.

Shotte of yron. For cannon – 1. For demy cannon – lx. For culveryn – lx. For demy culveryn – cxl. For sakers – lxxx. For fawcon – lx. For slyng – xl. For demy slyng – xl. For qwarter slyng – 1. Dyce of yron for hayle shotte – [*blank*].

Shotte of stoen and leade. For porte pecys – cc. For fowlers – clxx. For toppe pecys – xx. For baessys, shotte of leade – iiij^c. For handgonnes, shotte of leade – j^{ml}.

Bowes, bowestrynges, arrowes, morrys pyckes, byllys, daertes for toppis. Bowes of yough – ccl. Bowestrynges – vj groce. Lyvere arrowes in shevis – cccc. Morrys pykes – cl. Byllys – cl. Daertes for toppys in doussens – xl.

Munitions. Pyckehamers – xij. Sledgys of yron – viij. Crowes of yron – xij. Comaunders – xij. Tampions – iiij^{ml}. Canvas for cartowches – xx^{ti} ellys. Paper ryall for cartowches – j qwayer. Fourmes for cartowches – vj.

Habillimentes for warre. Ropis of hempe for woling and brechyng – x coylles. Naylis of sundere sortes – j^{ml}. Bagges of ledder – viij. Fyrkyns with pursys – vj. Lyme pottes – x doussen. Spaer whelys – iiij payer. Spaer truckelles – iiij payer. Spaer extrys – vj. Shepe skynnys for spongys – xij. Tymber for forlockes and koynnys – c foete.

The Peter

Tunes – vj^c.

Men {souldiours – clxxxv; marrynars – clxxxv; gonnars – xxx^{ti}}: iiij^c.

For the Peter. Ordenaunce, artillary, munitions, habillimentes for the warre, for the armyng and in the deffence of the sayd shyppe to the see.

Gonnes of brasse. Demy cannons – ij. Culveryns – ij. Demy culveryns – iiij. Sakers – iiij. Fawcons – ij. Somma – xiiij.

Gonnes of yron. Porte pecys – xvj. Demy slynges – ij. Quarter slynges – ij. Fowlers – iiij. Baessys – lxvj. Toppe pece – ij. Hayle shotte pecys – xx^{ti}. Handgonnes complete – xl.

Gonnepowder. Serpentyn powder – ij lastes. Corne powder in barrelles – ij.

Shotte of yron. For demy cannons – 1. For culveryns – 1. For demy culveryns – lxxx. For sakers – j^c. For fawcons – lx. For demy slynges – xx. For qwarter slynges – xl. Dyce of yron for hayle shotte – m^l.

Shotte of stoen and leade. For porte pecys – iiij^c. For fowlers – lx. For toppe pece – xl. For baessys, shotte of leade – vij^c. For handgonnes, shot of leade – j^{ml}.

Bowes, bowestrynges, arrowes, morrys pyckes, byllys, daertes for toppys. Bowes of yough – cc. Bowestrynges – vj groce. Lyvere arrowes in shevis – ccc. Morrys pykes – cc. Byllys – cc. Daertes for toppis – xxx doussen.

Munitions. Pyckehamers – xij. Sledgys of yron – x. Crowes of yron – x. Comaunders – xij. Tampions – iij^{ml}. Canvas for cartowches – xx^{ti} ellys. Paper ryall for cartowches – ij qwayers. Fourmes for cartowches – v.

Habillimentes for warre. Ropis of hempe for woling [and] brechyng – viij coyles. Naylis – vij^c. Bagges of ledder – viij. Fyrkyn with pursys – vj. Lyme pottes – vj doussen. Spaer whelis – iiij payer. Spaer truckelles – iiij payer. Spaer extrys – vj. Shepe skynnys – xij. Tymber for forlockes – lxxx foet.

44

Donnepollder · Shotte of yron · Shotte of stoen · Bowes · Bowestryng

4

5

[pp. 10–11]

The Matthew

Tunnes – vj^c.

Men {souldiours – cxxxviij; marrynars – cxxxviij; gonnars – xxiiij}: iij^c.

For the Matthew. Ordenaunce, artillary, munitions, habillimentes for warre, for the armyng and in the defence of the sayd shippe to the see.

Gonnes of brasse. Demy cannons – ij. Demy culveryns – v. Sakers – iij.

Gonnes of yron. Porte pecys – xvj. Slynges – ij. Quarter slynges – ij. Baessys – xlviij. Top pecys – ij. Hayle shott pecys – ij. Handgonnes – xx.

Gonnepowder. Serpentyn powder – j last di. Grosse corne powder in barrelles – ij. Fyne corne powder – xl^{lb}.

Shotte of yron. For demy cannons – lx. For demy culveryns – cl. For sakers – c. For slynges – xl. For quarter slynges – xl. Crosse barre shott – xx. Dyce of yron for hayle shott – j^{ml}.

Shotte of stoen and leade. For porte pecys – ccc. For tope pece – xl. For baessys, shott of leade – vj^c. For handgonnes, shott of leade – v^c.

Bowes, bowestrynges, arrowes, morryse pykes, byllys and daertes for toppys. Bowes of yough – cc. Bowestrynges – iiij groce. Lyvere arrowes in shevys – ccc. Morrys pyckes – cl. Byllys – cl. Daertes for toppys – ccc.

Munitions. Pyckhamers – x. Sleggys – vj. Crowes of yron – vj. Comaunders – viij. Tampions – j^{ml}. Canvas for cartowchys – viij elles. Paper ryall for cartowche – j quayer. Fourmes for cartowchys – vj.

Habillimentes for the warre. Hempen ropys^a for woling and brechyng – viij coyles. Naylis of sundere sortes – ij^{ml}. Bagges of ledder – vj. Fyrkyn with pursys – iiij. Lyme pottes^b – vj doussen. Spaer whelys – ij payer. Spaer truckelles – iij payer. Spaer extrys – vj. Shepe skynnys for spongys – xij. Tymber for forlockes – 1 foet.

The Greate Barcke

Tunnes – v^c.

Men {souldiours – cxxxvj; marrynars – cxxxviij; gonnars – xxvj}: iiij^c.

For the Greate Barke. Ordenaunce, artillary, munitions, habillimentes for the warre, for the armyng and in the deffence of the sayd shyppe to the see.

Gonnes of brasse. Demy cannons – v. Culveryns – ij. Demy culveryns – iij. Sakers – ij.

Gonnes of yron. Porte pecys – x. Slynges – ij. Demy slynges – ij. Fowlers – vj. Baessys – xxx. Tope pece – j. Hayle shott peces – xx. Handgonnes complet – xx.

Gonnepowder. Serpentyn powder in demy barrelles – xxx. Grosse corne powder – ij barrelles. Fyne corne powder, demy barrelles – ij.

Shotte of yron. For demy cannons – c. For culveryns – l. For demy culveryns – lxx. For sakers – lxx. For slynges – xl. For demy slynges – xl. Dyce of yron for hayle shott – j^{ml}.

Shotte of stoen and leade. For porte pecys – clx. For fowlers – cxx. For tope pece – xx. For baessys, shott of leade – v^c. For handgonnes – ccc.

Bowes, bowestrynges, arrowes, morrys pykes, byllys and daertes for toppys. Bowes of yough – cl. Bowestrynges – iij groce. Lyvere arrowes in shevys – ccxxv. Morrys pyckes – c. Byllys – c. Daertes for toppis – ccc.

Munitions. Pyckhamers – viij. Sleggys – vj. Crowes of yron – vj. Comaunders – vj. Tampions – viij^c. Canvas for cartowchys – xij ellys. Paper ryall for cartowchys – j qwayer. Fourmes for cartowchys – iiij.

Habillimentes for the warre. Hempen ropys for woling and brechyng – vj coyles. Naylis of sundere sortes – v^c. Bagges of ledder – vj. Fyrkyn with pursys – iiij. Lyme pottes – iiij doussen. Spaer whelys – ij payer. Spaer truckelles – iij payer. Spaer extrys – viij. Shepe skynnys – viij. Tymber for forlockes and koynnys – 1 foete.

^{a} MS 'robys'. ^{b} MS 'pootes'.

besus of
ke temes viij c

Son dion
Marryn
Gonnar

6

cey
mel

Son dion
Marryn
Gonnar

[pp. 14–15]

The Jhesus of Lubeke

Tunnes – vij^c.

Men {souldiours – cxviij; marrynars – clviij; gonnars – xxiiij}: iij^c.

For the Jhesus of Lubeke. Ordenaunce, artillary, munitions, habillimentes for the warre, for the armyng and in the deffence of the sayd shyppe to the see.

Gonnes of brasse. Cannons – ij. Culveryns – ij. Sakers – ij.

Gonnes of yron. Porte pecys – iiij. Slynges – x. Fowlers – iiij. Baessys – xij. Tope pecys – ij. Hayle shott pecys – xx. Handgonnes complet – xx.

Gonnepowder. Serpentyn powder – j last. Grosse corne powder – j barel. Fyne corne powder – xl^{lb}.

Shotte of yron. For cannons – l. For culveryns – lx. For sakers – lx. For slynges – cc. Dice of yron for hayle shott – vj^c.

Shotte of stoen and leade. For porte pecys – c. For fowlers – $^{xx}_{iiij}$. For tope pecys – xl. For baessys, shott of leade – ccxl. For handgonnes – iiij^c.

Bowes, bowestrynges, arrowes, morrys pykes, byllys and daertes for toppis. Bowes of yough – c. Bowestrynges – iij groce. Lyvere arrowes in shevys – cl. Morrys pykes – c. Byllys – c. Daertes for toppys – ccc.

Munitions. Pyckhamers – iiij. Sledgys – iiij. Crowes of yron – iiij. Comaunders – iiij. Tampions – vj^c. Canvas for cartowchys – x ellys. Paper ryall – j qwayer. Fourmes for cartowchys – iij.

Habillimentes for the warre. Hempen ropys for woling and brechyng – viij coyles. Naylis of sundere sortes – iiij^c. Bagges of ledder – iiij. Fyrkyns with pursys – iij. Lyme pottes – iiij doussen. Spaer whelys – ij payer. Spaer truckelles – iiij. Spaer extrys – iiij. Shepe skynnys – vj. Tymber for forlockes – xl foet.

The Pawncey

Tunnes – iiij^{c}l.

Men {souldiours – cxxxvj; marrynars – cxl; gonnars – xxiiij}: iij^c.

For the Pawncey. Ordenaunce, artillary, munitions, habillimentes for warre, for the armyng and in the defence of the sayd shyppe to the see.

Gonnes of brasse. Demy cannons – iiij. Culveryns – ij. Demy culveryns – ij. Sakers – iiij.

Gonnes of yron. Porte pecys – xij. Demy slynges – ij. Fowlers – ix. Baessys – xxiiij. Tope pece – j. Hayle shott peces – xx. Handgonnes complet – xx.

Gonnepowder. Serpentyn powder in demy barrelles – xxx. Grosse corne powder, demy barrelles – ij. Fyne corne powder – xl^{lb}.

Shotte of yron. For demy cannons – c. For culveryns – l. For demy culveryns – lx. For sakers – c. For demy slynges – cxx. Dyce of yron for hayle shott – vj^c.

Shotte of stoen and leade. For porte pecys – cc. For fowlers – c. For top pece – xx. For baessys, shott of leade – vj^c. For handgonnes – ccl.

Bowes, bowestrynges, arrowes, morrys pykes, byllys and daertes for toppis. Bowes of yough – cc. Bowestrynges – iiij groce. Lyvere arrowes in shevys – ccc. Morrys pykes – c. Byllys – c. Daertes for toppys – ccc.

Munitions. Pyckhamers – viij. Sledgys – vj^a. Crowes of yron – iiij. Comaunders – vj. Tampions – m^l. Canvas for cartowchys – xij ellys. Paper ryall – j qwayer. Fourmes for cartowchys – iiij.

Habillimentes. Ropis of hempe for woling and brechyng – vj coyles. Naylis of sundere sortes – v^c. Bagges of ledder – xij. Fyrkyns with pursys – vj. Lyme pottes – iiij doussen. Spaer whelys – ij payer. Spaer truckelles – iiij payer. Spaer extrys – vj. Shepe skynnys – xij. Tymber for forlockes – l foet.

---

^{a} Corrected from 'iij' or vice-versa.

8

9

[pp. 18–19]

The Murrian

Tunnes – v^c.

Men {souldiours – cxxxviij; marrynars – cxlij; gonnars – xx}: iij^c.

For the Murrian. Ordenaunce, artillary, munitions, habillimentes for warre, for the armyng and in defence of the sayd shyppe to the see.

Gonnes of brasse. Culveryns – ij. Sakers – ij.

Gonnes of yron. Porte pecys – iiij. Demy slynges – iiij. Baessys – xij. Tope pece – j. Hayle shott pecys – vj. Handgonnes complet – xij.

Gonnepowder. Serpentyn powder in barrelles – vij. Grosse corne powder – j di bar[rell]. Fyne corne powder – xxiiij^{lb}.

Shotte of yron. For culveryn – lx. For sakers – lx. For demy slynges – cxx. Dyce of yron for hayle shott – iiij^c.

Shotte of stoen and leade. For porte pecys – lxxx. For toppe pece – xx. For baessys, shott of leade – cc. For handgonnes – cc.

Bowes, bowestrynges, arrowes, morrys pykes, byllys and daertes for toppis. Bowes of yough – cl. Bowestrynges – iij groce. Lyvere arrowes in shevys – ij^cxxv. Morrys pykes – cl. Byllys – c. Daertes for toppys – iiij doussen.

Munitions. Pyckhamers – vj. Sledgys – iiij. Crowes of yron – iiij. Comaunders – vj. Tampions – m^l. Canvas for cartowchys – vj ellys. Paper ryall for cartowches – j qwayer. Fourmes for cartowche – ij.

Habillimentes. Hempen ropis for woling and brechyng – vj coyles. Naylis of sundere sortes – iiij^c. Bagges of ledder – vj. Fyrkyns with pursys – iiij. Lyme pottes – ij doussen. Spaer whelys – j payer. Spaer truckelles – ij payer. Spaer extryes – iiij. Shepe skynnys – iiij. Tymber for forlockes – xl foet.

The Struse

Tunnes – iiij^cl.

Men {souldiours – cxl; marrynars – lxxxxvj; gonnars – xiiij}: ij^cl.

For the Struse. Ordenaunce, artillary, munitions, habillimentes for warre, for the armyng and in the defence of the sayd shyppe to the see.

Gonnes of brasse. Culveryns – ij. Sakers – ij.

Gonnes of yron. Porte pecys – vj. Demy slynges – iiij. Fowlers – ij. Baessys – xij. Hayle shot pecys – xij. Handgonnes complet – xij. Topp pece – j.

Gonnepowder. Serpentyn powder in demy barrelles – xij. Grosse corne powder – j di barrell. Fyne corne powder – xxiiij^{lb}.

Shotte of yron. For culveryns – lx. For sakers – $\frac{xx}{iiij}$. For demy slynges – c. Dyce of yron for hayle shott – iii^c.

Shotte of stoen and leade. For porte pecys – cxx. For fowlers – xl. For toppe pece – xx. For baessys, shott of leade – ccl. For handgonnes – ccc.

Bowes, bowestrynges, arrowes, morrys pykes, byllys and daertes for toppis. Bowes of yough – c. Bowestrynges – ij groce. Lyvere arrowes in shevis – cl. Morrys pykes – c. Byllys – c. Daertes for toppis – iiij doussen.

Munitions. Pyckhamers – vj. Sledgys – iiij. Crowes of yron – ij. Comaunders – iiij. Tampions – v^c. Canvas for cartowchys – iiij ellys. Fourmes for cartowches – ij.

Habillimentes. Ropis of hempe for woling and brechyng – iiij coyles. Naylis of sundere sortes – iiij^c. Bagges of ledder – iiij. Fyrkyns with pursys – ij. Lyme pottes – ij doussen. Spaer whelis – j payer. Spaer truckelles – ij payer. Spaer extrys – iiij. Shepe skynnys – vj. Tymber for forlockes – xl foet.

10

11

[pp. 22–3]

The Mary Hambrough

Tunnes – iiij^c.

Men {souldiours – cxix; marrynars – cxj; gonnars – xvj}: ij^{c}xlvj.

For the Mary Hambrow. Ordenaunce, artillary, municions, habillymentes for warre, for the armyng and in defence of the sayd shyppe to the see.

Gonnes of brasse. Demy culveryns – ij. Sakers – ij. Fawcon – j.

Gonnes of yron. Porte pecys – vj. Demy slynges – ij. Fowlers – ij. Baessys – xij. Tope pece – j. Hayle shott pecys – xij. Handgonnes complet – xij.

Gonnepowder. Serpentyn powder in demy barrelles – xxvij. Grosse corne powder demy barell – j. Fyne corne powder – xxiiij^{lb}.

Shotte of yron. For demy culveryns – lx. For sakers – $^{xx}_{iij}$. For fawcon – xl. For demy slynges – l. Dyce of yron for hayle shott – iiij^c.

Shotte of stoen and leade. For porte pecys – cxx. For fowlers – xl. For tope pece – xx. For baessys, shott of leade – ccl. For handgonnes – iiij^c.

Bowes, bowestrynges, arrowes, morrys pykes, byllys and daertes for toppis. Bowes of yough – cxx. Bowestrynges – iij groce. Lyvere arrowes in shevis – clx. Morrys pykes – c. Byllys – c. Daertes for toppis – iiij doussen.

Munitions. Pyckhamers – iiij. Sledgys – ij. Crowes of yron – ij. Comaunders – ij. Tampions – v^c. Canvas for cartowches – iiij ellys. Paper ryall – j di qwayer. Fourmes for cartowches – ij.

Habillimentes. Hempen ropis for woling and brechyng – iiij coyles. Naylis of sundere sortes – iiij^c. Bagges of ledder – iiij. Fyrkyns with pursys – ij. Lyme pottes – iij doussen. Spaer whelis – j payer. Spaer truckelles – ij payer. Spaer extrys – iiij. Shepe skynnys for spongys – vj. Tymber for forlockes – xxx foet.

The Christoffer of Breame

[Tonnage not given]

Men {souldiours – cxix; marrynars – cxj; gonnars – xvj}: ij^{c}xlvj.

For the Christoffer of Breame. Ordenaunce, artillary, munitions, habillimentes for warre, for the armyng and in defence of the sayd shyppe to the see.

Gonnes of brasse. Culveryns – ij. Saker – j. Fawcon – j.

Gonnes of yron. Porte pecys – ij. Saker – j. Demy slynges – ij. Baessys – xij. Hayle shott pecys – xij. Handgonnes complet – xij.

Gonnepowder. Serpentyn powder in demy barrelles – xiiij. Fyne corne powder – xxiiij^{lb}.

Shotte of yron. For culveryns – l. For sakers – lx. For fawcon – l. For demy slynges – l. Dyce of yron for hayle shott – iiij^c.

Shotte of stoen and leade. For porte pecys – l. For toppe pece – xx. For baessys, shott of leade – iij^c. For handgonnes – ij^{c}l.

Bowes, bowestrynges, arrowes, morrys pykes, byllys and daertes for toppis. Bowes of yough – cc. Bowestrynges – iij groce. Lyvere arrowes in shevys – iij^c. Morrys pykes – c. Byllys – c. Daertes for toppys – vj doussen.

Munitions. Pyckhamers – iiij. Sledgys – ij. Crowes of yron – ij. Comaunders – ij. Tampions – iiij^c. Canvas for cartowches – iiij elles. Paper ryall – j di qwayer.

Habillimentes. Ropis of hempe for woling and brechyng – iiij coyles. Naylis of sundere sortes – iiij^c. Bagges of ledder – iiij. Fyrkyns with pursys – ij. Lyme pottes – iij doussen. Spaer whelis – j payer. Spaer truckelles – ij payer. Spaer extrys – iiij. Shepe skynnys – vj. Tymber for forlockes – xl foet.

12

13

[pp. 26–7]

The Trynite Harry

Tunnes – ccl.

Men {souldiours – c; marrynars – c; gonnars – xx}: ij^{c}xx.

For the Trinite Harry. Ordenaunce, artillary, munitions habillimentes for warre, for armyng and in deffence of the sayd shippe to the see.

Gonnes of brasse. Demy culveryn – j. Sakers – iiij.

Gonnes of yron. Demy culveryn – j. Porte pecys – x. Demy slynges – v. Fowlers – iiij. Baessys – xij. Hayle shott pece – xij. Handgonnes complet – xij. Toppe pece – j.

Gonnepowder. Serpentyn powder – j last. Grosse corne powder – j barrell. Fyne corne powder – xxiiij^{lb}.

Shotte of yron. For demy culveryns – $\frac{xx}{iiij}$. For sakers – cxx. For demy slynges – cxx. Dyce of yron for hayle shott – iiij^c.

Shotte of stoen and leade. For porte pecys – cc. For fowlers – $\frac{xx}{iiij}$. For baessys, shot of leade – cc. For handgonnes – ccl. For toppe pece, shot of stoen – xx.

Bowes, bowestrynges, arrowes, morrys pykes, byllys and daertes for toppis. Bowes of yough – c. Bowestrynges – j groce. Lyvere arrowes in shevis – cl. Morrys pykes – c. Byllys – c. Daertes for toppys – vj doussen.

Munitions. Pyckhamers – vj. Sledgys – vj. Crowes of yron – iiij. Comaunders – iiij. Tampions – v^c. Canvas for cartowchys – viij ellys. Paper ryall for cartowche – j di qwayer. Fourme for cartowche – ij.

Habillimentes. Hempen ropis for woling and brechyr – vj coyles. Naylis of sundere sortes – iiij^c. Bagges of ledder – iiij. Fyrkyns with pursys – ij. Lyme pottes – iiij doussen. Spaer whelis – j payer. Spaer truckelles – ij payer. Spaer extrys – iiij. Shepe skynnys – vj. Tymber for forlockes – xl foet.

The Smaell Barck

Tunnes – iiij^c.

Men {souldiours – cv; marrynars – cxxij; gonnars – xxiij}: ccl.

For the Smaell Barke. Ordenaunce, artillary, munitions habillimentes for warre, for the armyng and in deffence of the sayd shippe to the see.

Gonnes of brasse. Demy cannons – ij. Cannon perers – ij. Culveryn – j. Demy culveryn – j. Sakers – v.

Gonnes of yron. Porte pecys – xij. Demy slynges – v. Baessys – xlvj. Hayle shott pecys – xij. Handgonnes complet – xij. Tope pece – j.

Gonnepowder. Serpentyn powder – j. last. Grosse corne powder – j di barrell. Fyne corne powder – xxiiij^{lb}.

Shotte of yron. For demy cannons – l. For culveryn – xxx. For demy culveryn – xxx. For sakers – cxx. For demy slynges – cxx. Dyce of yron for hayle shott – v^c.

Shotte of stoen and leade. For porte pecys – ccxl. For cannons perers – l. For toppe pece – xx. For baessys, shott of leade – viij^c. For handgonnes – ccl.

Bowes, bowestrynges, arrowes, morrys pykes, byllys and daertes for toppis. Bowes of yough – cl. Bowestrynges – ij groce. Lyvere arrowes in shevys – ccxxv. Morrys pykes – c. Byllys – c. Daertes for toppis – viij doussen.

Munitions. Pyckhamers – vj. Sledgys – vj. Crowes of yron – iiij. Comaunders – iiij. Tampions – vj^c. Canvas for cartowches – xij ellys. Paper ryall – j qwayer. Fourmes for cartowches – iiij.

Habillimentes. Ropis of hempe for woling and brechyng – vj coyles. Naylis of sundere sortes – iiij^c. Bagges of ledder – vj. Fyrkyns with pursys – ij. Lyme pottes – iiij doussen. Spaer whelis – ij payer. Spaer truckelles – iij payer. Spaer extrys – vj. Shepe skynnys – xij. Tymber for forlockes – xl foet.

14

15

[pp. 30–1]

The Swypstake

Tunnes – iij^c.

Men {souldiours – c; marrynars – cix; gonnars – xxj}: ij^{c}xxx.

For the Swypstake. Ordenaunce, artillary, munitions, habillimentes for warre, for the armyng and in deffence of the sayd shippe to the see.

Gonnes of brasse. Demy cannons – ij. Culveryn – j. Demy culveryns – iij. Sakers – ij.

Gonnes of yron. Porte pecys – [*blank*]. Demy slynges – iiij. Fowlers – iiij. Tope pece – j. Baessys – xxix. Hayle shot pecys – xij. Handgonnes complet – xij.

Gonnepowder. Serpentyn powder – j last. Fyne corne powder – xxiiij^{lb}.

Shotte of yron. For demy cannons – l. For culveryn – xxx. For demy culveryns – c. For sakers $^{xx}_{iiij}$. For demy slynges – cl. Dyce of yron for hayle shott – iiij^c. Crosse barre shot – xij.

Shotte of stoen and leade. For porte pecys – [*blank*]. For fowlers – $^{xx}_{iiij}$. For tope pece – xx. For baessys, shott of leade – vj^c. For handgonnes – ccl.

Bowes, bowestrynges, arrowes, morrys pykes, byllys and daertes for toppys. Bowes of yough – cl. Bowestrynges – iij groce. Lyvere arrowes in shevis – ccxxv. Morrys pykes – cxl. Byllys – cxl. Daertes for toppis – vj doussen.

Munitions. Pyckhamers – xij. Sledgys – vj. Crowes of yron – iiij. Comaunders – iiij. Tampions – m^l. Canvas for cartowchys – xij ellys. Paper ryall – j qwayer. Fourmes for cartowches – iiij.

Habillimentes. Ropis of hempe for woling and brechyng – vj coyles. Naylis of sundere sortes – iiij^c. Bagges of ledder – vj. Fyrkyn with pursys – ij. Lyme pottes – iiij doussen. Spaer whelis – ij payer. Spaer truckelles – iij payer. Spaer extrys – vj. Shepe skynnys – xij. Tymber for forlockes – xl fcet.

The Mynnyon

Tunnes – iij^c.

Men {souldiours – c; marrynars – c; gonnars – xx}: ij^{c}xx.

For the Mynnyon. Ordenaunce, artillary, munitions, habillimentes for warre, for the armyng and in the deffence of the sayd shippe to the see.

Gonnes of brasse. Demy culveryn – j. Sakers – vj. Fawcons – ij.

Gonnes of yron. Porte pecys – xij. Slynges – iiij. Fowlers – ij. Tope pece – j. Baessys – xxxiij. Hayle shott pecys – xij. Handgonnes complet – xij.

Gonnepowder. Serpentyn powder – j last. Corne powder – xxiiij^{lb}.

Shotte of yron. For demy culveryn – xxx. For sakers – cl. For fawcons – c. For slynges – $^{xx}_{iiij}$. Dice of yron for hayle shott – iij^c.

Shotte of stoen and leade. For porte pecys – cclx. For fowlers – lx. For tope pece – xx. For baessys, shott of leade – v^c. For handgonnes – ccl.

Bowes, bowestrynges, arrowes, morrys pykes, byllys and daertes for toppis. Bowes of yough – cl. Bowestrynges – iiij groce. Lyvere arrowes in shevis – ccl. Morrys pykes – c. Byllys – c. Daertes for toppis – vij doussen.

Munitions. Pyckhamers – x. Sledgys – vj. Crowes of yron – iiij. Comaunders – iiij. Tampions – j^{ml}. Canvas for cartowchys – viij ellys. Paper ryall – j qwayer. Fourmes for cartowches – iij.

Habillimentes. Ropis of hempe for woling and brechyng – vj coyles. Naylis of sundere sortes – iiij^c. Bagges of ledder – vj. Fyrkyns with pursys – ij. Lyme pottes – iiij doussen. Spaer whelis – ij payer. Spaer truckelles – iij payer. Spaer extrys – vj. Shepe skynnys for sponges – xij. Tymber for forlockes – xxx foet.

16

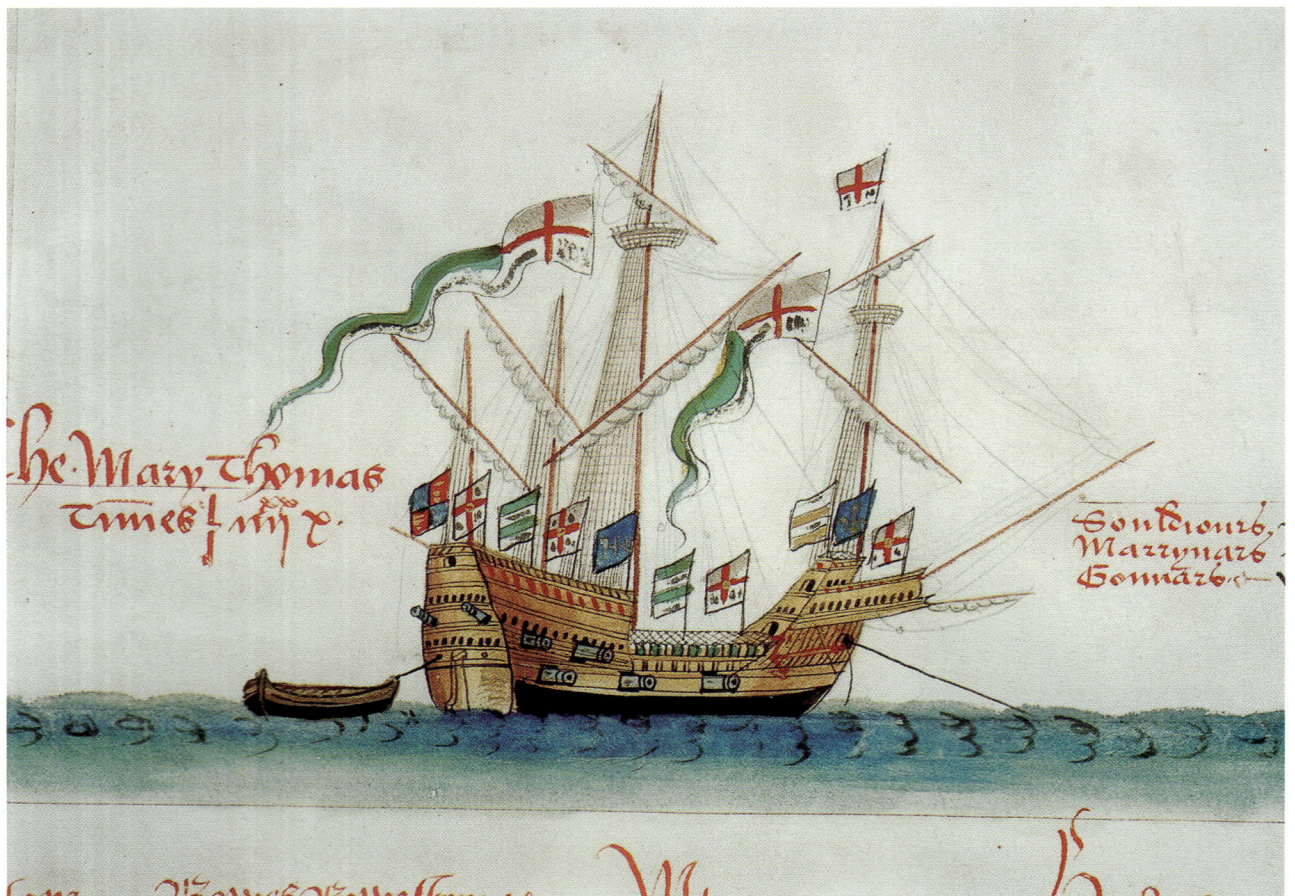

17

[pp. 34–5]

The Lartyque

Tunes – c.

Men {souldiours – lxxx; marrynars – lij; gonnars – viij}: cxl.

For the Lartyque. Ordenaunce, artillary, munitions, habillimentes for warre, for the armyng and in the defence of the sayd shippe to the see.

Gonnes of brasse. Mynnyon – j.

Gonnes of yron. Saker – j. Demy slynges – iij. Baessys – viij. Hayle shott pecys – iiij. Handgonnes complet – vj. Quarter slynges – iiij. Toppe pece – j.

Gonnepowder. Serpentyn powder in demy barrelles – x. Corne powder – xvj^{lb}.

Shott of yron. For the mynnyon – xl. For saker – xl. For demy slynges – lx. For qwarter slynges – $\frac{\text{xx}}{\text{iiij}}$. Dyce of yron for hayle shott – ccc.

Shott of stoen. For toppe pece – xx. For baessys, shott of leade – cc. For handgonnes, shott of leade – cl.

Bowes, bowestrynges, arrowes, morrys pykes, byllys and daertes for toppis. Bowes of yough – l. Bowestrynges – j groce. Lyvere arrowes in shevis – lxxv. Morrys pykes – l. Byllys – l. Daertes for toppys – iiij doussen.

Munitions. Sledgys – iiij. Crowes of yron – ij. Comaunders – ij. Tampions – iiij^c. Canvas for cartowches – iiij ellys. Fourmes for cartowches – ij.

Habillimentes. Hempen ropis for woling and brechyrg – vj coyles. Naylis of sundere sortes – iiij^c. Bagges of ledder – iiij. Fyrkyns with pursys – ij. Lyme pottes – ij doussen. Spaer truckelles – ij payer. Spaer extrys – ij. Shepe skynnes for sponges – ij. Tymber for forlockes – xx foet.

The Mary Thomas

Tunnes – $\frac{\text{xx}}{\text{iiij}}$x

Men {souldiours – xxv; marrynars – xlvij; gonnars – viij}: $\frac{\text{xx}}{\text{iiij}}$.

For the Mary Thomas. Ordenaunce, artillary, munitions, habillimentes for warre, for the armyng and in the defence of the sayd shippe to the see.

Gonnes of brasse. Mynnyon – j.

Gonnes of yron. Saker – j. Porte pecys – ij. Demy slynges – v. Baessys – x. Toppe pece – j. Hayle shott pecys – iiij. Handgonnes complet – x.

Gonnepowder. Serpentyn [powder]^a in demy barrelles – x. Fyne corne powder – xx^{lb}.

Shotte of yron. For mynnyon – l. For saker – lx. For demy slynges – c. Dice of yron for hayle shott – ccc.

Shotte of stoen and leade. For toppe pece – xx. For baessys, shott of leade – ccc. For handgonnes, shott of leade – ccc.

Bowes, bowestrynges, arrowes, morrys pykes, byllys and daertes for toppis. Bowes of yough – xl. Bowestrynges – j groce. Lyvere arrowes in shevis – lx. Morrys pykes – xxx. Byllys – xxx. Daertes for toppys – iiij doussen.

Munitions. Pyckhamers – iiij. Sledgys – ij. Crowes of yron – ij. Comaunders – ij. Tampions – cccc. Canvas for cartowches – ij ellys. Fourmes for cartowches – ij.

Habillimentes. Hempen ropis for woling and brechyng – vj coyles. Naylis of sundere sortes – iiij^c. Bagges of ledder – iiij. Fyrkyns with pursys – ij. Lyme pottes – ij doussen. Spaer truckelles – ij payer. Spaer extrys – iiij. Shepe skynnys for spongys – ij. Tymber for forlockes – xx foet.

---

^{a} Ellipsis in MS.

Hope Barcke
times f iiij

Men

Souldiours
Marroners
Gonnars

of   Gonnes of   Gonne powder.   Shotte of yron   Sh

18

The George
times fhe

Sould
Marry
Gonn

W

19

[pp. 38–9]

The Hoye Barcke

Tunnes – $\frac{xx}{iiij}$

Men {souldiours – xxviij; marrynars – xxviij; gonnars – iiij}: lx.

For the Hoye Barcke. Ordenaunce, artillary, munitions, habillimentes for warre, for the armyng and in the defence of the sayd shyppe to the see.

Gonnes of brasse. Fawcon – j.

Gonnes of yron. Porte pecys – ij. Fowlers – ij. Quarter slynges – ij. Baessys – vj. Hayle shott pecys – vj. Handgonnes complet – vj.

Gonnepowder. Serpentyn powder in demy barrelles – viij. Fyne corne powder – xvj^{lb}.

Shotte of yron. For fawcon – xl. For qwarter slynges – l. Dice of yron for hayle shott – cc.

Shotte of stoen and leade. For porte pecys – xl. For fowlers – xl. For baessys, shott of leade – c. For handgonnes, shott of leade – cxx.

Bowes, bowestrynges, arrowes, morrys pykes, byllys and daertes for toppis. Bowes of yough – lx. Bowestrynges – j groce. Lyvere arrowes in shevys – $\frac{xx}{iiij}$x. Morrys pykes – lx. Byllys – lx. Daertes for toppys – iij doussen.

Munitions. Pyckhamers – iiij. Sledgys – ij. Crowes of yron – ij. Comaunders – ij. Tampions – cc. Canvas for cartowches – ij ellys. Fourmes for cartowche – j.

Habillimentes. Ropis of hempe for woling and brechyn – iij coyles. Naylis of sundere sortes – ccc. Bagges of ledder – iij. Fyrkyn with purse – j. Lyme pottes – ij doussen. Spaer truckelles – j payer. Spaer extry – ij. Shepe skynnys – ij. Tymber for forlockes and koynnys – x foet.

The George

Tunnes – lx.

Men {souldiours – xviij; marrynars – xviij; gonnars – iiij}: xl.

For the George. Ordenaunce, artillary, munitions, habillimentes for warre, for the armyng and in the defence of the sayd shyppe to the see.

Gonnes of brasse. Demy culveryn – j. Saker – j.

Gonnes of yron. Porte pecys – ij. Demy slyng – j. Baessys – viij. Hayle shott pecys – iiij. Handgonnes complet – iiij.

Gonnepowder. Serpentyn powder in demy barrelles – v. Fyne corne powder – viij^{lb}.

Shotte of yron. For demy culveryn – xl. For saker – xl. Dyce of yron for hayle shott – cc. For demy slyng – xxx.

Shotte of stoen and leade. For porte pecys – xl. For baessys, shott of leade – clx. For handgonnes, shott of leade – clx.

Bowes, bowestrynges, arrowes, morrys pykes, byllys and daertes for toppis. Bowes of yough – xxx. Bowestrynges – j groce. Lyvere arrowes in shevis – xlv. Morrys pykes – xxx. Byllys – xxx. Daertes for toppys – iij doussen.

Munitions. Pyckhamers – iiij. Sledgys – ij. Crowes of yron – ij. Comaunders – ij. Tampions – cc. Canvas for cartowches – ij ellys. Fourmes for cartowches – ij.

Habillimentes. Ropis of hempe for woling and brechyn – iiij coyles. Naylis of sundere sortes – ccc. Bagges of ledder – iij. Fyrkyn with purse – j. Lyme pottes – ij doussen. Spaer truckelles – ij payer. Spaer extrys – iij. Shepe skynnys for spongys – ij. Tymber for forlockes and koynnys – xx foet.

20

[pp. 42–3]

The Mary Jamys

Tunnes – lx

Men {souldiours – xviij; marrynars – xviij; gonnars – iiij}: xl.

For the Mary Jamys. Ordenaunce, artillary, munitions, habillimentes for the warre, for the armyng and in the deffence of the sayd shyppe to the see.

Gonnes of brasse. Mynnyon – j.

Gonnes of yron. Saker – j. Porte pecys – ij. Demy slynges – v. Baessys – x. Hayle shotte pecys – iiij. Handgonnes complete – x.

Gonnepowder. Serpentyn powder in demy barrelles – ix. Fynne corne powder – xx^{lb}.

Shotte of yron. For mynnyon – l. For saker – lx. For demy slynges – c. Dyce of yron for hayle shotte – iij^c.

Shotte of stoen and leade. For porte pecys – lx. For baessys, shotte of leade – ij^c. For handgonnes, shott of leade – ij^c.

Bowes, bowestrynges, arrowes, morrys pykes, byllys and daertes for toppis. Bowes of yough – xl. Bowestrynges – j groce. Lyvere arrowes in shevis – lx. Morrys pykes – xxx. Byllys – xxx. Daertes for toppis – iij doussen.

Munitions. Pyckhamers – ij. Sledgys of yron – ij. Crowes of yron – ij. Comaunders – ij. Tampions – iiij^c. Canvas for cartowches – ij ellys. Fourmes for cartowches – ij.

Habillimentes for the warre. Ropis of hempe for brechyng – iiij coyles. Naylis – cc. Bagges of ledder – ij. Fyrkyns with purses – j. Lyme pottes – iij doussen. Spaer truckelles – ij payer. Spaer extrys – ij. Shepe skynnys – ij. Tymber for forlockes – xx foet.

[*Summary of first roll. In MS arranged below section headings for last ship, here repeated*]

[**Gonnes of brasse**] Somma. Cannons – viij. Cannon perers – iiij. Demy cannons – xxij. Culveryns – xxij. Demy culveryns – xxxj. Sakers – xlvj. Mynnyons – iij. Fawcons – ix. Totalis – cxlv pecys of brasse.

[**Gonnes of yron**] Somma. Porte peces – clx. Slynges – xx. Demy culveryns – j. Sakers – vj. Demy slynges – lvij. Quarter slynges – ix. Fowlers – liiij. Baessys – iiij$^{xx}_{iiij}$xj. Top peces – xxij. Hayle shot pecys – ij^{c}lxxij. Handgonnes – iij^{c}xij. Totalis – j^{ml}iiij^{c}iiij.

[**Gonnepowder**] Somma. Serpentyn powder – xx last j$^{c[lb]}$. Corne powder ij last di, viij^{c}xxiiij^{lb}. Totalis – xxij last di, ix^{c}xxiiij^{lb}.

[**Shotte of yron**]. Somma. For cannon – ij^c. For demy cannon – v^{c}xxx. For culveryn – vj^{c}x. For sakers – xv^{c}l. For demy culveryns – ix^c. For mynyons – cxl. For fawcons – iij^{c}x. For slynges – vj^c. For demy slynges – xj^{c}xl. For qwarter slynges – ij^{c}lx. Crosse barre shotte – cxij. Totalis – vj^{ml}iiij^{c}ij. Dyce of yron – xj^{ml}iiij^c.

[**Shotte of stoen and leade**] Somma. For cannon perer – lxxx. For porte pecys – iij^{ml}lxx. For fowlers – ix^{c}lxx. For toppe pecys – iiij^{c}xx. Totalis – iiij^{ml}v^{c}xl yron shotte; leadon shotte – xvij^{ml}j^{c}xxx.

[**Bowes, bowestrynges, arrowes, morrys pykes, byllys and daertes for toppis**]
Somma. Bowes – ij^{ml}ix^{c}xl. Bowestry[n]ges – lxj groce. Arrowes in shevis – iiij^{ml}iiij^{c}xl. Morrys pykes – j$^{mlxx}_{iiij}$x. Byllys – ij^{ml}xl. Toppe daertes in doussens – iij^{c}xxxj.

[**Munitions**] Somma. Pyckhamers – cxxxviij. Sledgys – cj. Crowes – $^{xx}_{iiij}$j. Comaunders – j^c. Tampions – xxij^{ml}iiij^c. Canvas – clxvj ellys. Paper ryall in qwayers – xij. Fourmes for cartowces – lxiiij.

[**Habillimentes for the warre**] Somma. Ropis of hempe – cxxij coyles. Naylis – x^{ml}ix^c. Bagges of ledder – cxj. Fyrkyns with pursys – lx. Lyme potes – $^{xx}_{iiij}$xvj doussen. Spaer whelys – xxxij payer. Spaer truckelles – lj payer. Spaer extrys – $^{xx}_{iiij}$x. Shepe skynnys – j^{c}lxij. Tymber – xvij lode.

Men. Somma {souldiours – ij^{ml}iiij^{c}xlvij; marrynars – ij^{ml}iiij^{c}xxiiij; gonnars – iij^{c}lxxxvij}: v^{ml}lviij.

Your Majesties poure and humble servaunt. Par me Anthony Anthony.

The Second Roll

BL, Add. MS 22047

21

22

[m. 1] In thys the second*ᵃ* rolle declaryng the nombre of the Kynges Majesties owne galliasses, with every galliasse and galliasse naem [with theyr tunage and nombre of *ᵇ*men; as also the ordenaunce, [artillary, munitions and habillimentes for]*ᶜ* warre for the armyng and deffence of the sayd galliasses agaynst theyr ennymys upon the see, as followeth. That ys to say:

The Graunde Masterys

Tunnes – iiij^{c}l.

Men {souldiours, marrynars – ccxx; gonnars – xxx}: ij^{c}l.

For the Graunde Masterys. Ordenaunce, artillary, munitions, habillimentes for the warre, for the armyng and in the deffence of the sayd galias to the see.

Gonnes of brasse. Demy cannons – ij. Culveryns – iiij. Saker – j. Somma – vij.

Gonnes of yron. Porte pecys – ij. Demy slynges – ij. Fowlers – ij. Baessys – xij. Tope pece – j. Hayle shott pecys – xij. Handgonnes complet – xij. Somma – xliij.

Gonnpowder. Serpentyn powder in barrelles – x. Fyre corne powder – xxiiij^{lb}.

Shott of yron. For demy cannons – lx. For culveryns – cxx. For saker – xl. For demy slynges – lx. Dyce of yron for hayle shott – iiij^c. Somma – vj$^{cxx}_{iiij}$x.

Shotte of stoen and leade. For porte pecys – lx. For fowlers – lx. For tope pece – xx. For baessys, shott of leade – v^c. For handgonnes, shott of leade – iij^c. Somma – viij^{c}xl.

Bowes, bowestrynges, arrowes, morrys pykes, byllys and daertes. Bowes of yough – cl. Bowestrynges – ij groce. Lyvere arrowes in shevis – ccxxv. Morrys pykes – c. Byllys – c. Daertes for toppis – vj doussen.

Munitions. Pyckhamers – vj. Sledgys – iiij. Crowes of yron – iiij. Comaunders – iiij. Tampions – vj^c. Canvas for cartowches – xx ellys. Fourmes for cartowche – ij.

Habillimentes for warre. Ropis of hempe for woling and brechyn – vj coyles. Naylis of sundere sortes – vj^c. Bagges of ledder – iiij. Fyrkyns with pursys – ij. Lyme pottes – iiij doussen. Spaer whelis – ij payer. Spaer truckelles – ij payer. Spaer extrys – iiij. Shepe skynnys for spongys – iiij. Tymber for forlockes – xxx foet.

The Anne Gallante

Tunnes – iiij^{c}l.

Men {souldiours, marrynars – ccxx; gonnars – xxx}: ii^{c}l.

For the Anne Gallante. Ordenaunce, artillary, munitions, habillimentes for the warre, for the armyng and in the deffence of the sayd galias to the see.

Gonnes of brasse. Long culveryns – ij. Short culveryns – ij. Demy culveryns – ij. Curtall – j. Somma – vij.

Gonnes of yron. Slyng – j. Baessys – xij. Hayle shott pecys – xij. Handgonnes complet – xij. Toppe pece – j. Somma – xxxviij.

Gonnpowder. Serpentyn powder – ij last. Fyne corne powder – xxiiij^{lb}.

Shott of yron. For long culveryns – c. For short culveryns – lx. For demy culveryns – lx. For curtall – xx. For the slyng – xxx. Dice of yron for hayle shott – iiij^c. Somma – vj^{c}lxx.

Shott of stoen and leade. For toppe pece – xx. For baessys, shott of leade – iiij^c. For handgonnes, shott of leade – iij^c.

Bowes, bowestrynges, arrowes, morrys pykes, byllys and daertes. Bowes of yough – cxl. Bowestrynges – ij groce. Lyvere arrowes in shevis – ccx. Morrys pykes – c. Byllys – c. Daertes for toppis – vj doussen.

Munitions. Pyckhamers – ij. Sledgys – iij. Crowes of yron – iiij. Comaunders – iiij. Tampions – iij^c. Canvas for cartowches – xx ellys. Fourmes for cartowches – iiij.

Habillimentes for warre. Ropis of hempe for woling and brechyng – vj coyles. Nailis of sundere sertes – vj^c. Bagges of ledder – iiij. Fyrkyn with pursys – ij. Lyme pottes – iiij doussen. Spaer whelis – ij payer. Spaer truckelles – ij payer. Spaer extrys – iiij. Shepe skynnys for spongys – iiij. Tymber for forlockes and koynnys – xxx foet.

ᵃ Two words inserted.   *ᵇ–ᶜ* MS illegible. Bracketed words supplied from heading to first roll.

23

24

The Harte

Tunnes – iij^c.

Men {souldiours, marrynars – clxx; gonnars – xxx}: ij^c.

For the Harte. Ordenaunce, artillary, munitions, habillimentes for the warre, for the armyng and in the deffence of the sayd galias to the see.

Gonnes of brasse. Demy cannon – j. Culveryns – iij. Somma – iiij.

Gonnes of yron. Demy culveryns – iij. Sakers – ij. Porte pecys – iiij. Slynges – ij. Baessys – xij. Hayle shotte pecys – xij. Handgonnes complete – xij. Toppe pece – j. Somma – xlviij.

Gonnepowder. Serpentyn powder in barrelles – xij. Grosse corne powder in barrelles – ij. Fynne corne powder – xxiiij^{lb}.

Shotte of yron. For demy cannon – lx. For culveryns – cl. For demy culveryns – cxx^{ti}. For sakers – lx. For slynges – lx. Dyce of yron for hayle shotte – iiij^c. Crosse barre shotte – xij. Somma – vij^clxij.^a

Shotte of stoen and leade. For porte pecys – lxxx. For toppe pece – xx^{ti}. For baessys, shotte of leade – ccc. For handgonnes, shotte of leade – cc. Somma – vj^c.

Bowes, bowestrynges, arrowes, morrys pykes, byllys and daertes for toppis. Bowes of yough – c. Bowestrynges – ij groce. Lyvere arrowes in shevis – cl. Morrys pykes – c. Byllys – c. Daertes for toppis – vj doussen.

Munitions. Pyckehamers – vj. Sledgys of yron – iiij. Crowes of yron – vj. Comaunders – iiij. Tampions – vj^c. Canvas for cartowches – xiiij ellys. Fourmes for cartowches – iiij.

Habillimentes for the warre. Ropis of hempe for woling and brechyng – vj coyles. Naylis of sundre sortes – vj^c. Bagges of ledder – iiij. Fyrkyns with pursys – ij. Lyme pottes – ij doussen. Spaer whelys – ij payer. Spaer truckelles – ij payer. Spaer extrys – iiij. Shepe skynnys – iiij. Tymber for forlockes and koynnys – xxx foet.

The Antelop

Tunnes – iij^c.

Men {souldiours, marrynars – clxx; gonnars – xxx}: ij^c.

For the Antelop. Ordenaunce, artillary, munitions, habillimentes for the warre, for the armyng and in the deffence of the sayd galias to the see.

Gonnes of brasse. Demy cannon – j. Culveryns – iij. Somma – iiij.

Gonnes of yron. Demy culveryns – iij. Sakers – ij. Porte pecys – iiij. Slynges – ij. Baessys – xij. Handgonnes complete – xij. Toppe pece – j. Hayle shotte pecys – viij. Somma – xliiij.

Gonnepowder. Serpentyn powder in barrelles – x. Grosse corne powder in barrelles – ij. Fynne corne powder – xxiiij^{lb}.

Shotte of yron. For demy cannon – l. For culveryns – cl. For demy culveryns – cxx^{ti}. For sakers – lxxx. For slynges – lx. Dyce of yron for hayle shotte – iiij^c. Crosse barre shotte – xij. Somma – viij^clxxij.

Shotte of stoen and leade. For porte pecys – lxxx. For toppe pece – xx^{ti}. For baessys, shotte of leade – iij^c. For handgonnes, shotte of leade – iij^c. Somma – vij^c.

Bowes, bowestrynges, arrowes, morrys pykes, byllys and daertes for toppis. Bowes of yough – c. Bowestrynges – ij groce. Lyvere arrowes in shevis – cl. Morrys pykes – c. Byllys – c. Daertes for toppys – vj doussen.

Munitions. Pyckehamers – vj. Sledgys of yron – iiij. Crowes of yron – vj. Comaunders – iiij. Tampions – vj^c. Canvas for cartowches – xij elles. Fourmes for cartowches – iiij.

Habillimentes for the warre. Ropis of hempe for woling and brechyng – viij coyles. Naylis of sundre sortes – vj^c. Bagges of ledder – vj. Fyrkyns with pursys – ij. Lyme pottes – iij doussen. Spaer whelis – ij payer. Spaer truckelles – ij payer. Spaer extrys – iiij. Shepe skynnys – iiij. Tymber for forlockes and koynnys – xxx foet.

^a Corrected from 'viij^clxij'.

25

26

The Tegar

Tunnes – ij^c.

Men {marrynars – c; gonnars – xx}: cxx^{ti}.

For the Tegar. Ordenaunce, artillary, munitions, habillimentes for the warre, for the armyng and in the deffence of the sayd galias to the see.

Gonnes of brasse. Culveryn – j. Demy culveryns – ij. Somma – iij.

Gonnes of yron. Demy culveryns – iiij. Porte pecys – iiij. Quarter slynges – ij. Baessys – xij. Hayle shotte pecys – iiij. Handgonnes complete – xij. Somma – xxxviij.

Gonnepowder. Serpentyn powder in demy barrelles – xij. Grosse corne powder, demy barrell – j. Fynne corne powder – xxiiij^{lb}.

Shotte of yron. For culveryns – lx. For demy culveryns – cxx^{ti}. For quarter slynges – xl. Dyce of yron for hayle shotte – iij. Somma – vj^cxx.

Shotte of stoen and leade. For porte pecys – lxxx. For baessys, shotte of leade – iij^c. For handgonnes, shotte of leade – ij^c. Somma – v^clxxx.

Bowes, bowestrynges, arrowes, morrys pykes, byllys and daertes for toppis. Bowes of yough – lx. Bowestrynges – j groce. Lyvere arrowes in shevis – c. Morrys pykes – l. Byllys – l. Daertes for toppis – iiij doussen.

Munitions. Pyckehamers – vj. Sledgys of yron – iiij. Crowes of yron – iiij. Comaunders – iiij. Tampions – v^c. Canvas for cartowches – viij ellys. Fourmes for cartowches – ij.

Habillimentes for the warre. Ropis of hempe for woling and brechyng – vj coyles. Naylis of su[n]dre sortes – iiij^c. Bagges of ledder – iiij. Fyrkyns with pursys – ij. Lyme pottes – iiij doussen. Spaer whelis – j payer. Spaer truckelles – ij payer. Spaer extrys – iiij. Shepe skynnys – iiij. Tymber for forlockes and koynnys – xx foet.

[m. 3]

The Bulle

Tunnes – ij^c.

Men {marrynars – c; gonnars – xx}: cxx^{ti}.

For the Bulle. Ordenaunce, artillary, munitions, habillimentes for the warre, for the armyng and in the deffence of the sayd galias to the see.

Gonnes of brasse. Culveryns – ij. Demy culveryns – ij. Saker – j. Somma – v.

Gonnes of yron. Demy culveryns – iiij. Porte pecys – iiij. Quarter slynges – ij. Baessys – xij. Hayle shotte pecys – iiij. Handgonnes complete – viij. Somma – xxxiiij.

Gonnepowder. Serpentyn powder in demy barrelles – xij. Grosse corne powder in demy barrell – j. Fynne corne powder – xvj^{lb}.

Shotte of yron. For culveryns – lx. For demy culveryns – cl. For saker – xl. For quarter slyng – xl. Dyce of yron for hayle shotte – iij^c. Somma – v^{c xx}_{iiij}x.

Shotte of stoen and leade. For porte pecys – lxxx. For baessys, shotte of leade – iij^c. For handgonnes, shotte of leade – ij^cl. Somma – vj^cxxx.

Bowes, bowestrynges, arrowes, morrys pykes, byllys and daertes for toppis. Bowes of yough – lx. Bowestrynges – j groce. Lyvere arrowes – c shevis. Morrys pykes – l. Byllys – l. Daertes for toppis – iiij doussen.

Munitions. Pyckehamers – vj. Sledgys of yron – iiij. Crowes of yron – iiij. Comaunders – vj. Tampions – iiij^c. Canvas for cartowches – viij ellys. Fourmes for cartowches – ij.

Habillimentes for the warre. Ropis of hempe for woling and brechyng – vj coyles. Naylis of sundre sortes – iiij^c. Bagges of ledder – iiij. Fyrkyns with pursys – ij. Lyme pottes – ij doussen. Spaer whelis – j payer. Spaer truckelles – ij payer. Spaer extrys – iiij. Shepe skynnys – ij. Tymber for forlockes and koynnys – xxx foet.

70

27

28

The Salamander

Tunnes – iij^c.

Men {marrynars – cc; gonnars – xx}: ccxx^{ti}.

For the Salamander. Ordenaunce, artillary, munitions, habillimentes for the warre, for the armyng and in the deffence of the sayd galias to the see.

Gonnes of brasse. Culveryns – ij. Demy culveryns – ij. Sakers – iiij. Somma – viij.

Gonnes of yron. Porte pecys – viij. Demy slynges – ij. Fowlers – iiij. Baessys – xvij. Hayle shotte pecys – xij. Handgonnes complete – xij. Tope pece – j. Somma – lv.

Gonnepowder. Serpentyn powder – j last. Fynne corne powder – xxiiij^{lb}.

Shotte of yron. For culveryns – lx. For demy culveryns – lxxx. For sakers – c. For demy slynges – l. Dyce of yron for hayle shotte – iij^c. Somma – v^c$_{iiij}^{xx}$x.

Shotte of stoen and leade. For porte pecys – clx. For toppe pece – xx. For fowlers – lx. For baessys, shotte of leade – iij^c. For handgonnes, shotte of leade – ij^c. Somma – vij^{c}xl.

Bowes, bowestrynges, arrowes, morrys pykes, byllys and daertes for toppis. Bowes of yough – c. Bowestrynges – ij groce. Lyvere arrowes in shevis – cl. Morrys pykes – c. Billys – c. Daertes for toppis – vj doussen.

Munitions. Pyckehamers – vj. Sledgys of yron – iiij. Crowes of yron – iiij. Comaunders – vj. Tampions – v^c. Canvas for cartowches – xij ellys. Fourmes for cartowches – ij.

Habillimentes for the warre. Ropis of hempe for woling and brechyng – vj coyles. Naylis of sundre sortes – iiij^c. Bagges of ledder – iiij. Fyrkyns with pursys – ij. Spaer whelis – ij payer. Spaer truckelles – ij payer. Spaer extrys – iiij. Shepe skynnys – iiij. Tymber for forlockes and koynnys – xx^{ti} foet. Lyme pottes – iiij doussen.

The Unicorne

Tunnes – ij^{c}xl.

Men {marrynars – cxxiiij; gonnars – xvj}: cxl.

For the Unicorne. Ordenaunce, artillary, munitions, habillimentes for the warre, for the armyng and in the deffence of the sayd galias to the see.

Gonnes of brasse. Culveryns – j. Demy culveryns – j. Cannon perer – j. Sakers – ij. Somma – v.

Gonnes of yron. Saker – j. Porte pecys – ij. Demy slynges – iij. Fowlers – ij. Baessys – xij. Hayle shotte pecys – viij. Handgonnes complete – viij. Toppe pece – j. Somma – xxxvij.

Gonnepowder. Serpentyn powder in barrelles – vj. Grosse corne powder in demy barrell – j. Fynne corne powder – xvj^{lb}.

Shotte of yron. For culveryns – xxx. For demy culveryns – xl. For sakers – lxxx. For demy slynges – lx. Dyce of yron for hayle shotte – iij^c. Somma – v^{c}x.

Shotte of stoen and leade. For cannon perer – xx. For porte pecys – xl. For fowlers – xl. For toppe pece – xx^{ti}. For baessys, shotte of leade – iij^c. For handgonnes, shotte of leade – ij^c. Somma – vj^{c}xx.

Bowes, bowestrynges, arrowes, morrys pykes, byllys and daertes for toppis. Bowes of yough – lxxx. Bowestrynges – ij groce. Lyvere arrowes in shevis – cxx^{ti}. Morrys pykes – l. Byllys – l. Daertes for toppis – iiij doussen.

Munitions. Pyckehamers – vj. Sledgys of yron – iiij. Crowes of yron – iiij. Comaunders – iiij. Tampions – v^c. Canvas for cartowches – vj ellys. Fourmes for cartowches – iiij.

Habillimentes for the warre. Ropis of hempe for woling and brechyng – vj coyles. Naylis of sundre sortes – iiij^c. Bagges of ledder – iiij. Fyrkyns with pursys – ij. Lyme pottes – iiij doussen. Spaer whelis – j payer. Spaer truckelles – ij payer. Spaer extrys – iiij. Shepe skynnys – iiij. Tymber for forlockes and koynnys – xx foet.

29

30

[m. 4]

The Swallowe

Tunnes – ccxl.

Men {marrynars – cxxx; gonnars – xxx}: clx.

For the Swallowe. Ordenaunce, artillary, munitions, habillimentes for the warre, for the armyng and in the ceffence of the sayd galias to the see.

Gonnes of brasse. Demy cannon – j. Demy culveryn – j. Sakers – iiij. Somma – vj.

Gonnes of yron. Demy culveryn – j. Porte pecys – vj. Demy slynges – iiij. Baessys – xx. Tope pece – j. Hayle shotte pecys – xij. Handgonnes complete – xij. Somma – lv.

Gonnepowder. Serpentyn powder in barrelles – xxiij. Fynne corne powder – xxx^{lb}.

Shotte of yron. For demy cannon – l. For demy culveryn – lx. For demy slynges – lxx. For sakers – cxx. Dice of yron for hayle shotte – iiij^c. Crosse barre shott – xx. Somma – vij^{c}xx.

Shotte of stoen and leade. For porte pecys – cxx. For the tope pece – xx. For baessys, shott of leade – iiij^c. For handgonnes, shott of leade – ij^c. Somma – vj^{c}xl.

Bowes, bowestrynges, arrowes, morrys pyckes, byllys, daertes for toppys. Bowes of yough – c. Bowestrynges – ij groce. Lyvere arrowes in shevis – cl. Morrys pykes – l. Byllys – l. Daertes for toppis – vj doussen.

Munitions. Pyckhamers – vj. Sledgys – iiij. Crowes of yron – iiij. Comaunders – iiij. Tampions – v^c. Canvas for cartowches – xij ellys. Fourmes for cartowche – iij.

Habillimentes for warre. Ropis of hempe for woling and brechyng – vj coyles. Naylis of sundere sortes – iiij^c. Bagges of ledder – iiij. Fyrkyn with pursys – ij. Lyme pottes – iiij doussen. Spaer whelis – j payer. Spaer truckelles – iiij. Spaer extrys – iiij. Shepe skynnys – iiij. Tymber for forlockes – xxx foet.

The Galie Subtille

Tunnes – cc.

Men {marrynars – ccxlij; gonnars – viij}: ccl.

For the Galie Subtille. Ordenaunce, artillary, munitions, habillimentes for the warre, for the armyng and in the deffence of the sayd galie to the see.

Gonnes of brasse. Cannon – j. Sakers – ij. Somma – iij.

Gonnes of yron. Fowlers – ij. Baessys – xiiij. Hayle shott pecys – xij. Handgonnes complete – l. Somma $\frac{xx}{iiij}$xij.^{a}

Gonnpowder. Serpentyn powder in demy barrelles – xviij. Fynne corne powder, demy barrell – j.

Shotte of yron. For cannon – l. For sakers – $\frac{xx}{iiij}$. Dice of yron for hayle shotte – v^c. Somma – vj^{c}xxx.

Shotte of stoen and leade. For fowlers – xl. For baessys, shott of leade – v^c. For handgonnes, shotte of leade – iiij^c. Somma – viij^{c}xl.

Bowes, bowestrynges, arrowes, morrys pyckes, byllys, daertes for toppis. Bowes of yough – c. Bowestrynges – ij groce. Lyvere arrowes in shevis – cl. Morrys pykes – lx. Byllys – lx. Daertes for toppis – ij doussen.

Munitions. Pyckhamers – iij. Sledgys – iij. Crowes of yron – ij. Comaunders – ij. Tampions – iiij^c. Canvas for cartowches – vj ellys. Fourmes for cartowche – iij. Paper ryall – j qwayer.

Habillimentes for warre. Ropis of hempe for woling and brechyng – j coyle. Naylis of sundre sortes – ij^c. Bagges of ledder – ij. Fyrkyn with pursys – j. Lyme pottes – iiij doussen. Spaer truckelles – ij. Spaer extrys – ij. Shepe skynnys – iiij.

^{a} *Recte* 78.

31

32

The Newe Barcke

Tunnes – cc.

Men {marrynars – cxxiiij; gonnars – xvj}: cxl.

For the Newe Barcke. Ordenaunce, artillary, munitions, habillimentes for warre, for the armyng and in the defence of the sayd galias to the see.

Gonnes of brasse. Demy culveryn – j. Cannon perer – j. Sakers – iij. Somma – v.

Gonnes of yron. Porte pecys – ix. Demy slyng – j. Fowlers – vj. Baessys – xx. Hayle shotte pecys – vj. Toppe pece – j. Handgonnes complete – xij. Somma – lv.

Gonnepowder. Serpentyn powder in demy barrelles – xij. Grosse corne powder, demy barrell^a –j. Fynne corne powder – xxiiij^{lb}.

Shotte of yron. For demy culveryn – xxx. For sakers – $\frac{xx}{iiij}$. For demy slyng – xx. Dice of yron for hayle shotte – iiij^c. Somma – v^{c}xxx.

Shotte of stoen and leade. For cannon perer – xx. For porte pecys – viij^{xx}. For fowlers – cxx. For toppe pece – xx. For baessys, shotte of leade – iiij^c. For handgonnes, shotte of leade – ij^c. Somma – ix^{c}xx.

Bowes, bowestrynges, arrowes, morrys pykes, byllys, daertes for toppys. Bowes of yough – lxxx. Bowestrynges – ij groce. Lyvere arrowes in shevis – cxx^{ti}. Morrys pykes – l. Byllys – lx. Daertes for toppis – iiij doussen.

Munitions. Pyckhamers – vj. Sledgys – iiij. Crowes of yron – iiij. Comaunders – iiij. Tampions – v^c. Canvas for cartowches – vj ellys. Fourmes for cartowche – iij.

Habillimentes for warre. Ropis of hempe for woling and brechyng – vj coyles. Naylis of sundre sortes – iiij^c. Bagges of ledder – iiij. Fyrkyn with pursys – ij. Lyme pottes – iiij doussen. Spaer whelis – j payer. Spaer truckelles – iiij. Spaer extrys – iiij. Shepe skynnys – iiij. Tymber for forlockes – xx foet.

[m. 5]

The Graye Hounde

Tunnes – cc.

Men {marrynars – cxxiiij; gonnars – xvj}: cxl.

For the Graye Hounde. Ordennaunce, artillary, munitions for the warre, for the armyng and in the defence of the sayd shippe to the see.

Gonnes of brasse. Culveryn – j. Cannon perers – ij. Sakers – ij. Fawcons – ij. Fawconnet – j. Somma – viij.

Gonnes of yron. Demy slynges – ij. Baessys – xij. Hayle shott pecys – vj. Handgonnes complet – xij. Toppe pece – j. Somma – xxxiiij.

Gonnepowder. Serpentyn powder in demy barrelles – xx. Grosse corne powder, demy barrell – j. Fyne corne powder – xxiiij^{lb}.

Shotte of yron. For culveryn – lx. For sakers – c. For fawcons – lx. For fawconnet – xxx. For slynges – lxxx. Dice of yron for hayle shotte – ij^c. Somma – vj^{c}xxx.

Shotte of stoen and leade. For cannon perer – lx. For baessys, shott of leade – ij^c. For handgonnes – ij^c. For toppe pece, shotte of stoen – xx^{ti}. Somma – v^{c}lxxx.

Bowes, bowestrynges, arrowes, morrys pykes, byllys and daertes for toppis. Bowes of yough – cl. Bowestrynges – iij groce. Lyvere arrowes in shevis – ij^{c}xx. Morrys pykes – c. Byllys – c. Daertes for toppis – vj doussen.

Munitions. Pyckhamers – iiij. Sledgys – iiij. Crowes of yron – iiij. Comaunders – ij. Tampions – iiij^c. Canvas for cartowchys – vj ellys. Paper ryall – j di qwayer. Fourmes for cartowche – iij.

Habillimentes. Ropis of hempe for woling and brechyng – iiij coyles. Naylis of sundere sortes – ij^c. Bagges of ledder – iiij. Fyrkyn with pursys – ij. Lyme pottes – iiij doussen. Spaer whelis – ij payer. Spaer truckelles – ij payer. Spaer extrys – iiij. Shepe skynnys – iiij. Tymber for forlockes – xv foet.

---

^{a} Two words inserted.

76

33

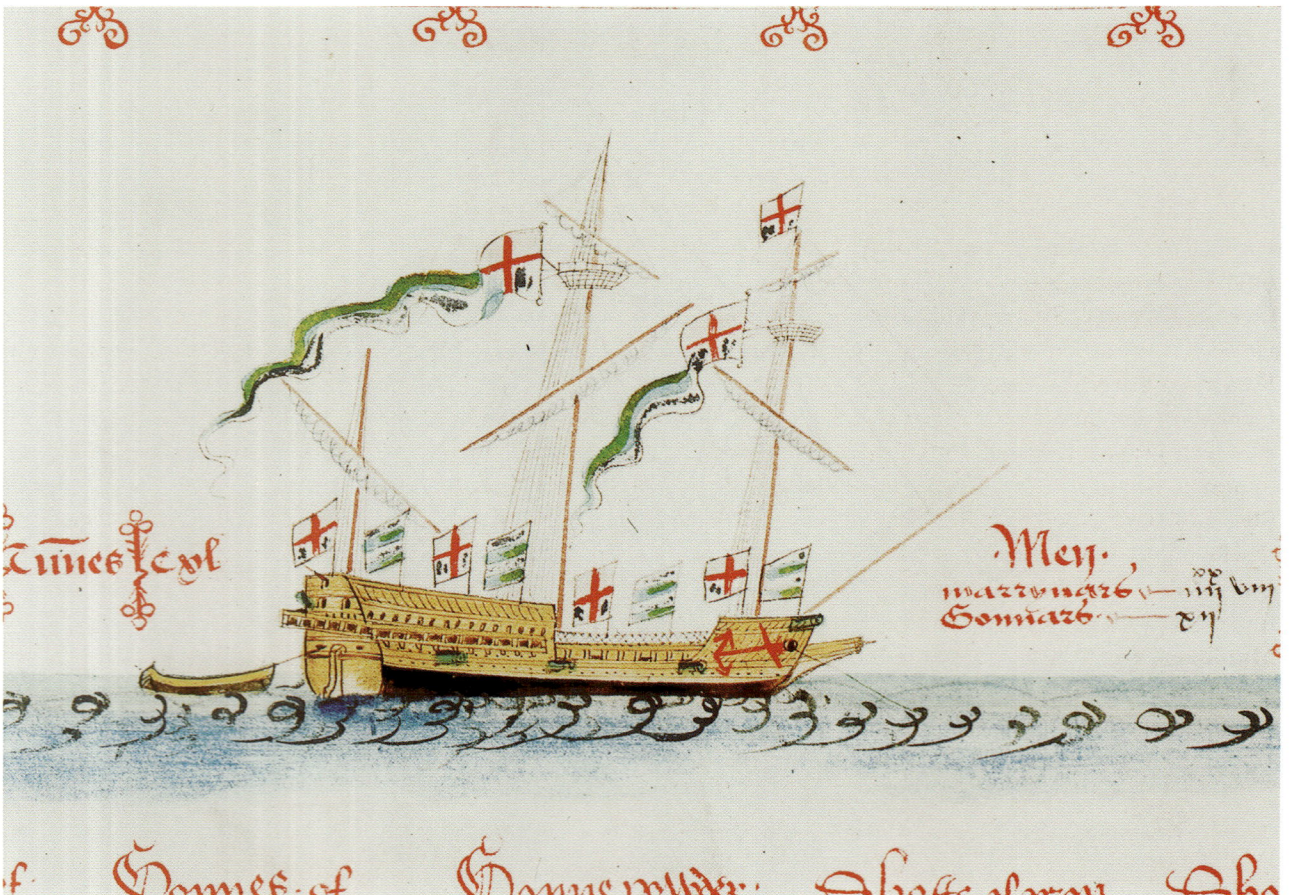

34

The Jennet

Tunnes – clxxx.

Men {marrynars – cvj; gonnars – xiiij}: cxx^{ti}.

For the Jennet. Ordenaunce, artillary, munitions, habillimentes for the warre, for the armyng and in the defence of the sayd shippe to the see.

Gonnes of brasse. Culveryn – j. Sakers – ij. Somma – iij.

Gonnes of yron. Demy culveryn – j. Sakers – ij. Baessys – x. Hayle shott pecys – vj. Handgonnes complet – xij. Toppe pece – j. Somma – xxxij.

Gonnepowder. Serpentyn powder, demy barrelles*a* – x. Fyne corne powder – xxiiij^{lb}. Somma – [*blank*]*b*.

Shotte of yron. For culveryn – xxx. For demy culveryns – xxx. For sakers – lxxx. Dice of yron for hayle shotte – iij^c. Somma – iiij^cxl.

Shotte of stoen and leade. For toppe pece – xx. For baessys, shott of leade – ij^c. For handgonnes – ij^c. Somma – iiij^cxx.

Bowes, bowestrynges, arrowes, morrys, pykes, byllys and daertes for toppis. Bowes of yough – l. Bowestrynges – j groce. Lyvere arrowes in shevys – lxxv. Morrys pykes – l. Byllys – l. Daertes for toppis – iij doussen.

Munitions. Pyckhamers – ij. Sledgys – ij. Crowes of yron – ij. Comaunders – ij. Tampions – j^c. Canvas for cartowchys – v ellys. Fourmes for cartowche – ij.

Habillimentes. Ropis of hempe for woling and brechyng – iij coyles. Naylis of sundere sortes – ij^c. Bagges of ledder – iiij. Fyrkyn with pursys – ij. Lyme pottes – ij doussen. Spaer whelis – j payer. Spaer truckelles – ij payer. Spaer extrys – ij. Shepe skynnys for spongys – ij. Tymber for forlockes – x foet.

The Lyon

Tunnes – cxl.

Men {marrynars – $\frac{xx}{iiij}$viij; gonnars – xij}: c.

For the Lyon. Ordenaunce, artillary, munitions, habillimentes for the warre, for the armyng and in the defence of the sayd shippe to the see.

Gonnes of brasse. Sakers – ij. Fawcon – j. Somma – iij.

Gonnes of yron. Porte pecys – viij. Quarter slynges – ij. Fowlers – ij. Baessys – xviij. Hayle shott pecys – iiij. Handgonnes complet – viij. Somma – xliiij.

Gonnepowder. Serpentyn powder in demy barrelles – xx^{ti}. Fyne corne powder – xvj^{lb}.

Shotte of yron. For sakers – lx. For fawcon – xxx. For qwarter slynges – xl. Dice of yron for hayle shott – ij^c. Somma – iij^cxxx.

Shotte of stoen and leade. For porte pecys – cl. For fowlers – lx. For baessys, shott of leade – iij^c. For handgonnes – ij^c. Somma – vij^cx.

Bowes, bowestrynges, arrowes, morrys pykes, byllys and daertes for toppis. Bowes of yough – $\frac{xx}{iiij}$. Bowestrynges – ij groce. Lyvere arrowes in shevis – cxx. Morrys pykes – xl. Byllys – xl. Daertes for toppis – ij doussen.

Munitions. Pyckhamers – iiij. Sledgys – iiij. Crowes of yron – iiij. Comaunders – ij. Tampions – v^c. Canvas for cartowches – iij ellys. Fourmes for cartowche – ij.

Habillimentes. Ropis of hempe for woling and brechyng – iiij coyles. Naylis of su[n]dere sortes – ij^c. Bagges of ledder – iiij. Fyrkyn with pursys – ij. Lyme pottes – ij doussen. Spaer truckelles – iiij. Spaer extrys – iiij. Shepe skynnys – ij. Tymber for forlockes – xx foet.

---

a Two words inserted. *b* Entry begun in error.

The dragon tyme

Men marrymars gonmars

35

[m. 6]

The Dragon

Tunnes – cxl.

Men {marrynars – $\frac{xx}{iiij}$xviij; gonnars – xij}: cx.

For the Dragon. Ordenanunce, artillary, munitions, habillimentes for the warre, for the armyng and in the deffence of the sayd shyppe to the see.

Gonnes of brasse. Saker – j. Double baesse – j.

Gonnes of yron. Sakers – ij. Demy slynges – iiij. Fowlers – ij. Baessys – xx. Hayle shott pecys – vj. Handgonnes complet – x.

Gonnepowder. Serpentyn powder in demy barrelles – xvj. Fynne corne powder – xx^{lb}.

Shotte of yron. For sakers – c. For demy slynges – c. Dice of yron for hayle shott – iiij^c.

Shotte of stoen and leade. For fowlers – xl. For baessys, shotte of leade – iiij^c. For handgonnes, shotte of leade – ij^c.

Bowes, bowestrynges, arrowes, morrys pykes, byllys, daertes for toppis. Bowes of yough – $\frac{xx}{iiij}$. Bowestrynges – ij groce. Lyvere arrowes in shevis – cxl. Morrys pykes – lx. Byllys – lx. Daertes for toppys – iiij doussen.

Munitions. Pyckhamers – iiij. Sledgys – iiij. Crowes of yron – iiij. Comaunders – ij. Tampions – iiij^c. Canvas for cartowches – iiij ellys. Fourmes for cartowche – ij.

Habillimentes for warre. Ropis of hempe for woling and brechyng – iiij coyles. Naylis of sundere sortes – iij^c. Bagges of ledder – iiij. Fyrkyns with pursys – ij. Lyme pottes – iij doussen. Spaer truckelles – iiij. Spaer extrys – ij. Shepe skynnys – ij. Tymber for forlockes – xxx foet.

[Summary of second roll. In MS arranged below section headings for last ship, here repeated]

[**Gonnes of brasse**] Somma. Cannon – j. Cannon perers – iiij. Demy cannons – vj. Culveryns – xxj. Demy culveryns – xij. Sakers – xxiiij. Fawcons – ij. Fawconnetes – ij. Totalis – lxxiij pecys of brasse.

[**Gonnes of yron**] Somma. Porte pecys – lj. Slynges – viij. Demy slynges – xv. Quarter slynges – vij. Fowlers – xvij. Sakers – vij. Demy culveryns – xviij. Tope pecys – x. Baessys – ccxv. Hayle shott pecys – cxxiiij.^{a} Handgonnes – cciiij. Totalis – vj^{c}lxxv pecys of yron.

[**Gonnepowder**]. Somma. Serpentyn powder in barrelles – lxxxij. Grosse corne powder in barrelles – iiij; in demy barrelles – v. Fynne corne powder in poundes – ij^c$\frac{xx}{iij}$x^{lb}. Serpentyn powder in demy barrelles – j^{c}xx. Totalis – xix last di, iiij^c$\frac{xx}{iiij}$x^{lb}.

[**Shotte of yron**] Somma. For cannon – l. For demy cannon – ij^{c}xl. For culveryn – viij^c$\frac{xx}{iiij}$. For demy culveryn – viij^{c}x. For sakers – ix^{c}xxx. For fawcons – $\frac{xx}{iiij}$x. For fawconnetes – xxx. For demy slynges – ij^{c}xxx. For demy slynges^b – ij^{c}lx. For qwarter slynges – j^{c}xx. Crosse barre shott – xliiij. Totalis – iiij^{ml}vij^{c}lxxxiiij shot of yron. Dyce of yron – v^{ml}ij^c.

[**Shotte of stoen and leade**] Somma. For porte pecys – xj^{c}x. For fowlers – iiij^{c}xx. For toppe pecys – ij^c. Totalis – j^{ml}vij^{c}xxx.

Somma. For baessys, shot of leade – v^{ml}j^c. For handgons – iij^{ml}iiij^c. Totalis – viij^{ml}c.

[**Bowes, bowestrynges, arrowes, morrys pykes, byllys, daertes for toppis**] Somma. Bowes – j^{ml}iiij^{c}xxx. Bowestrynges – xxviiij groce. Arrowes in shevis – ij^{ml}j^{c}lxxv. Morrys pykes – j^{ml}lx. Byllys – j^{ml}lxx. Daertes for toppys – lxx doussen.

[**Munitions**] Somma. Pyckhamers – lxxiiij. Sledgys – lv. Crowes – lviij. Comaunders – lvj. Tampions – vj^{ml}vij^c. Canvas – j^{c}xlij ellys. Fourmes for cartowces – xlvj.

[**Habillimentes for warre**] Somma. Ropis of hempe – lxxv coyles. Naylis – v^{ml}viij^c. Bagges of ledder – lx. Fyrkyns with pursys – xxviij. Lyme potes – liiij doussen. Spaer whelis – xviij payer. Spaer extrys – lv. Shepe skynnys – liiij. Tymber for forlockes – ij^{c}xxv foet. Spaer truckelles – liiij.

Men {souldiers and marrynars – ij^{ml}ij^{c}xvj; gonnars – iiij^{c}iiij}: ij^{ml}v^{c}xx^{ti}.

Youre Majesties humble and poure servaunt. Par me Anthony Anthony.

---

^{a} Corrected from 'cxxiij'. ^{b} Repeated words *sic*.

The Third Roll

Pepys 2991

r the Armyng and deffence of the sayd pynnasses agaynst th

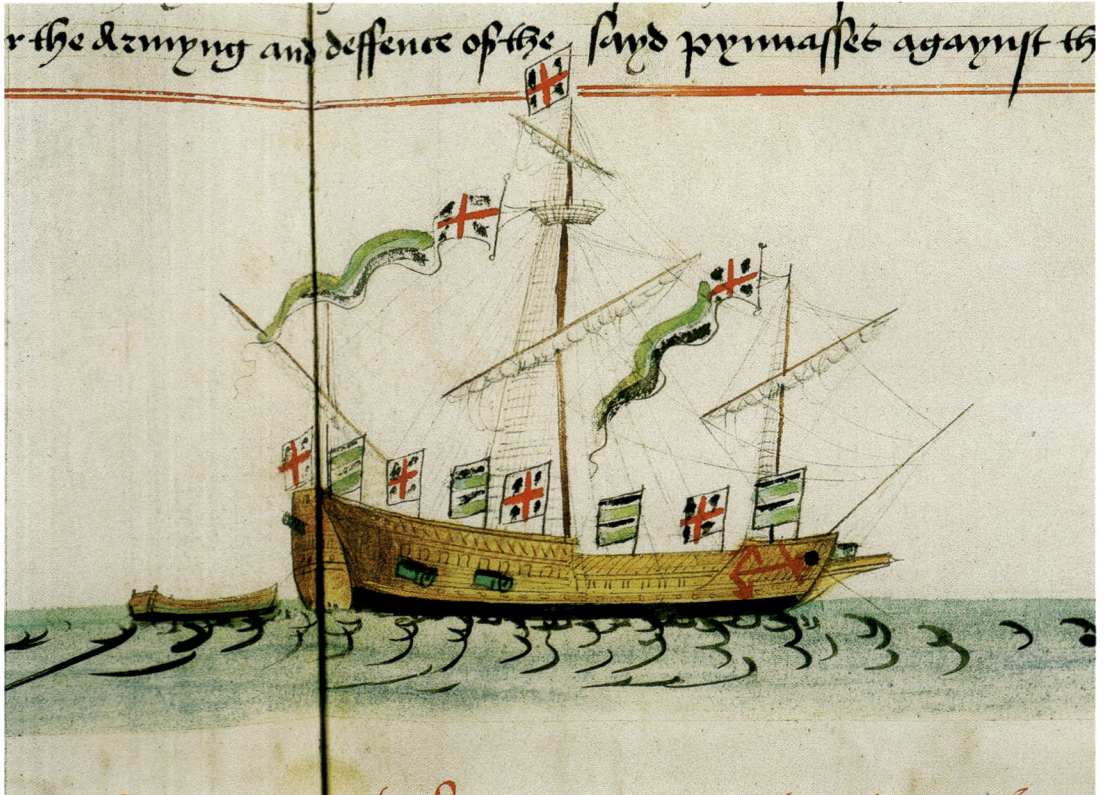

36

37

[pp. 54–5] In thys the thyrde roolle declaryng the nombre of the Kynges Majestys pynnasses with every pynras and pynnas naem with theyr tunage and nombre of men, as also the ordenaunce, artillary, munitions and habillimentes[a] for the warre for the armyng and deffence of the sayd pynnasses agaynst theyr ennymys apon the see.

The Phawcon

Tunnes – $\frac{xx}{iiij}$.

Men {marrynars – liiij; gonnars – vj}: lx.

For the Phawcon. Ordenaunce, artillary, munitions, habillimentes for the warre, for the armyng and in the deffence of the sayd pynnas to the see.

Gonnes of brasse. Sakers – iiij.

Gonnes of yron. Demy slynges and qwarter slynges – ij. Double baessys and demy baessys – xx^{ti}. Hayle shott pecys – iiij. Handgonnes complete – vj.

Gonnepowder. Serpentyn powder in demy barrelles – viij. Fynne corne powder – xij^{lb}.

Shotte of yron. For sakers – c. For demy and quarter slynges – lxxx. Dyce of yron for hayle shotte – iij^c.

Shotte of stoen and leade. For baessys, shotte of leade – iiij^c. For handgonnes, shotte of leade – j^{c}xx^{ti}.

Bowes, bowestrynges, arrowes, morrys pykes, byllys and daertes for toppis. Bowes of yough – xl. Bowestrynges – j groce. Lyvere arrowes in shevis – lx. Morrys pykes – xxx^{ti}. Byllys – xxx^{ti}. Daertes for toppys – ij doussen.

Munitions. Sledgys of yron – iiij. Crowes of yron – ij. Tampions – iiij^c. Canvas for cartowches – iiij ellys. Fourmes for cartowche – j.

Habillimentes for the warre. Ropis of hempe for woling – iij coyles. Naylis – ij^c. Bagges of ledder – iij. Fyrkyn with purse – j. Lyme pottes – iij doussen. Spaer truckelles – ij. Spaer extrys – ij. Shepe skynnys – ij. Tymber for forlockes – x foet.

The Sacar

Tunnes – $\frac{xx}{iiiij}$.

Men {marrynars – liiij; gonnars – vj}: lx.

For the Sacar. Ordenaunce, artillary, munitions, habillimentes for the warre, for the armyng and in the deffence of the sayd pynnas to the see.

Gonnes of brasse. Sakers – ij.

Gonnes of yron. Fowlers – ij. Baessys – xij. Hayle shotte pecys – ij. Handgonnes complete – iiij.

Gonnepowder. Serpentyn powder in demy barrelles – viij. Fynne corne powder – viij^{lb}.

Shotte of yron. For saker – lxxx. Dyce of yron for hayle shotte – ij^c.

Shotte of stoen and leade. For fowlers – xl. For baessys, shott of leade – ij^{c}xl. For handgonnes, shotte of leade – c.

Bowes, bowestrynges, arrowes, morrys pykes, byllys and daertes for toppis. Bowes of yough – xxv. Bowestrynges – j groce. Lyvere arrowes in shevis – xxxvj. Morrys pykes – xx. Byllys – xx. Daertes for toppys – iiij doussen.

Munitions. Pyckhamers – iiij. Sledgys of yron – ij. Crowes of yron – ij. Comaunders – j. Tampions – iij^c. Canvas for cartowches – ij ellys. Fourme for cartowches – j.

Habillimentes for the warre. Ropis of hempe for brechyng – j coyle. Naylis – j^c. Bagges of ledder – ij. Fyrkyn with purse – j. Lyme pottes – ij doussen. Spaer truckelles – ij. Spaer extrys – ij. Shepe skynnys – ij. Tymber for forlockes – v foet.

---

[a] 'im' conflated.

38

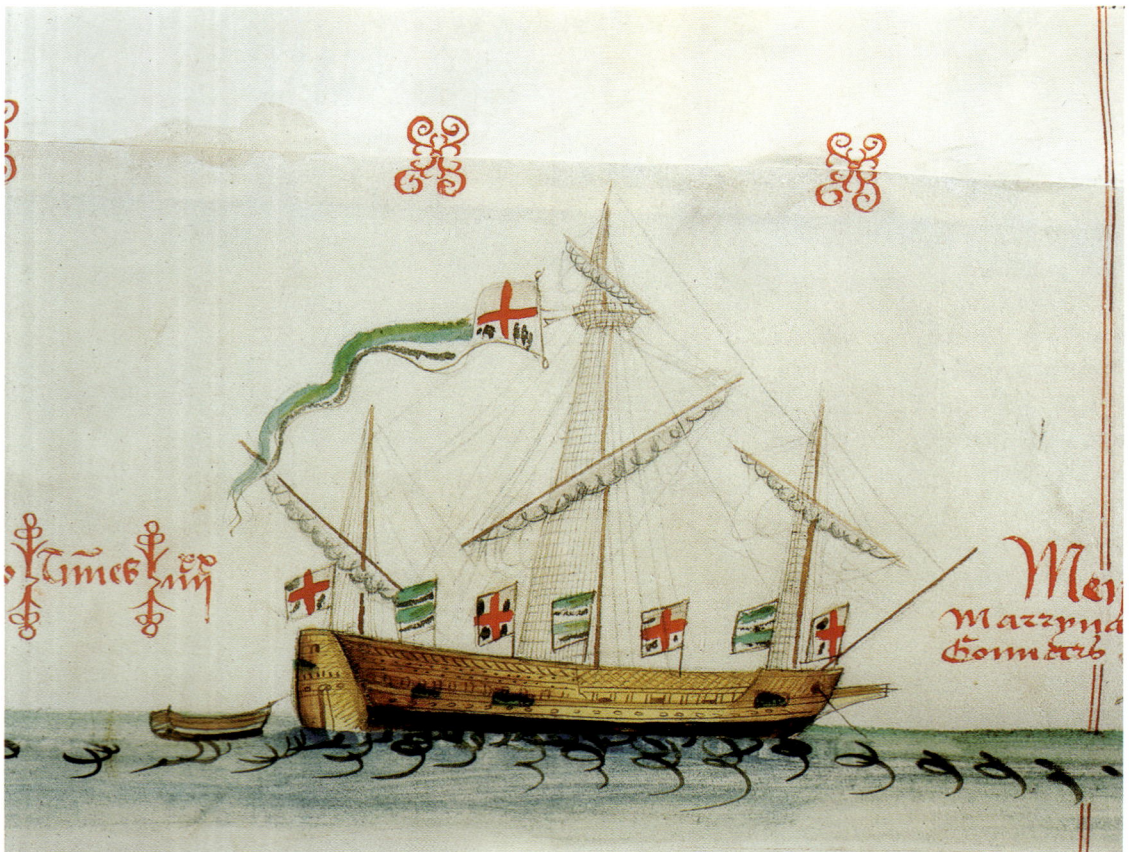

39

[pp. 58–9]

The Hynde

Tunnes – $\frac{xx}{iiij}$.

Men {marrynars – liiij; gonnars – vj}: lx.

For the Hynde. Ordenaunce, artillary, munitions, habillimentes for the warre, for the armyng and in the deffence of the sayd pynnas to the see.

Gonnes of brasse. Saker – j.

Gonnes of yron. Quarter slynges – ij. Baessys – xiiij. Hayle shot peces – iiij. Handgonnes complete – vj.

Gonnepowder. Serpentyn powder in demy barrelles – vj. Fynne corne powder – xij^{lb}.

Shotte of yron. For saker – xxx. For quarter slynges – c. Dyce of yron for hayle shotte – iiij^c.

Shotte of stoen and leade. For baessys, shotte of leade – iij^c. For handgonnes, shotte of leade – cxx^{ti}.

Bowes, bowestrynges, arrowes, morrys pykes, byllys and daertes for toppis. Bowes of yough – xl. Bowestrynges – j groce. Lyvere arrowes in shevis – lx. Morrys pykes – xxx. Byllys – xx. Daertes for toppis – iij doussen.

Munitions. Sledgys of yron – ij. Crowes of yron – ij Tampions – iiij^c. Canvas for cartowches – iij ellys. Fourme for cartowche – j. Comaunders – ij.

Habillimentes for the warre. Ropis of hempe for woling and brechyng – iij coyles. Naylis of sundre sortes – ij^c. Bagges of ledder – ij. Fyrkyn with purse – j. Lyme pottes – ij doussen. Spaer truckelles – ij. Spaer extrys – ij. Shepe skynnys for sponges – ij.

The Roo

Tunnes – $\frac{xx}{iiij}$.

Men {marrynars – xlvj; gonnars – iiij}: l.

For the Roo. Ordenaunce, artillary, munitions, habillimentes for the warre, for the armyng and in the deffence of the sayd pynnas to the see.

Gonnes of brasse. Culveryn perer – j. A chamber peces [*sic*] – ij. Demy culveryns – ij.

Gonnes of yron. Baessys – xij. Hayle shotte pecys – vj. Handgonnes complete – vj.

Gonnepowder. Serpentyn powder in demy barrelles – viij. Fynne corne powder – xij^{lb}.

Shotte of yron. For demy culveryns – lx. Dyce of yron for hayle shott – iiij^c.

Shotte of stoen and leade. For culveryn perer – xxx. For chamber pecys – lx. For baessys, shotte of leade – iiij^c. For handgonnes, shotte of leade – j^c.

Bowes, bowestrynges, arrowes, morrys pykes, byllys and daertes for toppis. Bowes of yough – xxx. Bowestrynges – j groce. Lyvere arrowes in shevis – xlv. Morrys pykes – xx. Byllys – xxx. Daertes for toppis – iij doussen.

Munitions. Pyckehamers – iiij. Sledgys of yron – ij. Crowes of yron – ij. Comaunders – iiij. Tampions – v^c. Canvas for cartowches – iiij ellys. Fourmes for cartowches – ij.

Habillimentes for the warre. Ropis of hempe for woling and brechyng – iij coy[les]. Naylis of sundre sortes – ij^c. Bagges of ledder – iiij. Fyrkyn with purse – ij. Lyme pottes – iij doussen. Spaer truckelles – ij. Spaer extrys – ij. Shepe skynnys – ij. Tymber for forlockes – xxx fo[et].

40

41

[pp. 62–3]

The Phenyx

Tunnes – xl.

Men {marrynars – xlvj; gonnars – iiij}: l.

For the Phenyx. Ordenaunce, artillary, munitions, habillimentes for the warre, for the armyng and in the deffence of the sayd pynnas to the see.

Gonnes of brasse. Sakers – ij.

Gonnes of yron. Porte pecys – ij. Quarter slynges – i. Baessys – x. Hayle shotte pecys – iiij. Handgonnes complete – vj.

Gonnepowder. Serpentyn powder in demy barrelles – vj. Fynne corne powder – xij^{lb}.

Shotte of yron. For sakers – lxxx. For quarter slynges – l. Dyce of yron for hayle shotte – ij^c.

Shotte of stoen and leade. For porte pecys – xl. For baessys, shotte of leade – ij^c. For handgonnes, shotte of leade – j^c.

Bowes, bowestrynges, arrowes, morrys pykes, byllys and daertes for toppis. Bowes of yough – xxv. Bowestrynges – j groce. Lyvere arrowes in shevis – xxxvj. Morrys pykes – xx^{ti}. Byllys – xx^{ti}. Daertes for toppis – iij doussen.

Munitions. Pyckhamers – iiij. Sledgys of yron – ij. Crowes of yron – ij. Comaunders – ij. Tampions – iij^c. Canvas for cartowches – ij ellys. Fourmes for cartowches – j.

Habillimentes for the warre. Ropis of hempe for woling and brechyng – ij coyles. Naylis of sundre sortes – ij^c. Bagges of ledder – iij. Fyrkyn with purse – j. Lyme pottes – ij doussen. Spaer truckelles – ij. Spaer extrys – ij. Shepe skynnys – j. Tymber for forlockes – x foet.

The Marlion

Tunnes – xl.

Men {marrynars – xlvj; gonnars – iiij}: l.

For the Marlion. Ordenaunce, artillary, munitions, habillimentes for the warre, for the armyng and in the deffence of the sayd pynnas to the see.

Gonnes of brasse. Mynnyons – iij. Fawcon – j.

Gonnes of yron. Baessys – viij. Hayle shotte pecys – iiij. Handgonnes complete – vj.

Gonnepowder. Serpentyn powder in demy barrelles – vj. Fynne corne powder – xij^{lb}.

Shotte of yron. For the mynnyons – lxxx. For fawcons – xxx. Dyce of yron for hayle shotte – ij^c.

Shotte of stoen and leade. For baessys, shotte of leade – ij^c. For handgonnes, shotte of leade – j^{c}xx.

Bowes, bowestrynges, arrowes, morrys pykes, byllys and daertes for toppys. Bowes of yough – xxx. Bowestrynges – j groce. Lyvere arrowes in shevis – xlv. Morrys pykes – xx^{ti}. Byllys – xx^{ti}. Daertes for toppis – ij doussen.

Munitions. Sledgys of yron – ij. Crowes of yron – ij. Comaunders – ij. Tampions – ij^c. Canvas for cartowches – iiij ellys. Fourmes for cartowches – ij.

Habillimentes for the warre. Ropis of hempe for brechyng – ij coyles. Naylis – j^c. Bagges of ledder – ij. Fyrkyn with purse – j. Lyme pottes – ij doussen. Spaer truckelles – ij. Spaer extrys – ij. Shepe skynnys – ij. Tymber for forlockes – x foet.

42

43

[pp. 66–7]

The Lesse Pennas

Tunnes – xl.

Men {marrynars – xl; gonnars – iiij}: xliij.

For the Lesse Pennas. Ordenaunce, artillary, munitions, habillimentes for the warre, for the armyng and in defferce of the sayd pennas to the see.

Gonnes of brasse. Fawcon – j.

Gonnes of yron. Saker – j. Fawconnet – j. Fowlers – ij. Baessys – vj. Hayle shott pecys – iij. Handgonnes complete – iiij.

Gonnepowder. Serpentyn powder in demy barrelles – viij. Fynne corne powder – viij^{lb}.

Shotte of yron. For saker – xl. For fawcon – lxxx. Dyce of yron for hayle shott – ij^c.

Shotte of stoen and leade. For fowlers – xl. For baessys, shotte of leade – cxx. For handgonnes, shotte of leade – lxxx.

Bowes, bowestrynges, arrowes, morrys pykes, byllys and daertes for toppis. Bowes of yough – xxx. Bowestrynges – j groce. Lyvere arrowes in shevis – xlv. Morrys pykes – x. Byllys – x. Daertes for toppis – ij doussen.

Munitions. Sledgys of yron – ij. Crowe of yron – j. Comaunders – ij. Tampions – iiij^c. Paper rayll for cartowches – j qwayer. Fourme for cartowches – ij.

Habillimentes for the warre. Ropis of hempe for brechyng – ij coyles. Naylis – ij^c. Bagges of ledder – ij. Fyrkyn with purse – j. Spaer truckelles – ij. Spaer extrys – ij. Shepe skynnys – ij. Tymber for forlockes – x foet. Lyme pottes – ij doussen.

The Bryggendyn

Tunnes – xl.

Men {marrynars – xl; gonnars – iiij}: xliiij.

For the Bryggendyn. Ordenaunce, artillary, munitions, habillimentes for the warre, for the armyng and in the deffence of the sayd pynnas to the see.

Gonnes of brasse. Fawcon – j. Fawconnetes – ij.

Gonnes of yron. Baessys – x. Hayle shotte pecys – ij. Handgonnes complete – vj.

Gonnepowder. Serpentyn powder in demy barrelles – iiij. Fynne corne powder – xij^{lb}.

Shotte of yron. For fawcon – xl. For fawconnet – lxxx. Dyce of yron for hayle shotte – j^c.

Shotte of stoen and leade. For baessys, shott of leade – ij^c. For handgonnes, shotte of leade – j^{c}xx^{ti}.

Bowes, bowestrynges, arrowes, morrys pykes, byllys and daertes for toppis. Bowes of yough – xx. Bowestrynges – j di groce. Lyvere arrowes in shevis – xxx. Morrys pykes – xx. Byllys – x. Daertes for toppis – j doussen.

Munitions. Sledgys of yron – ij. Crowes of yron – ij. Comaunders – [*blank*]. Tampions – ij^c. Canvas for cartowches – iiij ellys. Fourmes for cartowches – ij.

Habillimentes for the warre. Ropis of hempe for brechyng – ij coyles. Naylis – j^c. Bagges of ledder – ij. Fyrkyn with purse – j. Lyme pottes – ij doussen. Spaer truckelles – ij. Spaer extrys – ij. Shepe skynnys – ij. Tymber for forlockes – x foet.

44

45

[pp. 70–1]

The Hare

Tunnes – xv.

Men {marrynars – xxviij; gonnars – ij}: xxx.

For the Hare. Ordenaunce, artillary, munitions, habillimentes for the warre, for the armyng and in the deffence of the sayd pynnas to the see.

Gonnes of brasse. Saker – j.

Gonnes of yron. Baessys – xij. Hayle shott pecys – iiij. Handgonnes complete – vj.

Gonnepowder. Serpentyn powder in demy barrelles – vj. Fynne corne powder – xij^{lb}.

Shotte of yron. For saker – xl. Dyce of yron for hayle shotte – ij^c.

Shotte of stoen and leade. For baessys, shotte of leade – ij^c. For handgonnes, shotte of leade – cxx^{ti}.

Bowes, bowestrynges, arrowes, morrys pykes, byllys and daertes for toppis. Bowes of yough – xx^{ti}. Bowestrynges – j di groce. Lyvere arrowes in shevis – xl. Morrys pykes – xx. Byllys – xx. Daertes for toppis – ij doussen.

Munitions. Sledgys of yron – ij. Crowes of yron – ij. Tampions – iiij^c. Paper ryall for cartowches – di qwayer. Fourme for cartowche – j.

Habillimentes for the warre. Ropis of hempe for brechyng – j coyle. Naylis – j^c. Bagges of ledder – ij. Fyrkyr with purse – j. Lyme pottes – ij doussen. Spaer extrys – ij. Shepe skynnys – ij. Tymber for forlockes – x foet.

The Trego Ronnyger

Tunnes – xx.

Men {marrynars – xxiiij; gonnars – j}: xxv.

For the Trego Ronnyger. Ordenaunce, artillary, munitions, habillimentes for the warre, for the armyng and in the deffence of the sayd pynnas to the see.

Gonnes of brasse [*blank*].

Gonnes of yron. Baessys – xij. Hayle shotte pecys – iiij. Handgonnes complete – vj.

Gonnepowder. Serpentyn powder in demy barrelles – iiij. Fynne corne powder – xij^{lb}. Dyce of yron for hayle shotte – ij^c.

Shotte of stoen and leade. For baessys, shotte of leade – iiij^c. For handgonnes, shotte of leade – cxx^{ti}.

Bowes, bowestrynges, arrowes, morrys pykes, byllys and daertes for toppis. Bowes of yough – xvj. Bowestrynges – j di groce. Lyvere arrowes in shevis – xxiiij. Morrys pykes – xij. Byllys – xij. Daertes for toppis – j doussen.

Munitions. Sledgys of yron – ij. Crowes of yron – ij. Tampions – iiij^c. Paper ryall for cartowches – j di qwayer. Fourme for cartowche – j.

Habillimentes for the warre. Ropis of hempe for brechyng – j coyle. Naylis – j^c. Bagges of ledder – ij. Fyrkyn with purse – j. Lyme pottes – ij doussen. Spaer extrys – ij. Shepe skynne – ij. Tymber – x foet.

46

[pp. 74–5]

Here After insuyth the Kynges Majesties owne roo baergys, with every roo barge and roo baergys naem, with theyr tunage and nombre of men, as also the ordenaunce, artillary, munitions and habillimentes for warre for the armyng and deffence of the sayd roo baergys agaynst theyr ennemys apon the see. That ys to say:

The Double Rose

Tunnes – xx^{ti}.

Men {marryners – xxxix; gonnars – iiij}: xliij.

For the Double Rose. Ordenaunce, artillary, munitions, habillimentes for warre, for the armyng and in the defence of the sayd shyppe to the see.

Gonnes of brasse. Demy culveryn – j.

Gonnes of yron. Baessys – vj. Hayle shott pecys – iiij. Handgonnes complet – vj.

Gonnepowder. Serpentyn powder in demy barrelles – ij. Grosse corne powder demy barrelles – ij. Fyne corne powder – xij^{lb}.

Shotte of yron. For demy culveryn – lxxx. For saker – lxxx. Dice of yron for hayle shott – iij^c.

Shotte of stoen and leade. For baessys, shot of leade – ij^c. For handgonnes, shott of leade – j^cxx.

Bowes, bowestrynges, arrowes, morrys pykes, byllys, daertes for toppis. Bowes of yough – xx. Bowestrynges – j di groce. Lyvere arrowes in shevis – xxx. Morrys pykes – xij. Byllys – xij. Daertes for toppe – j doussen.

Munitions. Sledgys – ij. Crowes of yron – ij. Tampions – ij^c. Canvas for cartowches – v ellys. Paper ryall – j di qwayer. Fourmes for cartowches – ij.

Habillimentes for the warre. Ropis of hempe for brechyng – j coyle. Naylis – j^c. Bagges of ledder – ij. Fyrkyn with purse – j. Lyme pottes – ij doussen. Shepe skynnys – j. Spaer extrys – ij. Tymber for koynnys – v foet.

94

47

48

[pp. 78–9]

The Flowre deluce

Tunnes – xx^{ti}.

Men {marrynars – xxxix; gonnars – iiij}: xliij.

For the Flowre deluce. Ordenaunce, artillary, munitions, habillimentes for warre, for the armyng and in the deffence of the sayd shippe to the see.

Gonnes of brasse. Demy culveryn – j. Saker – j.

Gonnes of yron. Baessys – vij. Handgonnes complet – iiij. Hayle shott pecys – iiij.

Gonnepowder. Serpentyn powder in demy barreles – ij. Grosse corne powder in demy barrelles – iij. Fynne corne powder – xij^{lb}.

Shotte of yron. for demy culveryn – lxxx. For saker – j^c. Dice of yron for hayle shott – iij^c.

Shotte of stoen and leade. For baessys, shotte of leade – ij^c. For handgonnes, shotte of leade – j^{c}xx.

Bowes, bowestrynges, arrowes, morrys pykes, byllys, daertes for toppis. Bowes of yough – xx. Bowestrynges – j di groce. Lyvere arrowes in shevis – xxx. Morrys pykes – xl. Byllys – xx.

Munitions. Sledgys of yron – ij. Crowes – ij. Tampions – iiij^c. Canvas for cartowches – vj ellys. Paper ryall – j di qwayer. Fourmes for cartowches – ij.

Habillimentes for the warre. Ropis of hempe for brechyng – j coyle. Naylis – j^c. Bagges of ledder – ij. Fyrkyn with purse – j. Lyme pottes – ij doussen. Spaer extrys – ij. Shepe skynnys for sponges – ij. Tymber for koyns – v foet.

The Portquillice

Tunnes – xx^{ti}.

Men {marrynars – xxxiiij; gonnars – iiij}: xxxviij.

For the Portquillice. Ordenaunce, artillary, munitions, habillimentes for the warre, for the armyng and in the deffence of the sayd shyppe to the see.

Gonnes of brasse. Saker – j.

Gonnes of yron. Double baessys – ij. Demy baessys – iiij. Hayle shotte pecys – iiij. Handgonnes complet – iiij.

Gonnepowder. Serpentyn powder, demy barell – j. Grosse corne powder in demy barrelles – ij. Fynne corne powder – viij^{lb}.

Shotte of yron. For saker – lxx. Dice of yron for hayle shotte – iiij^c.

Shotte of stoen and leade. For baessys, shotte of leade – clx. For handgonnes, shotte of leade – c.

Bowes, bowestrynges, arrowes, morrys pykes, byllys, daertes for toppis. Bowes of yough – x. Bowestrynges – v doussen. Lyvere arrowes in shevis – xv. Morrys pykes – viij. Byllys – ij.

Munitions. Sledgys of yron – ij. Crowe of yron – j. Tampions – iiij^c. Canvas for cartowches – ij ellys. Paper ryall – j di qwayer. Fourme for cartowche – j.

Habillimentes for the warre. Ropis of hempe for brechyng – j coyle. Naylis – j^c. Bagges of ledder – ij. Fyrkyn with purse – j. Lyme pottes – ij doussen. Spaer extrys – ij. Shepe skynnys – j. Tymber for forlockes – v foet.

49

50

[pp. 82–3]

The Harpe

Tunnes – xx^{ti}.

Men {marrynars – xxxvj; gonnars – iiij}: xl.

For the Harpe. Ordenaunce, artillary, munitions, habillimentes for the warre, for the armyng and in the deffence of the sayd rowe barge to the see.

Gonnes of brasse. Saker – j.

Gonnes of yron. Baessys – vj. Hayle shotte pecys – iij. Handgonnes complete – iij.

Gonnepowder. Serpentyn powder, demy barrelles – j. Grosse corne powder, demy barrelles – ij. Fyne corne powder – vj^{lb}.

Shotte of yron. For saker – lxx. Dyce of yron for hayle shotte – iij^c.

Shotte of stoen and leade. For baessys, shotte of leade – c$_{iiij}^{xx}$. For handgonnes, shotte of leade – lx.

Bowes, bowestrynges, arrowes, morrys pykes, byllys, daertes for toppis. Bowes of yough – x. Bowestrynges – j di groce. Lyvere arrowes in shevis – xv. Morrys pykes – viij. Byllys – xij.

Munitions. Sledgys of yron – ij. Crowe of yron – j. Tampions – ij^c. Paper ryall for cartowche – j di qwayer. Fourme for cartowche – j.

Habillimentes for the warre. Rope of hempe for brechyng – j coyle. Naylis – j^c. Bagges of ledder – ij. Fyrkyn with purse – j. Lyme pottes – ij doussen. Spaer extrys – ij. Shepe skynnys – ij. Tymber for koynnys – v foet.

The Clowde in the Sonne

Tunnes – xx^{ti}.

Men {marrynars – xxxvj; gonnars – iiij}: xl.

For the Clowde in the Sonne. Ordenaunce, artillary, munitions, habillimentes for the warre, for the armyng and in the deffence of the sayd row barge to the see.

Gonnes of brasse. Demy culveryn – j. Saker – j.

Gonnes of yron. Quarter slyng – j. Baessys – vj. Hayle shotte pecys – iij. Handgonnes complet – iij.

Gonnepowder. Serpentyn powder, demy barrell – j. Grosse corne powder, [demy barrelles] – ij. Fynne corne powder – vj^{lb}.

Shotte of yron. For demy culveryn – lxxx. For saker – lxx. For quarter slyng – xxx. Dice of yron for hayle shott – iij^c.

Shotte of stoen and leade. For baessys, shotte of leade – clxxx. For handgonnes, shotte of leade – c.

Bowes, bowestrynges, arrowes, morrys pyckes, byllys, daertes for toppis. Bowes of yough – xv. Bowestrynges – j di groce. Lyvere arrowes in shevis – xxiij. Morrys pykes – x. Byllys – ij.

Munitions. Sledgys of yron – ij. Crowe of yron – ij. Tampions – cc. Canvas for cartowchys – iiij ellys. Paper ryall – j di qwayer. Fourmes for cartowches – ij.

Habillimentes for the warre. Rope of hempe for brechyng – j coyle. Naylis – j^c. Bagges of ledder – ij. Fyrkyn with purse – j. Lyme pottes – ij doussen. Spaer extry – j. Shepe skynne – j. Tymber for koynnys – v foet.

51

52

[pp. 86–7]

The Rose in the Sonne

Tunnes – xx^{ti}.

Men {marrynars – xxxvj; gonnars – iiij}: xl.

For the Rose in the Sonne. Ordenaunce, artillary, munitions, habillimentes for the warre, for the armyng and in the deffence of the sayd roo barge to the see.

Gonnes of brasse. Demy culveryn – j.

Gonnes of yron. Baessys – vj. Hayle shotte pecys – iiij. Handgonnes complete – iiij.

Gonnepowder. Serpentyn powder, demy barrelles – ij. Grosse corne powder, demy barrelles – ij. Fynne corne powder – viij^{lb}.

Shotte of yron. For demy culveryn – lxxx. Dice of yron for hayle shotte – iij^c.

Shotte of stoen and leade. For baessys, shotte of leade – clxxx. For handgonnes, shotte of leade – j^c.

Bowes, bowestrynges, arrowes, morrys pyckes, byllys, daertes for toppis. Bowes of yough – xx. Bowestrynges – j di groce. Lyvere arrowes in shevis – xxx^{ti}. Morrys pykes – xij. Byllys – xij.

Munitions. Sledgys of yron – ij. Crowes of yron – ij. Tampions – cc. Canvas for cartowches – iiij ellys. Fourme for cartowche – j.

Habillimentes for the warre. Rope of hempe for brechyng – j coyle. Naylis – j^c. Bagges of ledder – ij. Fyrkyn with purse – j. Lyme pottes – ij doussen. Spaer extrye – j. Shepe skynnes – ij. Tymber for koynys – v foet.

The Hawthorne

Tunnes – xx^{ti}.

Men {marrynars – xxxiiij; gonnars – iiij}: xxxviij.

For the Hawthorne. Ordenaunce, artillary, munitions, habillimentes for the warre, for the armyng and in the deffence of the sayd roo barge to the see.

Gonnes of brasse. Saker – j.

Gonnes of yron. Baessys – vj. Hayle shotte pecys – iij. Handgonnes complete – iij.

Gonnepowder. Serpentyn powder, demy barrell – j. Grosse corne powder, demy barrelles – ij. Fynne corne powder – vj^{lb}.

Shotte of yron. For saker – lxx. Dyce of yron for hayle shotte – iij^c.

Shotte of stoen and leade. For baessys, shotte of leade – clxxx. For handgonnes, shotte of leade – j^c.

Bowes, bowestrynges, arrowes, morrys pyckes, byllys, daertes for toppis. Bowes of yough – x. Bowestrynges – v doussen. Lyvere arrowes in shevis – xv. Morrys pykes – viij. Byllys – viij.

Munitions. Sledgys of yron – ij. Crowe of yron – j. Tampions – cc. Paper ryall for cartowches – j di qwayer. Fourme for cartowche – j.

Habillimentes for the warre. Rope of hempe for brechyng – j coyle. Naylis – j^c. Bagges of ledder – ij. Fyrkyn with purse – j. Lyme pottes – ij doussen. Spaer extrye – j. Shepe skynne for sponge – j. Tymber for koynys – v foet.

53

54

[pp. 90–1]

The Thre Ostrydge Fethers

Tunnes – xx^{ti}.

Men {marrynars – xxxiij; gonnars – iiij}: xxxvij.

For the Thre Ostrydge Fethers. Ordenaunce, artillary, munitions, habillimentes for the warre, for the armyng and in the deffence of the sayd roo barge to the see.

Gonnes of brasse. Saker – j.

Gonnes of yron. Baessys – vj. Hayle shotte pecys – iij. Handgonnes complete – iij.

Gonnepowder. Serpentyn powder, demy barrell – j. Grosse corne powder, demy barrelles – ij. Fynne corne powder – vj^{lb}.

Shotte of yron. For saker – lxx. Dyce of yron for hayle shotte – iij^c.

Shotte of stoen and leade. For baessys, shotte of leade – clxxx. For handgonnes, shotte of leade – c.

Bowes, bowestrynges, arrowes, morrys pyckes, byllys, daertes for toppis. Bowes of yough – xij. Bowestrynges – j di groce. Lyvere arrowes in shevis – xviij. Morrys pyxes – x. Byllys – x.

Munitions. Sledgys of yron – ij. Crowe of yron – j. Tampions – cc. Canvas for cartowches – iij ellys. Fourme for cartowche – j.

Habillimentes for the warre. Rope of hempe for brechyng – j coyle. Naylis – j^c. Bagges of ledder – ij. Fyrkyn with purse – j. Lyme pottes – ij doussen. Spaer extrye – j. Shepe skynne – j. Tymber for koynys – v foet.

The Fawcon in the Fetterlock

Tunnes – xx^{ti}.

Men {marrynars – xlj; gonnars – iiij}: xlv.

For the Fawcon in the Fetterlock. Ordenaunce, artillary, munitions, habillimentes for the warre, for the armyng and in the deffence of the sayd roo barge to the see.

Gonnes of brasse. Demy culveryns – j. Fawcons – ij.

Gonnes of yron. Baessys – viij. Hayle shotte pecys – iiij. Handgonnes complete – iiij.

Gonnepowder. Serpentyn powder, demy barrelles – i. Grosse corne powder, demy barrelles – ij. Fynne corne powder – viij^{lb}.

Shotte of yron. For demy culveryns – c. For fawcons – lxxx. Dyce of yron for hayle shotte – iiij^c.

Shotte of stoen and leade. For baessys, shotte of leade – cc. For handgonnes, shotte of leade – c.

Bowes, bowestrynges, arrowes, morrys pyckes, byllys, daertes for toppis. Bowes of yough – xx. Bowestrynges – j di groce. Lyvere arrowes in shevis – xl. Morrys pykes – xl. Byllys – xx.

Munitions. Sledgys of yron – ij. Crowes of yron – ij. Tampions – ccl. Canvas for cartowches – vj ellys. Paper ryall – j di qwayer. Fourmes for cartowches – ij.

Habillimentes for the warre. Rope of hempe for brechyng – j coyle. Naylis – j^c. Bagges of ledder – ij. Fyrkyn with purse – j. Lyme pottes – ij doussen. Spaer extrye – j. Shepe skynne – j. Lantarne – j. Tymber for koynnys – v foet.

55

56

The Mayden Hede

[pp. 94–5]

Men {marryrars – xxxiij; gonnars – iiij}: xxxvij.

For the Mayden Hed. Ordenaunce, artillary, muniticns, habillimentes for the warre, for the armyng and in the deffence of the sayd roo barge to the see.

Gonnes of brasse. Saker – j.

Gonnes of yron. Baessys – vj. Hayle shotte pecys – iij. Handgonnes complete – iij.

Gonnepowder. Serpentyn powder, demy barrell – j. Grosse corne powder, demy barrelles – ij. Fynne corne powder – vj^{lb}.

Shotte of yron. For saker – lxx. Dyce of yron for hayle shotte – iij^c.

Shotte of stoen and leade. For baessys, shotte of leade – clxxx. For handgonnes, shotte of leade – lx.

Bowes, bowestrynges, arrowes, morrys pyckes, byllys, daertes for toppys. Bowes of yough – x. Bowestrynges – v doussen. Lyvere arrowes in shevis – xv. Morrys pykes – x. Byllys – x.

Munitions. Sledgys of yron – ij. Crowe of yron – j. Tampions – cc. Paper ryall for cartowches – j di qwayer. Fourme for cartowche – j.

Habillimentes for warre. Rope of hempe for brechyng – j coyle. Naylis – j^c. Bagges of ledder – ij. Fyrkyn with purse – j. Lyme pottes – ij doussen. Spaer extrye – j. shepe skynne for sponge – j. Tymber for koynys – v foet.

The Rose Slype

Tunnes – xx^{ti}.

Men {marryrars – xxxiij; gonnars – iiij}: xxxvij.

For the Rose Slype. Ordenaunce, artillary, munitions habillimentes for the warre, for the armyng and in the deffence of the sayd roo barge to the see.

Gonnes of brasse. Saker – j.

Gonnes of yron. Baessys – vj. Hayle shotte pecys – iij. Handgonnes complete – iij.

Gonnepowder. Serpentyn powder, demy barrell – j. Grosse corne powder, demy barrelles – ij. Fynne corne powder – vj^{lb}.

Shotte of yron. For saker – lxx. For hayle shott, dice of yron – iij^c.

Shotte of stoen and leade. For baessys, shotte of leade – clx. For handgonnes, shotte of leade – lx.

Bowes, bowestrynges, arrowes, morrys pyckes, byllys, daertes for toppys. Bowes of yough – x. Bowestrynges – v doussen. Lyvere arrowes in shevis – xv. Morrys pykes – viij. Byllys – viij.

Munitions. Sledgys of yron – ij. Crowe of yron – j. Tampions – cc. Paper ryall for cartowches – j di qwayer. Fourme for cartowche – j.

Habillimentes for the warre. Rope of hempe for brechyng – j coyle. Naylis – j^c. Bagges of ledder – ij. Fyrkyn with purse – j. Lyme pottes – j doussen. Spaer extrye – j. Shepe skynne – j. Tymber for koynys – v foet.

57

58

[pp. 98–9]

The Jyllyver Flowre

Tunnes – xx^{ti}.

Men {marrynars – xxxiiij; gonnars – iiij}: xxxviij.

For the Jllyver Flowre. Ordenaunce, artillary, munitions, habillimentes for the warre, for the armyng and in the deffence of the sayd roo barge to the see.

Gonnes of brasse. Saker – j.

Gonnes of yron. Baessys – v. Hayle shott pecys – iij. Handgonnes complete – iij.

Gonnepowder. Serpentyn powder, demy barrell – j. Grosse corne powder, demy barrelles – ij. Fynne corne powder – vj^{lb}.

Shotte of yron. For saker – lxx. Dyce of yron for hayle shott – iij^c.

Shotte of stoen and leade. For baessys, shotte of leade – clxxx. For handgonnes, shotte of leade – lx.

Bowes, bowestrynges, arrowes, morrys pyckes, byllys, daertes for toppis. Bowes of yough – xij. Bowestrynges – vj doussen. Lyvere arrowes in shevis – xviij. Morrys pykes – xij. Byllys – xij.

Munitions. Sledgys of yron – ij. Crowe of yron – j. Tampions – cc. Paper ryall for cartowches – j di qwayer. Fourme for cartowche – j.

Habillimentes for the warre. Rope of hempe for brechyng – j coyle. Naylis – j^c. Bagges of ledder – ij. Fyrkyn with purse – j. Lyme pottes – j doussen. Spaer extrye – j. Shepe skynne – j. Tymber for koynys – v foet.

The Sonne

Tunnes – xx^{ti}.

Men {marrynars – xxxvj; gonnars – iiij}: xl.

For the Sonne. Ordenaunce, artillary, munitions, habillmentes for the warre, for the armyng and in the deffence of the sayd roo barge to the see.

Gonnes of brasse. Saker – j. Fawcon – j.

Gonnes of yron. Baessys – vij. Hayle shotte pecys – iij. Handgonnes complete – iiij.

Gonnepowder. Serpentyn powder in demy barrelles – ij. Fynne corne powder – viij^{lb}.

Shotte of yron. For saker – xl. For fawcon – xl. Dyce of yron for hayle shotte – iij^c.

Shotte of stoen and leade. For baessys, shotte of leade – clx. For handgonnes, shott of leade – lxxx.

Bowes, bowestrynges, arrowes, morrys pyckes, byllis, daertes for toppis. Bowes of yough – xx. Bowestrynges – j groce. Lyvere arrowes in shevis – xxx. Morrys pykes – xiiij. Byllys – xij.

Munitions. Sledgys of yron – ij. Crowe of yron – j. Tampions – cc. Paper ryall for cartowches – j di qwayer. Fourme for cartowche – j.

Habillimentes for the warre. Rope of hempe for wolyng – j coyle. Naylis – j^c. Bagges of ledder – ij. Fyrkyn with purse – j. Lyme pottes – j doussen. Spaer extrye – j. Shepe skynne – j. Tymber for koynys – x foet.

[Summary of third roll. In MS arranged below section headings for last ship, here repeated]

[**Gonnes of brasse**] Somma. Demy culveryns – vij. Culveryns, perers – iij. Sakers – xxj. Fawcons – vj. Fawconnettes – ij. Mynnyons – iij. Totalis – xlij pecys of brasse.

[**Gonnes of yron**] Somma. Porte peces – ij. Demy slynges – j. Quarter slynges – vij. Fowlers – iiij. Fawconnet – j. Baessys – c$_{iiij}^{xx}$xvij. Hayle shot pecys – lxxxij. Handgonnes – $_{iiij}^{xx}$ viij.

[**Gonnepowder**]. Somma. Serpentyn powder in demy barrelles – $_{iiij}^{xx}$ xij. Grosse corne powder, demy l[astes] – xix. Fynne corne powder – ij^{c}x^{lb}. Totalis – iiij last di v^{c}x^{lb}.

[**Shotte of yron**] Somma. For demy culveryns – iij^c$_{iiij}^{xx}$. For saker – vij^{c}l. For fawcon – ij^{c}lxx. For fawconnet – $_{iiij}^{xx}$. For mynyons – $_{iiij}^{xx}$. For demy slynges – $_{iiij}^{xx}$. For qwarter slynges – j^{c}lxxx. Totalis – j^{ml}viij^{c}xx. Dyce of yron – vj^{ml}ij^c.

[**Shotte of stoen and leade**] Somma. For porte pecys – xl. For culveryn, perer – xxx. For baessys, shot of leade – iiij^{ml}ix^c. For handgonnes, shot of leade – ij^{ml}ij^{c}lx. For fowlers – $_{iiij}^{xx}$. Totalis – vij^{ml}iij^{c}x.

[**Bowes, bowestrynges, arrowes, morrys pyckes, byllis, daertes for toppis**] Somma. Bowes of yough – iiij^{c}lxv. Bowestrynges – xv groce. Lyvere arrowes in shevis – vij^{c}x. Morrys pykes – iij^c$_{iiij}^{xx}$xiiij. Byllys – iij^{c}xxxij. Daertes for toppys – xxv doussen.

[**Munitions**] Somma. Pyckhamers – xij. Sledgys – xlix. Crowes – xxxvij. Comaunders – xj. Tampions – vj^{ml}l. Canvas – lij ellys. Paper ryall – vij quayer di. Fourmes – xxx.

[**Habillimentes for the warre**] Somma. Ropis of hempe – xxxiij coyles. Naylis – iiij^{ml}viij^c. Bagges – xlix. Fyrkyns with pursys – xxiiij. Lyme potes – xlv doussen. Spaer truckelles – xix. Spaer extrys – xxxviij. Shepe skyns – xxxvj. Tymber for forlockes – clxxvj foet.

Men. {Somma. Marrynars – viij^{c}lxxxxvj. Gonnars – $_{iiij}^{xx}$xiij}   ix^c$_{iiij}^{xx}$ ix.

Youre Majesties humble poure servaunt. Par me Anthony Anthony.

Part Two

The Inventory of 1514

Introduction
D.M. Loades

Ship inventories of the kind which are here presented are not particularly rare. In 1982 Dr Susan Rose edited for the society a number taken from the accounts of William Soper, keeper of the king's ships between 1422 and 1427.[1] At that time such records were kept in a lowly but practical form of Latin, with the exception of the names of the ships and some, but not all, of the technical words, such as 'hedrope' or 'stetynges'. At some point between then and 1485, when Thomas Rogers inventoried the ships which he took into his custody on behalf of King Henry VII, Latin was abandoned in favour of English. All Rogers' inventories of that year, and his other accounts, were kept in the vernacular. It was the normal practice to inventory the contents of a ship when it was handed over from one manager to another, and a further series survives from the autumn of 1495 when Robert Brygandyne, then the clerk of the ships, resumed into his custody those vessels which had been at sea in the king's service during the summer. The clerk was only responsible for the ships when they were not in use, and it was important for the master to obtain his discharge by ensuring that the clerk acknowledged receipt of everything which was actually in the vessel at the time of handover. Rogers' inventories of 1485, and Brygandyne's of 1495 have also been edited for the society, in this case by Michael Oppenheim in 1895.[2]

However, these inventories from 1514 are distinctive in a number of ways. Henry VIII's war with France, from 1512 to 1514 had seen the navy adopt a somewhat different role to that which had been customary hitherto. Under the energetic command of Sir Edward Howard it had undertaken a limited, and not particularly successful, function as an independent military arm. In previous conflicts the king's ships had escorted troop carriers, supported the sieges of coastal towns, and patrolled the Channel; but in August 1512 Howard had taken the initiative with a fleet or 25 ships and attacked the French fleet assembling at Brest. The French were surprised by this unorthodox manoeuvre, but the resulting engagement was inconclusive, being best known for the spectacular self-destruction of the *Regent* and the *Cordelière*, two of the largest vessels engaged.[3] However, Henry had prepared for this war by both buying and building large ships in significant numbers, and had also increased the naval infrastructure from the extremely modest level at which it had existed during the previous reign. Robert Brygandyne was still clerk of the ships, but in 1512 a new storehouse had been built at Erith on the Thames estuary. Shortly afterwards two new offices were created, that of keeper of the storehouses, and that of clerk controller. John Hopton, a gentleman usher of the chamber, accounted for the latter office from February 1513, and was additionally appointed keeper at Erith and Deptford in January 1514.[4] By the summer of 1514, when the war was clearly coming to an end, the king had to decide what to do with the large fleet (over 30 ships of various sizes) which he had assembled. Custom suggested that the majority of them should be sold, or otherwise disposed of, leaving no more than half a dozen or so for the king's normal peace time business. However, Henry decided otherwise for reasons which are not entirely clear, but perhaps because he had no intention of remaining at peace for long. Some ships were released, but the great majority were retained, some to be 'mothballed' and some kept in active service. A number of documents connected with this operation are calendared in *Letters and Papers ... Henry VIII* under the general, and somewhat misleading, title 'Survey of the navy'.[5]

The 13 ships here listed, including most of the great ships then in service, were decommissioned. Their rigging was dismantled and handed over to John Hopton, the clerk controller, presumably for storage, although whether at Erith or elsewhere is not clear. Most of the armament was similarly handed over to John Millet and Thomas Elderton, representing the ordnance office, and the rest was left on board in the custody of the masters and pursers. It is this last provision which is most interesting. Not only does it indicate that the masters and pursers were to continue to look after their decommissioned ships, but also that small numbers of ship keepers would also be recruited to assist them, which was the normal practice by Elizabethan times. The inventories themselves do not differ much from those of twenty years earlier, but in some cases the location of the armament is given, indicating how the ships fought, and this is unusual information. The two galleys, the *Katherine* and the *Rose* were much smaller than the others listed, being of no more than 60 tons burthen, and sometimes described as 'barques'. The *Trinity Sovereign*, is almost certainly the old *Sovereign*, which was still in service. However, it has to be admitted that the inventory of the rigging does not bear much resemblance to the 1495 inventory of the same ship.[6] Since it was almost twenty years old, it may have been extensively rebuilt, or at any rate re-rigged.

With the exception of the galleys and the *Christ of Greenwich*, these were all Great Ships of 400 tons and upwards, and most were newly built or recently purchased. These inventories list not only the guns, ammunition and other weapons carried in each ship (which provides an interesting comparison with those of the Anthony Roll), but also every item of rigging and other equipment, from kettles and frying pans to pickaxes. Three ships appear in both 1514 and 1546, the *Henry Grace à Dieu*, the *Mary Rose* and the *Peter Pomegranate*; the first had been rebuilt in 1539, and the other two in 1536.

E36/13 is a handsomely written bound quarto volume of 100 pages, and appears to have been the formal copy of which many drafts and preliminary documents survive. The inventory of the *Henry Grace à Dieu* was printed from this document by Oppenheim as Appendix A to his study of naval administration.[7]

Notes

1. S. P. Rose, ed., *The Navy of the Lancastrian Kings: Accounts and Inventories of William Soper, Keeper of the King's Ships, 1422–1427* (NRS CXXIII, 1982).
2. M. Oppenheim, ed., *Naval Accounts and Inventories of the Reign of Henry VII, 1485–8 and 1495–7* (NRS VIII, 1896).
3. A. Spont, ed., *Letters and Papers relating to the War with France, 1512–1513* (NRS X, 1897), esp. pp. 52–3. For a recent appraisal of this campaign see Rodger, *Safeguard of the Sea*, pp. 170–2.
4. *LP* I, ii, nos 2617 (12), 3318.
5. *LP*, I, ii, no. 3137. The calendar summary brings together material from several PRO documents, now classified as SP 1/9, SP 1/230, E 101/52/1, and (the text here printed) E 36/13. The title assigned by the *LP* editors was probably suggested by the first item listed ('Expenses of Sir Henry Wyat, Sir Andrew Wyndsore, Sir Thomas Wyndham, George Dalison, and Thomas Tamworth, commissioners for viewing such tackle, &c., as remained in the great ships at Erith, Wolwich and other places in the Themmes "after their arrival", viz., from Wednesday 26 July 6 Hen. VIII. to 11 Aug. following.'). This is, however, only the first of 16 independent sub-entries to no. 3137 in the calendar, in which the E 36/13 document is no. 3137(6).
6. Oppenheim, *Accounts and Inventories*, pp. 187–218
7. Oppenheim, *History*, pp. 372–81

Editorial Note: Collation of E 36/13 with certain other PRO documents.

Those original indentures which survive in SP 1/230, and related matter in E101/57/2, are cited in the textual notes of this edition where they provide significant additions to or variations from the text of E36/13.

E = E 101/57/2 (a file of loose papers, without foliation or pagination)
SP = SP 1/230

	old fols	new fols
ordnance indentures:		
Gabriel Royal	223	201
Katherine galley	224	202
Erith storehouse	227	205
Trinity Sovereign	225	203
Katherine Fortileza	226	204
rigging indentures:		
Great Elizabeth	228	206
Mary Rose	229	208
Christ of Greenwich	230	210
Peter Pomegranate	231	209

[Drafts and rough copies of both inventories and indentures survive in SP 1/9, as follows: *Great Nicholas* (ordnance), f. 185; *Gabriel Royal* (tackle and ordnance), f. 186; *Trinity Sovereign* (ordnance), f. 187; *Katherine Fortileza* (ordnance and tackle), f. 188; *Mary Rose* (ordnance), f. 196; *Great Barbara* [*Magdalene*] (tackle and ordnance), f. 200; *Great Elizabeth* (ordnance), f. 202]

The Inventory of 1514

PRO, E 36/13

[The first two pages blank]

[p. 3]

The Kynges Shippes

Here ensuyth an inventorie or boke of all such stuff, tacle, apparell, ordynaunce, artillarie and habillamentes for the warre as remayned in our soveraigne lord the Kynges shippes the xxvij day of July the vjth yere of his reigne. By a vewe taken by Sir Henry Wyat Sir Andrewe Wyndsore knyghtes George Dalyson and Thomas Tamworth commissioners in that behalf appoynted.[1] Which stuff, tacle, apparell, ordynaunce, artillarie and habillamentes for the warre was delyverd into the charge and kepyng of severall persones hereaftyr particulerly named to our seid soveraigne lord the Kynges use by indenture thereof made[a] and also billes signed with the handes of the seid commissioners in the custodie of the seid persones remaynyng, that is to sey:

The Kynges Shipp called the *Henry Grace de dewe*

Stuff tacle and apparell of the seid ship delyverd by the seid commissioners into the charge of John Hopton[2] by indenture, that is to sey:

Fyrst the foremast of the seid shippe	j
Shrowdes to the same	xvj
Dedemens hyes to the same	xvj
Tacles to the foremast	iiij
Doble polles with shyvers of brasse	iiij
Single polles with shivers of brasse	iij
Single polles with acolk of brasse	j
Swyfters to the foremaste	vj
Doble polles with colkes of brasse	ij
Polles with[b] shyvers of wode	ij
Polles with v colkes of brasse and oone of wode	vj
Garnettes to the foremast with iiij poles	ij
Garnet with ij polles and shyvers of brasse	j
Garnet with a shever of brasse and an other of tymber	j
Trusses to the foremast	ij
Drynges to the same	j
Doble polles for the trusses with colkes of brasse	ij
Single poles of tymber	ij

[a]Word inserted.
[b]MS 'whuch'.

1. Sir Henry Wyatt was master of the mint and controller of the jewel house, and had been a trusted servant of Henry VII. Sir Andrew Windsor was master of the great wardrobe.
2. Hopton, a gentleman usher of the chamber, became the first clerk controller in 1513. He was succeeded by Thomas Spert in 1524.

[p. 4]

Yet the Henry Grace de Dew

Yet stuff and tacle delyverd to John Hopton by indenture as aforeseid, that is to sey:

Drynges with a doble pole with acolk of brasse and oone single pole of wode	j
Halyers to the foremast	ij
Shyvers of brasse to the brest of the forecastell	iiij
Ramehedes with ij shevers of brasse	j
Shetes to the foresayle	ij
Pollies with shevers of brasse to the same	ij
Lyftes to the foresayle	ij
Doble polies with shyvers of brasse to the same	ij
Single polies with colkes of brasse	ij
Shetes to the toppe sayle	ij
Single polies with woden pynnes to the same	ij
Tackes to the foresayle	ij
Stodynges to the foreyerd	ij
Pollies to the same with woden pynnes	ij
Cranelynnes to the foremast	j
Single poles with ashyver of brasse	ij
Bowelynnes to the foreyerd with the poleis and dede manes hies and oone doble pole with ashever of brasse	j
Stayes to the foreyerd with iiij dedemens heies	ij
Sprete sayle yerdes	j
Halyers to the same	ij
Single poleis with shyvers of brasse to the same	ij
Lyftes to the sprete sayle with iij single polies and woden pynnes	j
Grapilles with the cheyne hangyng apon the bowspret with apole havyng acolk of brasse	j
Knyghtes longyng to the lyftes of the foresayle with ij shevers of brasse	ij
The fore topmast	j
Shrowdes to the same	xij
Halyers with adoble polie and acolk of brasse ij single poleis with woden pynnes	ij

[p. 5]

Yet the Henry Grace de Dewe

Yet stuff and tacle delyverd to John Hopton by indenture as aforeseid that is to sey:

Bowlynes to the foretop sayle yerd with pawes and dedemens hyes to the same	ij
Brasses for the foretopsayle yerd ij single poles with pynnes of wode	ij
Lyftes to the foretopsayle yerd with iiij poleis with woden pynnes	ij
Shetes to the foretopsayle with ij woden poles	ij
Stayes to the foretopmast	j
Sayle yerdes to the foretop	j
Toppe galant apon the foretop mast	j
Mastes to the same	j
Shrowdes to the same	viij
Halyers with ij single poles with woden pynnes	ij
Brasses to the same with ij single poleis and wodepynnes and dedemens hyes to the same	ij
Bowlynes to the topgalant yerd the power and dedemens hies to the same	ij
Lyftes to the foretopgalant yerd with single polies with woden pynnes	ij
Shetes with ij single poles with woden pynnes	ij
Stayes to the foretopgalant mast	j
Shevers of brasse for the cattes in the forecastell	iiij
Davettes with iiij shevers of brasse	ij
Smale davettes with oone shever of brasse	j
The mayne mast	j
Shrowdes with cheynes of yron and dedemens hies to the same	xl
Bote tacles of stereborde syde with iiij doble poles and viij single poleis with xvj shyvers of brasse	iiij
Shifters over the samesyde with vij doble poleis and vij single polies with colkes of brasse and ij poles of tymber pynnes	viij
Garnettes with ij single poles with shivers of brasse	j

[p. 6]

Yet the Henry Grace de Dew

Yet stuff and tacle delyverd to John Hopton by indenture as aforeseid that is to sey:

Garnettes with ij single polies with colkes of brasse	j
Garnettes with oone single pole with ashever of brasse and an other pole with acolk of brasse	j
Stodynges[a] with asingle polie with a shever of brasse	j
Bote tacles oon ladbordsyde with iiij doble polies and viij single polies with xvj shevers of brasse	iiij
Bretayn tacles with ij single polies and shevers of brasse to the same	j
Swyfters with vij doble polies with colkes of brasse and viij single poles with colkes of brasse	viij
Garnettes wherof oone with ij single polies and ij shevers of brasse an other with ij single poleis with ij colkes of brasse and an other with a shever of brasse	iij
Stodynges with ashever of brasse	j
Tymbre polies for the shutes	ij
The mayne yerde with the mayne parell	j
Single poleis with ashever of brasse to wynde up the mayne parell	j
Trusses with iiij doble polleis and iiij single polies with xij shevers of brasse	iij
Drynges with ij doble polies and iiij shevers of brasse	ij
Single poleis of tymbre to the same	ij
Tyes	j payer
Whele ropes	j
Geers with vj single poleis wherof iiij with shevers of brasse and ij of tymbre	iij
Knyghtes belongyng to the same with ij shevers of brasse	iij
Single poles for the topsayle	iiij
Shutes with iiij shevers of brasse	ij
Knyghtes with ij shevers of brasse	ij
The mayne yerd	j

[a]MS 'scodynges'.

[p. 7]

Yet the Henry Grace de Dew

Yet stuff and tacle delyverd to John Hopton by indenture
as aforeseid that is to sey:

Lyftes with ij doble poleis and ij single with vj shevers of brasse to the same	ij
Knyghtes with ij shevers of brasse	ij
Shutes	ij
Tackes	ij
Bowlynes with brydelles and dedemens hies	ij
Poleis to the mayne bowlyne with ij shevers of brasse	j
Mayne stayes with viij dedemens hies	iiij
Brasses with ij single poles and colkes of brasse*a*	ij
The mayne top	j
The mayne top mast and acoler of yron	j
Shrowdes to the same with dedemens hies*b*	xiiij
The mayne top sayle yerd	j
Tyes	j
Halyers with a doble and asingle polie with iij shevers of brasse	j
Brases with iiij poles	ij
Lyftes with iiij polies and colkes of brasse	ij
Cranelynnes with asingle pole and acolk of brasse	j
Steyes to the mayne top mast	j
Bowlynes with dedemens hies	ij
The top galant apon the mayne topmast	j
Mastes for the same	j
Rynges of yron for the same	j
Shrowdes to the same with dedemens hies	x
Sayle yerdes to the same	j
Stayes to the same	j
Bowlynes	ij
Brases with ij poles to the same	ij
Shutes	ij
Gravulles with cheynes to the same	ij
Poleys apon the mayne yerd for the gravulles	ij

[p. 8]

Yet the Henry Grace de Dew

Yet stuff and tacle delyverd to John Hopton by indenture
as aforeseid that is to sey:

Spare knyghtes sta[n]dyng by the mast with ij shevers of brasse	ij
The mayne meson mast	j
Shrowdes with xj doble poles and xj single poles and doble and single pole with colkes of brasse	xij
Swyftyers with vj doble poles and vj single poles with colkes of brasse	vj
Tacles with ij doble poles of tymbre	ij
Single poles oone of tymbre the other with acolke of brasse	ij
Steyes	j
Shutes	j
Single poles oon of tre the other with acolke of brasse for the same shutes	ij
Cranelynes with asingle polie and acolke of brasse	j
Brases with ij single poles	ij
Teyes	ij
Halyers	ij
The rame hede	j
Knyghtes with iij shevers of brasse	j
The yerd to the meson sayle	j
Lyftes with iij poles and dedemens hies	j
Trusses with adoble and asingle polie with colkes of brasse	j
Toppe	j
Topmast to the same	j
Rynges of yron	j
Shrowdes with dedemens hies	x
The sayle yerd	j
Tyes	j
Poles to the same	ij
Lyftes with iij poles and dedemens hies	j

a'with … brasse' inserted.
*b*Three words inserted.

[p. 9]

Yet the Henry Grace de Dew

Yet stuff and tacle delyverd to John[a] Hopton by indenture that is to sey:

The top galant of the mayne meson	j
The mast to the same	j
Shrowdes to the same	vj
Lyftes with iij poleis and dedemens hies	j
The sayle yerd	j
Tyes to the same	j
Halyers	j
The boneaventure mast	j
Shrowdes with x doble poles and x single poleis	x
Saylee yerdes	j
Tyes	j
Halyers with adoble pole	ij
Knyghtes with iiij shevers of brasse	j
Shutes with ij poleis to the same	j
The boneaventure top	j
Mastes to the same	j
Sayle yerdes	j
Shrowdes	viij
Steys	j
In the storehouse of the ship viij single pendant polies with shivers of brasse	viij
Smale single garnet poleis with shevers of brasse	ij
Doble lyft poleis with shevers of brasse	iiij
Doble poleanker poleis with shevers of brasse	iiij
Snach polleis with gret shevers of brasse	iiij
Single poleis with shevers of wode	xiiij
Doble poleis with shevers of wode	ij
Doble poleis with acolk of brasse	j
Single poleis with acolk of brasse	j
Pottes called piche pottes	j
Ketilles to melt in pyche	j

[p. 10]

Yet the Henry Grace de Dew

Yet stuff and tacle delyverd to John Hopton by indenture as aforeseid that is to sey:

Boyes for ankers	x
Boy ropes	x
Shevers of brasse without poleis	iij
Leddern bokettes	xii doss'
Love hokes	iiij
Lynch hokes	iij
Coper ketill not sett in furnes weying by estimacon ccc	j

Cables and cablettes of
- xiij ynch compas — j
- xvij ynch compas — ij
- xv ynch compas — ij
- ix ynch compas — j
- viij ynch compas — j

} vij

Hawsers of
- iiij ynch compas — iiij
- vj ynch compas — iij
- vj ynch di compas — j
- v ynch compas — j
- viij ynch compas — j
- iiij ynch compas — j
- ij ynch compas — j
- v ynch compas — j
- iiij ynch compas — vij
- iij ynch compas — j
- iij ynch di compas — j

} xxij

Smale lyne	ij peces
Bygger lyne for lanyers	ij peces
Brayle ropes with iij poles to the same	j
Grete doble blockes ether of them [with] ij shyvers of brasse	ij
Single blokes with ij shevers of brasse	ij

[a]Word repeated.

[p. 11]

Yet the Henry Grace de Dew

Yet stuff and tacle delyverd to John Hopton by indenture
as aforeseid that is to sey:

Large ores for the grete bote	lx
Tarre	ij barelles
Ores for the cocke bote	xxiij
Standart staves	lix
Stremers	viij
Lytle flagges	c
Top armours	vij
Targettes	xx doss'
Large flagges	lx

To the mayne sayle acorse and ij bonettes doble	j mayne sayle
Mayne topsayles	j
Topgalant sayle	j
The meson sayle	j
The boneaventure sayle	j
The foresayle acorse and abonet doble and abonet single an other corse and iij bonettes single in all	ij foresayles
The fore topsayle	j
The foretopgalant seyle	j
The bowspret seyle	j
The mayne sayle for the gret bote acorse and ij bonettes single	j sayle
The foreseyle acorse and ij bonettes single	j
Top seyle	j
The meson seyle	j
The boneaventure sayle	j
An old corse of a hulkes sayle	j

	sterbord bowers	ij	
	ladbord bowers	ij	
	destrelles of sterbord	ij	
Ankers called	destrelles over ladbord	ij	xix
	shot ankers	j	
	caggers	j	
	spare ankers	x	

[p. 12]

Yet the Henry Grace de Dew

Yet stuff and tacle delyverd to John Hopton by indenture
as aforeseid that is to sey:

Trene platters	iiij doss'
Trene cuppes	v doss'
Tankerdes	iij doss'
Lantrons	vj
Grete lantrons	j
Middellantrons	ij
Coper ketilles in furnos	iiij
Lede in oone pece by estimacon	d[1]
Grete belles in the seid ship of brasse	j
The grete botes mayne mast	j
Shrowdes to the same	xiiij
Polles to the same	xxviij
Tacles oone with adoble pole and colkes of brasse the other with asingle pole and a shever of tymbre	ij
Single poles with ashever of brasse	j
Mayne yerdes and the parell	j
Trusses with ij poleis and shevers of tymbre	j
Tyes	j
Halyers with adoble pole and shever of brasse	j
Single poleis on of them with a shever of brasse and other of tymbre	ij
Shutes	ij
Tackes	ij
Bowlynes with apole and shever of tymbre	ij
Lyftes with ij single poleis	ij
Topsayle shotes with ij single poleis	ij
Yerde ropes	ij
The mayne stey with ij doble poleis	j
The toppe	j
The topmast	j
Shrowdes to the same	vj
Sayle yerdes	j
Tyes	j

---

1. 5 cwt.

[p. 13]

Yet the Henry Grace de Dew

Yet stuff and tacle delyverd to John Hopton by indenture as aforesaid that is to sey:

Parell to the sayle yerd	j
Bowlynes	ij
Lyftes	ij
Cranelynes	j
Brases	ij
The fore mast	j
Shrowdes to the same	vj
The sayle yerd	j
The parell	j
Teyes	j
Syngle halyers with apolie to the same	j
Shetes	ij
Tackes	i
Lyftes with ij poleys	ij
Steys	j
Bowlynes with apolie	j
Single trusses with apolie*a*	j
Bowspretes	j
Mayne meson mast	j
Shrowdes to the same	vj
The sayle yerd	j
The parell to the same	j
The tye	j
Single halyers with apole	j
Trusses with ij poles	j
Lyftes with iij poles	j
Brases with ij poles	ij
Steys with ij smale poles	j
The boneaventure mast	j
Shrowdes to the same	iiij
Tyes	j
Single halyers with oone pole	j

[p. 14]

Yet the Henry Grace de Dew

Yet stuff and tacle delyverd to John Hopton by indenture as aforeseid that is to sey:

The sayle yerd	j
The parell to the same	j
Ankers for the seid bote	iij
Cablettes of v ynch compas	ij
Cocke bote	j
Mastes for the same	j
Sayle yerdes	j
Shevers of brasse	ij
Ores to the same	xij
Bote hokes	j
The skyff otherwise called jolywat	j
Mastes to the same	j
Sayles	j
Ores to the same	vj
Shevers of brasse	j
Shevers of brasse called awyndyng shever for the rame hede	j
Hawsers of v ynch compas	j
Hawsers of vj ynch di compas	di hawser
Hawsers of v ynch compas	iij
Cables of ix ynch compas	j
Hawsers of vj ynch compas	di hawser
Soundynges ledes	vj

*a*Two words inserted.

[p. 15]

Yet the Henry Grace de Dew

Ordynaunce artillarie and habillamentes for warre delyverd to the charge and custodie of Thomas Spert master and William Bonytham purser[1] of the seid ship by indenture as aforeseid that is to sey:

Serpentynes of yron with miches boltes and forelockes	cxxij
Chambers to the same	ccxliiij
Stone gonnes of yron apon trotill wheles and all other apparell	iiij
Chambers to the same	iiij
Serpentynes of brasse apon wheles shod with yron	iij
Serpentynes of brasse apon wheles unshodd	j
Grete peces of yron of oon makyng and bygnes	xij
Chambers to the same	xxiiij
Grete yron gonnes of oone sort that come owt of Flaunders with myches boltes and forelockes	iij
Chambers to the same	vij
Grete Spanysh peces of yron of oone sorte	ij
Chambers to the same	iiij
Stone gonnes apon trotill wheles with miches boltes and forelockes to the same	xviij
Chambers to the same	xxxiiij
Smale vice peces of brasse apon shodd wheles of Symondes makyng[2]	j
Longe vice pece of brasse of the same makyng	iij
Fawcons of brasse apon trotill wheles	vj
A fayre pece of brasse of Arragows makyng[3]	j
A slyng of yron apon trotill wheles	j
Chambers to the same with other apparell	ij
Grete stone gonnes of yron	ij
Chambers to the same	iiij
Grete culverynes of brasse apon unshodd wheles of Symondes makyng	ij
Grete bumberds of brasse apon iiij trotill wheles of Herberd[4] makyng	j
Grete curtalles of brasse apon iiij wheles and of the same makyng[5]	j

[p. 16]

Yet the Henry Grace de Dew

Yet ordynaunce artillarie and habillamentes for warre delyverd to the seid master and purser of the foreseid ship by indenture that is to sey:

Hakebusshes of yron hole	c_{iiij}^{xx}xiij
Hakbusshes of yron broken	vij
Shott[a] of yron of dyverse sortes	dclx shott
Stone shott[b] of dyverse sortes in the balist of the ship agrete nombre not told	
In the grete bote of the seid ship remaynyng fyrst serpentynes of yron with myches boltes and forelockes	viij
Chambers to the same	xxv
Serpentynes of brasse apon shodd wheles	j
Fawcons of brasse apon shodd wheles	ij

In the storehouse of the shipp:

Bowes of ewe	cxxiiij
Chestes for the same	ij
Hole chestes of arrowes	iij
Billys	cxliiij
Morys pykes	$\overset{xx}{iiij}$
Backes and brestes of almyne ryvettes of ether	cc
Splentes	c_{iiij}^{xx}xviij payer
Salettes	cc
Standardes of mayle	cc
Javelyns	ix doss'
Dartes	lvij doss'
Chargyng ladylles for gonnes with staves	vj
Staves withowt ladelles	viij
Spare miches for gonnes	xiiij
Spare boltes	ij
Hamers for gonnes	xiiij
Crowes of yron	iiij
Stonepykes[c] of yron	xiiij
Lynch pynnes	iiij

[a]MS 'scott'.
[b]Idem.
[c]MS 'stokepykes'.

1. Spert later (1524) became clerk controller. He frequently served as vice-admiral, was knighted in 1535, and died in 1541. The purser, whose name appears in various forms [*LP*, I, ii, nos 2807, 3137(6), 3513, 3612 (p. 1507)] is undoubtedly the same as the separately indexed William Botham of *LP*, I, ii, no.2167.
2. Otherwise known as Simon Giles of Mechlin, gunfounder: *LP*, I, ii, no. 2831.
3. No person of this name can be traced; the meaning may be 'of Aragonese making'.
4. Probably Herbert, or Harbard, de Pole, 'gunfounder', paid (with Gyles) 'for making pieces of ordnance' on 14 March 1514: *LP*, I, ii, no. 2832 (v).
5. Oppenheim, *History*, p.380, citing *LP* [1st edn], I, ii, no. 4968 [*LP*, I, ii, no. 2807 in the revised and standard edition] gives the disposition of this ordnance. This reference relates to PRO SP 1/7, ff. 299–312, which is a draft inventory of the *Henry Grace à Dieu*, and includes a receipt by Bonytham to Cornelius Johnson 'the king's iron gun maker' for pieces of ordnance, but does not include any indication of distribution. Nor do the quantities correspond.

[p. 17]

The Kynges Ship called the *Trynitie Soveraigne*

Stuff tacle and apparell delyverd to John Hopton by indenture as aforeseid that is to sey:

The mayne mast of the seid ship	j
The mayne yerd	j
Shrehokes to the same	ij payer
Shrowdes	xxvj
Cheynes and dedemens hies to the same	xxvj
Halyers to the same	ij
Bote tacles of both sydes the mast	x
Poles with shevers of brasse to the same	xvj
Bowsers to the same	ij
Halyers to the same	ij
Swyftyng tacles and to every of them ij poles of wode	x
Halyers to the same	iiij
The mayne stey made of v cablettes*a*	j
Dedemens hies and cheynes to the same	†
Halyers to the same	iiij
Garnettes with iiij poles and iij shevers of brasse	ij
Lyftes for the mayne yerd with iiij poleis and vj shevers of brasse	ij
Tyes for the same	ij
Geres therto belongyng with iij poleis and iij shevers of brasse	j
Trusses for the mayne yerd with viij poles and viij shevers of brasse	iiij
The parell to the mayne yerd	j
The mayne seyle a new corse ij bonettes	j sayle
Bolt ropes to the same	ij
Shutes to the same	ij
Tackes to the same	ij
Bowlyns to the same	ij
Braces to the same	ij

[p. 18]

Yet the Trenitie Soveraigne

Yet stuff and tacle delyverd to John Hopton by indenture as aforeseid that is to say:

The mayne top	j
The topmast	j
The seyleyerd	j
Shrowdes with dedemens hies	xvj
Halyers to the same	ij
Lyftes to the same	ij
Braces with viij poles of wode to the same	ij
Tyes	ij
Halyers to the topsayle with ij poleis of wode	ij
The mayne top sayle	j
Bowlyns to the same	ij
Shutes with ij poleis and shyvers of brasse	ij
The top galant apon the mayne top with the apparell to the same	j
The foremast	j
Shrowdes with cheynes of yron and dedemens hies	xx
Halyers to the same	ij
Tacles of both sydes the mast with iiij poleis and shevers of wode	iiij
Bowsers to the same	ij
Halyers to the same	ij
Stayes to the foremast with dedemens hies	j
Halyers to the same	ij
Aforeyerd	j
Lyftes to the same	ij
Braces with vj poles and shevers of wode	ij
Tyes	ij
Halyers with ij poleis and iiij shevers of brasse	ij
Trusses with poles and shevers of wode	ij
The fore sayle the corse new oone bonet new and an other old in all	j sayle

---

a 'made ... cablettes' inserted.

[p. 19]

Yet the Trenitie Soveraigne

Yet stuff and tacle delyverd to John Hopton by incenture as aforeseid that is to sey:

Bowlyns to the same	ij
Tackes to the same	ij
Shutes with poleis and ij shevers of brasse	ij
The foretop	j
The foretop mast	j
Shrowdes to the same	x
The top*a* sayle yerde	j
Lyftes to the same	ij
Braces with smale poleis and shevers of wode	ij
The tye	j
Halyers to the same	ij
The foretop seyle	j
Bowlyns to the same	ij
Shotes with ij poleis and shevers of wode	ij
The bowsprete	j
Sherehokes to the same	ij
Bowlyne poleis with iiij shevers of brasse	ij
Floure delyces crowned of coper and gylt on the ende of the bowsprete	j
The sprete seyle	j
The sprete seyle yerde	j
The mayne meson mast	j
Shrowdes with cheynes of yron and dedemens hies	xij
Halyers to the same	ij
The mayne meson yerd	j
Tyes	j
Halyers with ij poleis and ij shevers of brasse	j
Lyftes with iij poleis and shevers of wode	j
The meson tope	j
The top mast	j
Shrowdes to the same	viij

*a*Word inserted

[p. 20]

Yet the Trenitie Soveraigne

Yet stuff and tacle delyverd to John Hopton by indenture as aforeseid that is to sey:

The boneaventure mast	j
Shrowdes to the same with smale poleis and shevers of wode	viij
The top galant apon the same topmast	j
The meson yerd	j
The meson seyle	j
The owtlygger	j
Shevers of brasse for the meson shott	j
Shevers of brasse for the lyftes	ij
Smale poles with ij shevers of brasse	ij
Smale doble poleis with iiij shevers of brasse	ij
Voyde shevers of brasse	j

Ankers called { shott ankers j / broken ankers ij / smaler ankers iiij / broken ankers remaynyng at Portesmouth iiij }   xj

Cables new	v
Old cables	iiij
Spare hawsers	iiij
Top armours	iiij
Stremers of lynen cloth steyned	iij
Baners of lynen cloth	ij
Baners of Seynt George of tuke beten in metall	j
Baners of the kynges armes beten in metall	j
Baners of the armes of England in metall	ij
Baners of the portcoles crowned in metall	ij
Baners of whit and grene with the rose of gold crowned	ij
Baners of murrey and blew with half rose and half pomegarnade with a crowne of gold	ij
Fyn Baners of blew tuke with iij crownes of gold	j
Grappers with acheyne of yron to the bowsprete	j

[p. 21]

Yet the Trenitie Soveraigne

Yet stuff and tacle delyverd to John Hopton by indenture as aforeseid that is to sey:

Davettes in the forecastell with ij shevers of brasse	j
Halfe hokes with ij shevers of brasse	ij
Lede in apece cont' by estimacon	m^{li}
The grete bote	j
Mastes to the same	j
Seyles to the same	j
Shevers of brasse in the bote hede	j
The cocke bote	j
Mastes	j
Seyles	j
Shevers of brasse in the botehede	j
The bote called the jolyvatt	j
Ores to the seid botes good and badd	iij dosen

[p. 22]

Yet the Trenitie Soveraigne

Ordynaunce artillarie and habillamentes for warre delyverd to John Millet and Thomas Elderton[1] by bill signed with thandes of the commissioners aforeseid. That is to sey:

Curtowes of brasse stocked apon trotill wheles	iij
Demy curtowe of brasse stoked apon trotill wheles	j
Half curtowes of brasse apon wheles shodd with yron	ij
Grete yron gonnes with myches boltes and forelockes	vij
Chambers to the same	xiiij
Culveryns of brasse without stock	j
Slynges of yron stocked	iiij
Chambers to the same	viij
Serpentynes of yron with myches boltes and forelockes^a	lxij
Chambers to the same	ccxxxiij
Culveryns of brasse stocked apon wheles shodd with yron	ij
Fawcons of brasse apon shodd wheles	ij
Spare miches for gonnes	xiij^b
Spare forelockes	lxj
Spare boltes	xlij
Wheles for curtowes wherof oon shodd with yron	ij payer
Gonne pounder in hole barelles and demy barelles	xxv barelles^c
Grete shott of yron	ccciiiixx
Smale shott of yron	cccxxxiiij
Shott of yron with pykes	iiij^{xx}x
Shott of stone of dyverse sortes	ccc$^{xx}_{iiij}$
Grete spare miches for grete gonnes	ij
Spare gonne chambers	iij
Broken hall of agonne	j
Old yron dyverse peces	†
Crowes^d of yron	iiij
Gonne laddelles of brasse	xj
Long boltes of yron for aship syde	j

^{a}SP adds 'whereof one is broken and oone withowt a stoke'.
^{b}SP gives 'xxiij'.
^{c}SP gives 'xiij hole barrelles of gonne powder xxiiij half barrelles of gonne powder'.
^{d}MS 'crownes'.

1.   John Millet was a clerk of the signet and a teller of the exchequer. Thomas Elderton was the undertreasurer of the war, assisting Sir John Daunce: *LP*, I, ii, no. 2546.

1.   1,000 lbs.

[p. 23]

Yet the Trenitie Soveraigne

Yet ordynance artillarie and habillamentes for the warre delyverd to John Millet and Thomas Elderton by bill signed as aforeseid that is to sey:

Dyce of yron	j barell
Pellettes of yron	ccxli
Pellettes of lede	di barell
Cusshons of lede for forelockes	xxiiij
Brestes of revettes	cclxiiij
Backes to the same	cc$^{xx}_{iiij}$vj
Splentes^a	ccxlvj payer
Salettes good and badd	ccxj^b
Standardes of mayle	ccxlix
Billes	dxxxj
Mores pykes	$^{xx}_{iiij}$xvij
Naves of brasse for curtow wheles	v
Dartes	j bondell
Stakes for the feld	vj bondelles
Chestes of arrowes	xix
Bowes of ewe	lxxviij
Chestes to the same	ij
Wiches haselle bowes	ij chestes

[p. 24]

The Kynges Ship called the *Gabryell Royle*

Stuff tacle and apparell delyverd to John Hopton by indenture made betwene the foreseid commissioners and the seyd John Hopton that is to sey:

The mayne mast	j
Steyes to the same	iij
Tacles with xxiiij poles iiij of them with shevers of brasse	viij
Shrowdes with dedemens hyes and cheynes^a	xxxij
Swyftyng tacles	vj
Poles to the same	xij
Garnettes	vj
Poleys to the same	xij
The mayne yerd	j
Trusses	ij
Drynges	ij
Poleis to the same	viij
The mayne parell	j
The mayne sayle acorse new and ij bonettes old	j
Tyes	ij
Ramehedes with ashever of brasse	j
Lyftes	ij
Poleys to the same ij of them with shevers of brasse^b	iiij
Shutes	ij
Tackes	ij
Geres with ij poles	j
A spare shever of brasse for the rame hede	j
Halyers for the mayne yerd	j
Braces with ij poleis	ij
Halyers for the same	ij
Warre tacles	ij
Loff hokes of yron	j
The mayne top	j
The top mast	j
Shrowdes to the same	x
Yerdes	j
Trusses	j
Lyftes with iiij poleys	ij

---

^{a}SP adds 'good and badde'.
^{b}SP gives 'cclxj'.

^{a} Two words inserted.
^{b} 'ij ... brasse' inserted.

[p. 25]

Yet the Gabriell Royall

Yet stuff and tacle delyverd to John Hopton by indenture
as aforeseid that is to sey:

Sayles to the top mast	j
Shutes with ij poles to the same	ij
Brases	ij
Bowlyns	ij
Tyes	j
Halyers to the same	ij
Parell to the sayle yerd	j
Trusses with ij poleys of wode	j
Steyes	j
The top galant	j
The mast to the same	j
The sayle yerd	j
Sayle with all that belongith therto made of calbens	j
The foremast	j
The stey	j
Tacles with xviij poles and oone shever of brasse	vj
Shrowdes with cheynes of yron and dedemens hies	xvj
Sayle yerdes	j
Sayles acorse and abonet new and an old bonet	j sayle
Lyftes with iiij poles to the same	ij
Brases with ij poles to the same	ij
Bowlynes with adoble pole	ij
Tackes	ij
Shetes old with ij poles	ij
Trusses with iiij poleis	ij
The foretop	j
The top mast	j
The sayle yerd	j
Olde sayle	j
Shrowdes to the topmast	viij
Shetes	ij

[p. 26]

Yet the Gabriell Royall

Yet stuff and tacle delyverd to John Hopton by indenture
as aforeseid that is to sey:

Bowlyns to the same olde	ij
Braces with ij poles	ij
Lyftes with iiij poleys to the same	ij
Steyes	j
The bowspret	j
The sayle yerd for the same	j
The sayle to the same old	j
Lyftes with iiij poleis	ij
Halyers with ij poleis	ij
The meson mast	j
Stayes to the same	j
Shrowdes	xij
Sayle yerdes	j
Sayles to the same old	j
Shutes	j
Poleis to the same	ij
Owtlyggers at sterne	j
Doble lyftes	ij
Tyes	j
Halyers	j
Knyghtes	j
The meson top	j
The top mast	j
Shrowdes to the same made of calbyns	vj
Sayle yerdes	j
Sayles to the same	j
An old corse to the meson sayle	j
An old corse to the foresayle	j
Cables old called jonkes	v
New cable of xvj ynch compas	iiij
Cathokes	ij
Brasyn shevers for the same	ij
Davettes with ij shevers of tymbre	j

[p. 27]

Yet the Gabriell Royall

Yet stuff and tacle delyverd to John Hopton by indenture
as aforeseid that is to sey:

Fyshe hokes		j
Grapper with acheyne of yron		j
Hawsers of v ynch compas		iij
Cablet with aboy		j

Ankers called	shott ankers	ij	
	sterbord bowers	j	
	ladbord*a* bowers	j	viij
	destrelles	ij	
	caggers	ij	

Coper ketilles sett in furnes	ij
Grete ketilles not sett	j
Lantrons	xiiij
Belles of brasse hole (j) and broken (j)	ij
Poldaves hole peces	vij
Pych ketilles	j
Boy ropes	iiij
Boyes of cork*b*	iij
Boyes of wode	iij

Grete bote	j
Mastes to the same	j
Sayles to the same	j
Ores	xvij
Botehokes	j
Shevers of brasse in the botehede	j
Davettes for the seid bote	j
Grape yrons	j

The cock bote	j
Mastes to the same	j
Seyles to the same	j
Shevers of brasse in the cockes hede	j

The jolywatt	j

Stremers for the mayne mast*c*	j
Stremers to the foremast with acrosse of seynt George in the same	j

[p. 28]

Yet the Gabriell Royall

Yet stuff and tacle delyverd to John Hopton by indenture
as aforeseid that is to sey:

Stremers of roses for the meson otherwise called the boneaventure	j
Baners of Seynt George and the crosse in metall	ij
Baners of Kyng Henry in metall	j
Baners with roses in metall	x
Baners of roses and pomegarnettes in metall	j
Baners of portcules in metall	ij
Baners of the castell in metall	j
Baners of Seynt George in metall	j

*a*MS 'ladbordbord'.
*b*Two words inserted.
*c*Four words inserted.

[p. 29]

Yet the Gabriell Royall

Ordynaunce artillarie and habillamentes for the warre delyverd to John Millet and Thomas Elderton by bill signed with thandes of the seid commissioners that is to sey:

Single serpentynes with miches boltes and forelockes	xv
Chambers to the same	xlvj
Facons of brasse apon shodd wheles	vj
Curtowes of brasse apon bare wheles	j
Grete culveryns of brasse apon shod wheles	j
Stone gonnes with miches boltes and forelockes	vij
Chambers to the same	vij
Murderers of yron	iiij
Chambers to the same	v
Slynges of yron	ij
Chambers to the same	iiij
Fawcons of yron	ij
Grete stone gonnes	ij
Chambers to the same	iiij
Organs apon iiij stokkes oon of the orgons broken	xij
Hakbusshes with v handelles broken	xxxvj
Shott of lede for fawcons	iiij
Grete shott of yron for curtowes	$\overset{xx}{vij}$
Shott of yron of alesser sort	cxxv
Shott of yron for fawcons	c
Shott of lede for culveryns	viij
Shott of lede for serpentynes	clxvj
Shott of lede for hakbushes	cclxxiiij
Shott of stone of dyverse sortes*a*	ccviij
Mouldes of brasse for culveryn shott*b*	j
Ladelles for meltynge of lede	ij
Hamours	v
Stone pykes for makyng of shott	vj
Crowes of yron	iiij
Ballez of wyldefyre with hokes of yron	v
Boltes of wyldefyre to cast at shippes*c*	lvj
Wyskers	vj

[p. 30]

Yet the Gabriell Royall

Yet ordynaunce artillarie and habillamentes for the warre delyverd to John Millet and Thomas Elderton by bill signed as aforeseid that is to sey:

Gonne powder	xxj barelles
Heyle shott	c cast
Dyce of yron	l
Billes	$cccc^{xx}_{iiij}viij$
Stakes for the feld	xx doss'
Mores pykes	ccccxx
Salettes	ccl
Brestes of revettes	cclxv
Backes	cclxxij
Standardes of mayle*a*	$c^{xx}_{iiij}v$
Splentes*b*	ccxxxvij payer
Bowes of ewe	cccxxxij
Chestes for the same	vj
Dartes	vj doss'
Arrowes	dcccclxiiij sheff
Chestes for the same	xxj
Chestes with wast and broken arrowes	j
Bowstrynges	d
Agrete*c* spare wheles shodd with yron	j
Colkes of brasse in the same	j
Wheles for fawcons shodd with yron	v
Javelynes	xl

*a*SP adds 'rugh and hewen'.
*b*SP adds 'with a handell of irone'.
*c*SP gives 'Cast of wyldefyre made lyke boltes' [same quantity].

*a*SP gives 'gorgeyttes' [same quantity].
*b*SP adds 'hole and broken'.
*c*Word inserted.

[p. 31]

The Kynges Ship called the *Kateryn Forteleza*

Stuff tacle and apparell delyverd unto John Hopton by indenture as aforeseyd that is to sey:

The mayne mast	j
The mayne yerd	j
Sherhokes to the same	iiij
Parell to the same	j
Trusses with xij poleis of wode	vj
S[t]eyes with ashyver	ij
Poleis with iiij shyvers of brasse ij dedemens hies and cheynes to the same	ij
Shrowdes to the mayne mast	xxviij
Dedemens hies with cheynes of yron	xxviij
Halyers to the same	iiij
Bote tacles on both sides the mast with pendauntes ronners [and] halyers to the same	ix
Poleis of wode wherof iiij with shevers of brasse	xxvij
Swyftyng tacles with xvj poleis of wode	viij
Garnettes with halyers and pendauntes	ij
Shevers of brasse to the same	iiij
Tyes	ij
Rame hedes with ashever of brasse	j
Halyers to the same	ij
Knyghtes with a*a* shever of brasse	j
Geres with iij poleis and iij shevers of brasse	j
Lyftes to the mayne yerd	ij
Shevers of brasse to the same	vj
The mayne sayle acorse abonet new doble and an other single	j
Olde mayne sayle acorse and ij bonettes single	j
Tackes	ij
Shutes	ij
Bowlyns with apole and ij shevers of brasse	ij
Braces with ij poleis of wode	ij

[p. 32]

Yet the Kateryn Forteleza

Yet stuff and tacle dylyverd to John Hopton by indenture as aforeseid that is to sey:

Mayne tope	j
Mayne topmast	j
The yerd	j
Lyftes with iiij poleis of wode	ij
Tyes with ahalyere to the same	j
Poleis of wode to the same	ij
Shrowdes with dedemens hies	xiiij
Potokes and halyers to the same	†
Sayles	j
Bowlyns	ij
Braces with poles of wode	ij
Trusses with potokes of wode	j
Shutes with ij poleis and ij shevers of brasse	ij
Top galant	j
Topgalant mast	j
Shrowdes to the same	vj
Yerdes with brases and bowlyns therto belongyng	j
Foremastes	j
Yerdes to the same	j
Sherhokes to the same	iiij
Parell to the same	j
Trusses with viij poleis of wode	iiij
Stayes with ij dedemens hies	j
Halyers to the same	j
Tyes to the seid foremast	ij
Ramehedes with ij shevers of brasse	j
Halyers to the same	j
Knyghtes with iij shevers of brasse	ij
Seyles acorse and abonet doble and abonet single	j
Shetes	ij
Tackes to the same	ij
Shrowdes with dedemens hies and chaynes of yron	xvj

a Replacing deletion.

[p. 33]

Yet the Kateryn Forteleza

Yet stuff and tacle delyverd to John Hopton by indenture as aforeseid that is to sey:

Halyers to the same	iiij
Tacles with xvj poleis of wode	viij
Bowlynes with apole of wode	ij
Braces with apole of wode	ij
Lyftes with iiij poleis of wode	ij
Aforetop	j
Topmastes	j
Shrowdes to the same	x
Dedemens hies with potokes and halyers to the seid shrowdes	x
Yerdes	j
Tyes	j
Halyers	j
Poleis of wode to the same	ij
Lyftes with iiij poleis of wode	ij
Trusse with ij poleis of wode	j
Braces with ij poleis of wode	ij
Foretop sayle	j
Bowlyns	ij
Stayes to the foretopmast*a*	j
Shutes with ij poleis of wode	ij
Bowsprettes	j
Sherehokes to the same	ij
Spret sayle with abonet	j
Yerdes	j
Tyes with ij poleis of wode	j
Lyftes with iiij poleis of wode	ij
Braces with ij poleis of wode	ij
Grapyrons with cheynes	ij
The meson mast	j
The top apon the same	j
Shrowdes with xx poleis of wode and halyers to the same	x

[p. 34]

Yet the Kateryn Forteleza

Yet stuff and tacle delyverd to John Hopton by indenture as aforeseid that is to sey:

Meson yerdes	j
Tyes with halyers to the same	j
Poleis of wode to the same	ij
Trusses	j
Parell	j
Seales to the meson mast acorse and abonet	j
Owtlyggers with ij poleis of wode	j
Shutes with ij poleis of wode	j
Ankers called shute ankers (j) and other ankers (iiij)	v
Cables of vij ynch compas	ij
Cables worne	j
Cables occupied	ij
Hawsers	ij
Doble hokes for ankers with ij shevers of brasse	ij
Devettes with ij shevers of brasse	ij
Fyshokes of yron	j
Ropes to the same	j
Lufhokes for the mayne seyle	iiij
Botes	j
Mastes to the same	j
Seyles to the same	j
Ores to the seid bote	xij
Shevers of brasse	j
Davettes with ashever of wode	j
Cokk botes	j
Mastes to the same	j
Seyles	j
Ores to the seid cock	viij
Shevers of yron	j
Jolyvattes	j
Ores to the same	iiij
Boltes of canvas	xij

*a*Altered from 'foremast'.

[p. 35]

Yet the Kateryn Forteleza

Yet stuff and tacle delyverd to John Hopton by indenture as aforeseid that is to sey:

Grapulles of yron with acheyne	j
Stremers	ij
Pendantes	xxiiij
Spanysh paveses	ij dos'di
Spare poles with iij brasen shevers	iij
Shovelles	xviij
Baners of Seynt George the feld sylver	vj
Baners of the armes of England in metall	iij
Baners of Seynt Edwardes armes in metall	iij
Baners of the armes of England and Castell	iiij
Baners of the same sort in colours	iiij
Baners of the Castell in metall	iiij
Baners of the rose crowned in metall	iij
Baners of the same sort in colours	j
Baners of the rose and pomegarnet crowned in metall	iij
Of the same sort in colours	ij
Baners of the portcules crowned in metall	iij
Baners of Seynt Anne in metall	j
Stremours of the dragon and greyhaund in colours	ij
Topp armours of cloth	iiij
Furnes of brasse	ij
Grete ketilles	j
Tarre ketilles	j
Lede	di sow

[p. 36]

Yet the Kateryn Forteleza

Ordynaunce artillarie and habillamentes for warre delyverd to John Millet and Thomas Elderton by billes signed with thande of the foreseid commissioners that is to sey:

Murderers grete and smale	xiiij
Chambers to the same hole (xxiiij) and broken (j)	xxv
Grete curtowes of brasse	j
Chambers to the same	ij
Fawcons of brasse	ij
Hakebusshes lying in stokkes	iiij
Hakebusshes without stokkes	xlix
Half^a slynges of yron	ij
Chambers to the same and all other apparell	iiij
Hole slynges of yron	iiij
Chambers to the same with all ther apparell	viij
Stone gonnes of yron	xij
Chambers to the same with all ther apparell	xxvij
Serpentynes of yron doble and single	xxvj
Chambers to the same with all ther apparell^b	liij
Hand gonnes lackyng ther apparell	xvij
Shott of lede of dyverse sortes	cclx^c
Shott of lede for hakbusshes	clxx
Shott of yron grete and smale	d$^{xx}_{iiij}$vij
Shott of yron with pykes	cxliiij
Shott of stone	cc$^{xx}_{iiij}$xv
Dyce of yron	dccxx
Crowes of yron	xj
Pykeaxes to hew stone	xvj
Hamers of yron	iij
Spare myches hole (x) and broken (iiij)	xiiij
Spare forelockes	xiiij
Spare boltes of yron	xij
Breches of yron for agonne	j
Ledder bagges for gonnepowder	iiij
Arrowes^d	xl sheff
Chestes to the same	ij

^{a}Word inserted.
^{b}SP adds 'onne broken and oone stoke broken'.
^{c}Replacing 'cxliiij' deleted.
^{d}SP gives 'xiij chestes of arrowes chest [sic] with xxvij sheff xl bowes of ewe cxix bowes of wychehasell' [see next column].

[p. 37]

Yet the Kateryn Forteleza

Yet ordynaunce artillarie and habillamentes for warre delyverd to John Millet and Thomas Elderton by indenture and bylles signed as aforeseid that is to sey:

Bowes of ewe	cl
Chestes to the same	ij
Bowes of wyche hasill	cxix
Chestes to the same	ij
Billes	ccciiij
Javelyns	c
Morys pykes	cccxliiij
Stakes for the feld	cccxij
Cross bowes hole and broken	v
Lytill crankett	j
Brestes of almyn revettes	ccviij
Backes	ccxi
Salettes	ccix
Standardes of mayle*a*	c$_{iiij}^{xx}$xviij
Splentes	cc payer
Gonnepowder	v barelles di
Lede	demy sow & awebbe
Old yron	†
Serpentynes of yron	xv
Chambers to the same with myches boltes and forelockes	xxxv

[p. 38]

The Kynges Ship called the *Grete Barbora*

Stuff tackle and apparell dyverse delyverd to John Hopton by indenture as aforeseid that*a* is to sey:

The mayne mast	j
Steyes to the same*b*	ij
Tackes with xiij poleis and shevers of wode	iiij
Shrowdes old with dedemens hies	xxvj
Cheynes of yron to the same	xxvj
The mayne yerd with trusse and dryng	j
Brest ropes	j
Tyes	j
Halyers with ij shevers of brasse	iiij
Lyftes	ij
Braces	ij
Mayne*c* sayle a corse and a bonet new and abonet old	j
Spare corse and abonet	j
Tackes	ij
Shutes	ij
Bowlyns with poles of wode	ij
The mayne top	j
The topmast	j
Shrowdes to the same	x
Halyers	ij
Tyes	ij
The sayle yerd	j
Brases	ij
Lyftes	ij
Top sayles new	j
Bowlyns	j
Shutes	ij
Poleis with shevers of wode	ij
Foremastes*d*	j
Spare mastes for the same*e*	j
Tacles with vj poleis of wode	ij
Shrowdes with dedemens hies	xiiij
Cheynes to the same	xiiij

*a*SP gives 'gorgettes' [same quantity].

*a*MS 'thay'.
*b*E adds 'old'.
*c*MS 'mayle'.
*d*E adds 'olde'.
*e*E adds 'new'.

[p. 39]

Yet the Grete Barbora

Yet stuff and tacle delyverd to John Hopton by indenture as aforeseid that is to sey:

Yerde to the seyle old and peced	i
Trusses with poleis to the same	ij
The foresayle acorse and ij new bonettes	j
Bowlyns with poleis to the same	ij
Lyftes	ij
Shutes	ij
Braces	ij
Shutes with ij poleis to the same	ij
The foretop	j
The foretopmast	j
Shrowdes to the same	viij
Yerdes to the seyle	j
Lyftes	ij
Braces	ij
Top seyles old	j
Top seyles new	j
Bowlyns and poleis to the same	ij
The bowspret	j
The stey	j
Poleis to the same	ij
Halyers	j
Sayles to the same bowspret old (j) and new (j)	ij
Bonettes to the same old	j
The meson mast	j
The seyle yerd	j
Shrowdes with dedemens hies	vj
Stayes	j
Trusses	ij
Polles to the same	ij
Tyes	j
Halyers	j
Doble poleis of wode	j

[p. 40]

Yet the Grete Barbora

Yet stuff and tacle delyverd to John Hopton by indenture as aforeseid that is to sey:

Baners of Spanysh work	x
Ankers called shet ankers (j) and other (iiij)	v
Broken ankers	j

Cables of	xiiij ynch compas	j	
	xij ynch compas	j	v
	ix ynch compas	j	
	old cables	ij	

Hawsers new and hole	ij
Hawsers cutt	ij
Old hawsers	j
A new bote	j
Mastes to the same	j
Seyles to the same	j
Ores to the same	xviij
Davettes	j
Hokkes of yron to the same	ij
Cock bote	j
Ores to the same	xiij
Ketilles smale	ij
Pech ketilles	j
Afurnes of coper	j

[p. 41]

Yet the Grete Barbora

Ordynaunce artillarie and habillamentes for warre left in the seid ship in the charge of John Restryk master and John Warwyk purser of the same by indenture that is to sey:

In the forecastell of the ship:

Serpentynes of yron	vij
Chambers to the same with myches boltes and foreclokes	xviij
Murderers of yron	ij
Chambers to the same	iiij

The upper lop of the seid ship:

Murderers of yron	ij
Chambers to the same	iiij

In the wast of the seid ship:

Serpentynes of yron	vj
Doble serpentynes in the brest of the ship	ij
Single serpentynes in the same place	j

In the holle[1] of the shipp:

Stone gonnes	ij
Serpentynes	ij
Chambers with other apparell except vj wa[n]ttyng their myches boltes and forelookes	xxiiij

In the barbican of the seid ship:

Murderers of yron	iiij
Chambers to the same with other apparell	vij

In the medill deck of the seid ship:

Fawcons of brasse apon shodd wheles	ij
Murderers of yron	ij
Chambers to the same and other apparell	iiij

In the hygh deck of the seid ship:

Fawconettes of brasse v of them apon trustelles and oon apon wheles with their apparell	vj

Mowldes of brasse	iij
Pyckes for stone shott	xij
Gonnehamers	v
Shott of stone	ccxxiij
Billes	xvj
Bowes of ewe	xij
Arrowes	xij sheff

[p. 42]

Yet the Grete Barbora

Artillary and habillamentes for warre delyverd to John Millet and Thomas Elderton by billes signed with the handes of the seid commissioners that is to sey:

Morys pykes	$cc_{iiij}^{xx}xj$
Shott of yron of dyverse sortes	cccxvj
Billes	cclxxv
Pellettes of lede for fawcons and fawconettes	$c_{iiij}^{xx}vj$
Javelyns	cl
Dyce of yron of dyverse sortes	cccc
Stakes for the feld	clxxj
Dartes	xiij doss' di
Bowes of ewe	clxij
Bowstrynges	xv doss'
Chestes with arrowes hole	x
Arrowes losse in acheff[1]	xx sheff
Handgonnes broken and hole	x
Crossebowes	xj
Bendes for the same	vij
Standards of mayle	cxxxiiij
Salettes	cxxx
Splentes	cxxix payre
Brygandynes	vij payere
Backes and brestes of almen revettes	clv payer
Hacbusshes	vij
Gonnepowder	di barell

---

1. The only deduceable meaning of this is 'hold', which would be a strange place to mount guns, unless the meaning is that they were unmounted and in store.

1. Presumably loose arrows in sheaves, perhaps meaning that the sheaves were not full.

[p. 43]

The Kynges Ship called the *Grete Nicholas*

Stuff tacle and apparell delyverd to John Hopton by indenture as aforeseid that is to sey:

The fore mast	j
Seyle yerdes to the same	j
Shrowdes with dedemens hies	xiiij
Cheynes to the same	xiiij
Tyes with poleis to the same	j
Halyers	ij
Tackelles	iiij
Poleis to the same	vj
Trusses with iiij polleis	ij
Lyftes with iiij poleis	ij
Stayes to the foremast	j
Bowlyns to the foresayle	ij
Braces with ii poleis*a*	ij
The foresayle acorse and ij bonettes	j
Shutes to the same	ij
Tackes	ij
Poleis to the shetes with thapparell	ij
Foretop	j
Foretop mastes	j
Sayles with all thapparell to the same	j
Mayne mastes	j
Yerdes to the same	j
Sayles acorse and ij bonettes	j
Shrowdes with dedemens hies	xxviij
Cheynes to the same	xxviij
Tacles with poleis and v shevers of brasse and j of yron*b*	xiiij
The mayne tyes	ij
Halyers to the same	iiij
Trusses	ij
Drynges with viij poleis	ij
Lyftes	ij
Mayne shutes	ij

[p. 44]

Yet the Grete Nicolas

Yet stuff and tacle delyverd to John Hopton by indenture as aforeseid that is to sey:

Tackes	ij
Mayne bowlyns	ij
Mayne top	j
Topmast	j
Topsayles	j
Lyftes	ij
Shutes with all other apparell	ij
Lyft poleis with iiij shevers of brasse	iiij
Poleis with ij shevers of tre	j
Mayne meson mastes	j
Sayle yerdes to the same	j
Tyes	j
Halyers to the same	j
Lyftes	j
Shrowdes	xij
Atope	j
Topmast	j
Shrowdes therto belongyng	viij
The boneaventure mast	j
Seyle yerdes to the same	j
Seyles	j
Tyes	j
Halyers with ij poleis	j
Shetes	j
Shrowdes*a*	vj
Sayles acorse and ij bonettes to the boneaventure	j
A bowspret	j
Yerdes to the same*b*	j
Seyles to the same	j
The parell with all other necessarie therto belongyng	j
Shevers of brasse to the doble hokkes	ij
Snach poleis with ashever of brasse	j

*a*E adds 'to the foresaile'.
b'and...yron' inserted.

*a*E adds 'for the mayne saile'.
*b*MS 'seyle'.

[p. 45]

Yet the Grete Nicolas

Yet stuff and tacle delyverd to John Hopton by indenture as aforeseid that is to sey:

Shevers of brasse for the mayne top seyle	ij
Spare shevers of brasse for store	vj

Ankers called	bowers	ij	
	destrelles	ij	vj
	caggers	j	
	shot ankers	j	

Cables of xiiij ynch compas*a*	iiij
Cables called junckes of xj ynch compas*b*	iiij
Bote	j
Botemast	j
Seyles	j
Ores to the same	x
Cock bote	j
Mastes to the same	j
Seyles	j
Ores to the same	iiij
Davettes	j
Shevers of yron on the botes hede	j
Hawsers new of v ynch compas	ij
Furnous of brasse*c*	j
Ketilles of brasse	j
Frying pannes	j
Spyttes	j
Gobyrons	ij
Pych ketilles	j
Terr ketilles*d*	j
Rackes for hangyng of ketilles	j
Clyphokes	j payer

[p. 46]

Yet the Grete Nicolas

Ordynaunce artillarie and habillamentes for warre delyverd to Richard Grey master and Robert Golsett purser of the same ship by indenture as aforeseid that is to sey:

In the forecastell of the seid ship:

Cast peces of yron	ij
Chambers to the same and other apparell	iiij

In the somer castell of the seid ship:

Serpentynes of yron wherof oon broken	xj
Chambres to the same with myches boltes and forelockes therto belongyng	xxvij
Murderers of yron grete apon trotill wheles	v
Chambres to the same with miches boltes and forelockes	x

In the somer deck of the seid ship:

Slynges of yron lying apon trotill wheles	ij
Chambres to the same with their apparell	iiij
Stone gonnes lying apon trotilles	j
Chambres to the same and his apparell	ij
Shott of stone rugh and hewen	clv
Morys pykes	vij
Billes	xij
Arrowes	xii sheff
Bowes of ewe	xij

---

*a*E gives 'ij new cabuls of xiiij ynches compas'.
*b*E adds 'iij of them and thother a small cagger'.
*c*E adds 'The cokerowme' [heading to this and following entries].
*d*E adds 'of brasse' [refers to both kettles].

[p. 47]
Yet the Grete Nicolas

Artillarie and habillamentes for warre delyverd to John Millet and Thomas Elderton by bill signed with thandes of the commissioners aforeseid that is to sey:

Yron shott of dyverse sortes	lxxvj
Shott of yron with pykes	iiij
Morys pykes	clx
Billes	cxxx
Bille hedes	v
Bowes of ewe	xliiij
Chestes to the same	j
Yet bowes of ewe	cviij
Chestes to the same	ij
Arrowes	cccxlviij
Chestes to the same	ix
Stakes for the feld	cxv
Splentes	clxiij payer
Brestes	clxij
Backes	clxiiij
Standardes of mayle	cxxvij
Salettes	clxiij
Gonnepowder	iiij barelles di
Mattockes	xiiij
Shott of lede for hacbusshes	cxxxij
Shott of lede for serpentynes	cxl
Dyce of yron of dyverse sortes	ccc
Bowstrynges	c
Arrowes of wyldfyre	v
Dartes of wyldfyre	viij
Spare miches hole (iiij) and broken (j)	iiij
Forelockes broken	j
Gonne hamers	v

[p. 48]

The Kynges Ship called the *John Baptist*

Yet stuff and tacle delyverd to John Hopton by indenture as aforeseid that is to sey:

The mayne mast	j
The mayne yerd	j
Sherehokes to the same	iiij
The mayne seyle acorse and abonett new and ij other bonettes old	j
A spare corse and abonet	j
Shutes	ij
Tackes	ij
Bowlyns	ij
Lyftes with iiij poleis and vj colkes of brasse	ij
Braces with ij poleis	ij
The mayne parell	j
Trusses	ij
Drynges	ij
Poleis to the same	iiij
Tyes	ij
Halyers	ij
Ramehedes with ashever of brasse	j
Knyghtes with ij shevers of brasse	j
Jeres with ij shevers of brasse	j
Mayne stayes made of iij cablettes	j
Dedemens hies with acolor and cheyne of yron	ij
Shrowdes with dedemens hies	xxvj
Cheynes of yron to the same	xxvj
Halyers to the same	iiij
Tacles with ix poleis and iiij shevers of brasse	j
Swyftyng tacles with viij poleis to the same	iiij
Tacles on sterbord with ix poleis to the same	iij
Breteyn tacles [with] iij shevers of brasse	j
Swyftyng tacles with viij poleis to the same	iiij
The mayne tope	j

[p. 49]

Yet the John Baptist

Yet stuff and tacle delyverd to John Hopton by indenture as aforeseid that is to sey:

Mayne top mastes	j
Garlandes of yron to the same	j
Shrowdes	xij
Parell to the topsayle	j
Tyes	j
Halyers to the same	ij
Braces with ij poleis	ij
Lyftes with iiij poleis	ij
Steyes	j
Bowlyns	ij
Sayles	j
Shutes with ij poleis	ij
Cranelynes with ij canvas bagges	j
Shevers of brasse in the deck hede	j
The mayne meson mast	j
Yerdes for the sayle	j
Shrowdes	x
Trusses with ij poleis and other apparell to the same	j
Tyes	j
Halyers with apole and ij colkes of brasse	ij
Doble poleis to the same	j
The mayne meson sayle	j
Lyftes with iiij poleis to the same	j
Topes	j
Topmastes	j
Garlandes of yron to the same	j
Shrowdes	vj
Sayle yerdes	j
Parell to the same	j
Lyftes to the same and other apparell	j
The boneaventure mast	j
Shrowdes to the same	vj
Yerdes	j

[p. 50]

Yet the John Baptist

Yet stuff and tacle delyverd to John Hopton by indenture as aforeseid that is to sey:

Parelles to the same	j
Sayles	j
Trusses with ij poleis	j
Shutes with ij poleis	j
Owtlyggers	j
The foremast	j
The yerd	j
The parell to the same	j
The sayle acorse and abonet and ij old bonettes	j
Bowlyns	ij
Lyftes	ij
Brasse with vj poleis to the same	ij
Shutes	ij
Tackes with ij poleis	ij
Tyes	ij
Halyers to the same	iiij
Poleis with ij shyvers of brasse	j
Shevers of brasse in the brest of the forecastell	ij
Trusses with iiij poleis	ij
Stayes with dedemens hies and halyers to the same	j
Shrowdes with dedemens hies	xvj
Cheynes to the same	xvj
Halyers to the same	iiij
Tacles with x poleis to the same	iiij
Swyftyng tacles with viij poleis to the same	iiij
Tope	j
Top mast	j
Garland of yron to the same	j
Shrowdes	x
Sayle yerdes	j
Tyes with halyers to the same	j
Lyftes with iiij poleis	ij
Braces with ij poleis	ij

[p. 51]

Yet the John Baptist

Yet stuff and tacle delyverd to John Hopton by indenture
as aforeseid that is to sey:

Stayes	j
Sayles	j
Bowlyns	ij
Shutes with ij poleis to the same	ij
Cranelynes with ij bagges of canvas to the same	j
Poledavies for a new foresayle	vj boltes
Bowsprettes	j
Doble poleis to the same with ij shivers of brasse	j
Doble polies	j
Yerdes	j
Lyftes with iiij poleis to the same	ij
Halyers	j
Braces with iiij poleis	ij
Sprete sayles old (j) and new (j)	ij
Hokes in the forecastell with shevers of yron	ij
Davettes with ij shevers of yron and halyers to the same	ij
Long devettes with ij shevers of yron	j
Fyshokes of yron with ij devettes of wode	ij

Cables of
- xiiij ynch compas — ij
- xiiij ynch di compas — ij
- ix ynch compas — j
- jonkes broken & hole — v
x

Halyers with oone doble pole and ij shevers of brasse iiij

Ankers called
- bowers — ij
- destrelles — ij
- shute ankers — j
- cagers — j
- spare ankers — j
vij

Boyes	iiij
Boye ropes	iiij

[p. 52]

Yet the John Baptist

Yet stuff and tacle delyverd to John Hopton by indenture
as aforeseid that is to sey:

Bote	j
Ores to the same	xviij
Botehokes	j
Mastes	j
Sayles	j
Skull	j
Davettes with ashever of brasse	j
Shevers of brasse in the botehede	j
The cocke bote	j
Mastes	j
Seyles	j
Ores for the same	xij
Shevers of yron in the cockes hede	j
The jolywat	j
Ores to the same	j
Cannehokes	j payer
Goodes of yron	ij
Soundyng lynes	ij
Soundyng ledes	ij
Compasses	ij
Rynnyng glasses	ij
Boltes of olrons for reparacon of seyles	ij
Olde cables	j
Crapnolles for the bote to ryde by	j
Pyche kettilles old	j
Loff hokes of yron to the mayne sayle	ij
Leche hokes	j
Breten tacles with iij shevers of brasse	j
Caldrons of coper set in furnos	ij
Kettilles to seth in fysh	j
Belles of ametely sise[1]	j

1 Sc. meetly (meaning of a moderate, or suitable) size.

[p. 53]

Yet the John Baptist

Ordynaunce artillarie and habillamentes for the warre left in the ship in the charge and custodie of John Kempe master and John Dobbys purser by indenture made as aforeseid that is to sey:

In the upper lop of the seid ship:

Grete gonnes of yron	iiij
Chambers to the same	vij

In the forecastell of the ship:

Serpentynes of yron	viij
Broken serpentynes with all apparell lackyng	j

In the somer castell of the seid ship:

Doble serpentynes of yron	xviij
Single serpentynes of yron	iiij

In the sterne of the seid ship:

Serpentynes of yron	iiij
Chambers to all the seid serpentynes with miches boltes and forelockes to them	lv
Grete gonnes of yron	v
Chamber to the same with miches boltes and forelockes	ix

In the middell deck of the seid ship:

[S]lynges of yron	ij
Chambers to the same with miches boltes and forelockes	iiij
Grete gonnes of yron	j
Chambers to the same and other apparell	ij
Cast peces of yron with all thapparell	j

In the upper deck of the seid ship:

Fawcons of brasse with all their apparell	j
Top gonnes of yron	ij
Chambers to the same with miches boltes and forelockes	viij
Shodd wheles for a fawcon	j payer

Morys pykes	viij
Billes	j

[p. 54]

Yet the John Baptist

Artillarie and habillamentes of warre delyverd to John Millet and Thomas Elderton by bill signed with thandes of the foreseid commissioners that is to sey:

Shott of stone of dyverse sortes	cciij
Shott of yron of dyverse sortes	clxvj
Pellettes of lede of dyverse sortes	dccclxij
Shott of yron with pykes	vj
Morys pykes	cclx
Billys	cxvij
Stakes for the feld	ccxvij
Arrowes	dlxi sheff
Chestes for the same	xij
Gonnepowder	xvij di barelles
Bowes of ewe	clj
Chestes to the same	j
Bowes of wich hasyll	$^{xx}_{iiij}$iiij
Chestes to the same	ij
Dartes	xviij doss'
Brestes of revett	cxxxix
Backes	cxlj
Splentes	cxxviij payer
Standardes of mayle	cvij
Salettes	cxxxvj
Gonnestone pykkes	xviij
Spare miches for gonnes	viij
Lede in apece cast by estimacon	cc
Spare boltes for gonnes	xvj
Bowstrynges	ccl

[p. 55]

The Kynges Ship called the *Mary Roose*

Stuff tacle and apparell delyverd to John Hopton by indenture as aforeseid that is to sey:

Mayne mastes	j
Mayne yerdes	j
Mayne sayles a corse and ij bonettes	j
Tackes	ij
Shutes	ij
Bowlyns	ij
Parell	j
Trusses	ij
Drynges	ij
Braces	ij
Tyes	j payer
Halyers to the same*a*	j
Lyftes	ij
Geres	j
Steyes*b*	j
Shyrwyns¹	j
Shrowdes*c*	xxvj
Cheynes of yron to the same	xxvj
Swyftyng tacles	viij
Panlankers	viij
Garlantes	iij
The mayne top	j
The top mast	j
Yerdes to the same	j
Top seyles*d*	j
Bowlyns	ij
Shutes	ij
Lyftes	ij
Braces	ij
Tyes	j
Halyers to the same	j
Stayes	j
Shrowdes	x

[p. 56]

Yet the Mary Roose

Yet stuff and tacle delyverd to John Hopton by indenture as aforeseid that is to sey:

Trusses	j
The top galant	j
Mastes to the same	j
Sayle	j
Yerdes to the same	j
Parell	j
Bowlyns	ij
Shutes	ij
Braces	ij
Lyftes	ij
S[t]eyes	j
Shrowdes	vj
Foremastes	j
Yerdes to the same	j
Parell	j
Seyles a corse and iij bonettes	j
Tackes	ij
Shutes	ij
Bowlynes	ij
Lyftes	ij
Braces	ij
Lyftes	ij
Trusses	ij
Shrowdes	xvj
Cheynes of yron with boltes to the same	xvj
Poleis	iiij
S[t]eyes	j
Tyes	ij
Halyers	j
Foretop	j
Topmast	j
Seyle yerdes	j
Seyles	j

*a*E gives 'a wyndyng halser'.
*b*E adds 'More to the mayne maste' [heading to this and following entries].
*c*E adds 'perteynyng to the mayne maste'.
*d*E follows with 'the parrell'.

1.   Unidentified.

[p. 57]

Yet the Mary Roose

Yet stuff and tacle delyverd to John Hopton by indenture as aforeseid that is to sey:

Bowlyns	ij
Shutes	ij
Lyftes	ij
Braces	ij
Tyes	j
Halyers to the same	j
Stayes	j
Parelles	j
Bowsprete	j
Yerdes	j
Spret sayles	j
Bonettes to the same	j
Trusse	j
Lyftes	ij
The mayne meson mast	j
Yerdes to the same	j
Parell	j
Sayles	j
Tyes	j
Halyers to the same	j
Trusse	j
Shutes	j
Braces	ij
Lyftes	j
Stayes	j
Shrowdes	xij
Yron cheynes with boltes to the same*a*	xij
The mayne meson top	j
Top mast	j
Seyle yerdes	j
Parell	j
Seyles	j

*a*E adds 'pertaynyng to the mayne myson maste'.

[p. 58]

Yet the Mary Roose

Stuff and tacle delyverd unto John Hopton by indenture as aforeseid that is to sey:

Trusse	j
Lyft	j
Shrowdes*a*	viij
Boneaventure mast	j
Yerdes to the same	j
Parell	j
Sayles	ij
Tyes	j
Halyers	j
Trusse	j
Shutes	j
Stayes	j
Shrowdes*b*	viij
Shevers of brasse to the halyers of the boneaventure mast	iiij
Shevers of brasse to the mayne meson mast	iiij
Shevers of brasse to the tacles on sterbord	iiij
Shevers of brasse for the garnettes of the same	j
Shevers of brasse in the ta[c]les of the ladbord side	xij
Shivers of brasse in the garnettes of the same	iiij
Shevers of brasse for the lyft poleis*c*	iij
Shivers of brasse for the topsayle shute*d*	j
Shivers of brasse in the knyghtes*e*	ij
Shivers of brasse in the ramehede	j
Shevers of brasse in the liftes*f*	iij
Shevers of brasse for the topsayle shut*g*	j
Shevers of brasse in the geres	iij
Shevers of brasse in the halyers of the foremast	iiij
Shivers of brasse in the tacles on both sydes	iiij
Shevers of brasse in the shutes*h*	ij
Shevers of brasse in the tye of the spret	j

*a*E adds 'pertaynyng to the mayne mysson toppe'.
*b*E adds 'pertaynyng to the boneawenture maste'.
*c*E adds 'off the same syde'.
*d*E adds 'off the same'.
*e*Replacing 'shutes' deleted.
*f*E adds 'a sterborde syde'.
*g*E adds 'off the same syde'.
*h*E adds 'of the fore sayle'.

[p. 59]

Yet the Mary Roose

Yet stuff and tacle delyverd to John Hopton by indenture as aforeseid that is to sey:

Shyvers of brasse for the mayne bowlyns	ij
Shevers of brasse in the davettes of the forecastell	ij
Shevers of brasse in the davettes of the destrelles	j
Shevers of brasse in the cattes	j
Shevers of yron in the cattes	j
Shevers of yron in the davettes	j
Spare shevers of brasse grete (ij) and smale (j)	iiij
Compas	iiij
Runnyng glasse[a]	ij
Soundyng ledes	ij
Soundyng lynes	j

Ankers called
- shut ankers — j[b]
- bowers — ij
- destrelles — ij
- caggers — j
- anew shut anker — j

vij

Cables
- new
  - for the shut ankers — ij
  - for the sterbordbowes — ij
  - for the ladbord — ij
- old
  - and worne — iiij
  - junckes — iiij
  - caggyng[c] cables — ij

xv

Cathokes	ij
Fyshokes	ij
Loffhokes	ij
Lech hokes	ij
Warpyng hawsers	vj
The bote	j
Mastes to the same	j
Sayles to the same	j
Ores to the same	xx
The cock with mast sayle and vj ores	j

[p. 60]

Yet the Mary Roose

Ordynaunce artillarie and habillamentes for the warre left in the seid ship in the charge and custodie of John Browne master and John Bryarley purser of the same by indenture as is aforeseid that is to sey:

Grete curtowes of brasse	v
Murderers of brasse	ij
Chambers to the same	iiij
Fawcons of brasse	ij
Fawconettes of brasse	iiij
Grete murderers of yron	j
Chambers to the same	j
Murderers of yron of an other sort	ij
Chambers to the same	iiij
Cast peces of yron	ij
Chambers to the same	iiij
Murderers of yron of an other sort	j
Chambers to the same	ij
Slynges of yron called demy slynges	ij
Chambers to the same	iiij
Stonegonnes	xxvj
Topgonnes	iiij
Chambers to the same	lxxv
Serpentynes of yron	xxviij
Chambers to the same	cvij
Forelockes for stonegonnes, topgons and serpentynes	iiij^{xx}xiiij
Myches for the same	iiij^{xx}
Shott of stone grete and smale	d
Alytell gonne of brasse without a chamber	j
Hammers for gonnes	xiij
Pykes for stone	xxij
Hede for arrowes of wyldefyre	viij
Hockes for arrowes of wyldefyre	xxix
Strynges	dc
Bagges of leder	ix
Parchement skynnes	xx
Lede ij sowes j quarter and certeyn cast	
Chargynge ladelles of coper	ij

[a]MS 'grasse'.
[b]Corrected from 'ij'.
[c]Ms. 'laggyng'.

[p. 61]

Yet the Mary Roose

Yet stuff and tacle delyverd to John Hopton by indenture as aforeseid that is to sey:

Ladelles of yron for castyng of pelettes	ij
Boltes of yron	xvij
Stremers for the top	iij
Gylt flagges	xviij
Smale flagges	xxviij
Top armours	iij
Standard stavers for flagges	xv
Trevettes of yron	iij
Spyttes of yron	j
Cobyrons	j
Gyrde yrons	j
Frying pannes	j
Tarre ketilles	j
Peche ketilles	j
Ketilles for the cockes rome	j
Cawdrons in furnos with their apparell	ij
Hoke for hangyng of ketilles	j
Cressettes of yron	j
Shovells	v
Skoppes	v
Ledder bokettes	iij
Baskettes	iiij
Lyme pottes	j
Bellys	j
Bowes	xx
Arrowes	xx
Billys	xx

[p. 62]

Yet the Mary Roose

Artillarie and habillamentes for the warre delyverd to John Millet and Thomas Elderton by bill signed with thandes of the foreseid commissioners that is to sey:

Hacbusshes	$\overset{xx}{iiij}$xj
Shott of yron of dyverse sortes	cccclvij
Shott of yron with crosse barres	cxx
Pellettes of lede grete & smale	m^l
Pellettes for hacbusshes	dcccc
Dyce of yron	m^{l}c
Arrowes of wyld fyre	lxxiiij
Balles of wyldfyre	ij
Salettes	c$\overset{xx}{iiij}$
Brestes	ccvj
Backes	ccvj
Gorgettes	cxlvj
Splentes	clxxiij payer
Gonnepowder	xxj di barelles
Cart tuches of gonnepowder	j chestfull
Charging ladelles for fawcons and curtowes	vij
Sponges to the same	vj
Stampes	iij
Crowes of yron	xiiij
Bowes of ewe	cxxiij
Chestes to the same	ij
Arrowes	diiij sheff
Chestes to the same	xj
Billes	ccxviij
Stakes for the feld	cxlix
Morys pykes	clix

[p. 63]

The Kynges Ship called the *Petyr Pome Granett*

Stuff tacle and apparell delyverd to John Hopton by indenture as aforeseid that is to sey:

The mayne mast	j
Shrowdes with dedemens hies	xxvj
Cheynes of yron to the same	xxvj
Pollankers with xij shevers of brasse	viij
Bowsyng tacles	viij
Breteyn tacles with ij shevers of brasse	j
The mayene stay	j
Garnettes with ij shevers of brasse	j
The rame hede with ashever of brasse	j
The knyghtes with ij shevers of brasse	ij
Tyes	ij
Halyers to the same*a*	ij
The mayne yerd	j
Seyles the corse and ij bonettes	j
Lyftes	ij
Braces	ij
Bowlyns	ij
Tackes	ij
Shutes	ij
Trusses	iiij
Smale garnettes	iiij
Cranelynes	j
The mayne top	j
The top mast	j
Garlandes of yron to the same	j
Shrowdes	xij
The top yerd	j
The top sayle	j
Shutes	ij
Lyftes	ij
Braces	ij

[p. 64]

Yet the Petyr Pome Granett

Yet stuff and tacle delyverd to John Hopton by indenture as aforeseid that is to sey;

Bowlyns	ij
Stayes	j
Tyes	j
Halyers to the same*a*	ij
Trusses	ij
Parell	j
The foremast	j
Shrowdes with dedemens hies	xiiij
Cheynes of yron to the same	xiiij
Tackes	ij
Shutes	ij
Bowlyns	ij
Lyftes	ij
Braces	ij
Pendantes with vij shevers of brasse	iiij
The foreyerd	j
The seyle acorse and ij bonettes	j
Tyes with halyers to the same	j
The parell	j
The foretop	j
The foretopmast	j
Shrowdes	viij
Lyftes	ij
Braces	ij
Top seyles	j
Shutes	ij
Bowlyns	ij
Tyes	j
Halyers	j
The parell	j
The bowsprett	j

*a*SP gives 'a halyard'.

*a*SP gives 'the halyard'.

[p. 65]

Yet the Petyr Pome Granett

Yet stuff and tacle delyverd to John Hopton by indenture as aforeseid that is to sey:

The sprete seyle	j
The yerde to the same	j
Lyftes	ij
Braces	ij
Tyes	j
Fyshokes	j
Lyche hokes of yron*a*	j
Luff hokes of yron for the mayne sayle	ij
Davettes with ii shevers of brasse*b*	ij
Cathokes with ii shevers of brasse	ij
Shevers of brasse in the ramehede	ij
The mayne meson mast*c*	j
Shrowdes with dedemens hyes	x
Cheynes of yron to the same	x
The yerd	j
The parell	j
Sayelles	j
Trusses	j
Tyes	j
Halyers to the same	j
Shevers of brasse to the same	iiij
Lyftes	j
Braces	ij
Shutes	j
Stayes	j
The meson top	j
The top mast	j
Shrowdes	viij
Garland of yron	j
Halyers	j
Stayes	j
Lyftes	j
Braces	ij

[p. 66]

Yet the Petyr Pome Granett

Yet stuff and tacle delyverd to John Hopton by indenture as aforeseid that is to sey:

Seyles yerdes	j
The boneaventure mast	j
Shrowdes to the same	viij
Yerdes	j
Sayles	j
Parelles	j
The trusse	j
The tye with halyers to the same	j
Shevers of brasse to the same	j
Shutes	j
Stayes	j
The owtlygger	j
The growntacle	j

Ankers called	sterbordebowers	j	
	ladbordbower	j	v
	destrelles	ij	
	shot ankers	j	

Cables old	for bowers	iiij	
	for destrelles	iij	ix
	for shutankers	ij	

New hawsers	iiij
The bote with a shever of brasse	j
The mast	j
Shrowdes	iiij
Yerdes	j
Seyelles	j
Parell	j
Stayes	j
Ores	xx
Roders	j
Helmes	j
Skolles	j

*a*SP adds 'for the mayn saill'.
*b*SP gives 'a davite'.
*c*SP adds 'The mayne meson' [heading to this and following entries].

[p. 67]

Yet the Petyr Pome Granett

Yet stuff and tacle delyverd to John Hopton by indenture as aforeseid that is to sey:

The cocke bote	j
Mastes to the same	j
Shrowdes	iiij
Yerdes	j
Sayles	j
Stayes	j
Parell	j
Shevers of brasse in the hede of the coke	j
An old corse of asayle and a bonett*a*	ij
Item for the forse say[le] acorse	j
Bonettes to the same	ij
Old ju[n]ckes	ij
Ollerons canvas	ix boltes
Top armours	iiij
Grete coper ketilles in furnous*b*	ij
Lede	⁓ sow
Smale ketilles of laten	j
Pych ketilles	j
Tarre ketilles	j
Spittes	j
Cobbe herdes	j
Fleshhokes	j
Frying pannes	j
Tonges	j payer
Salthides¹	v
Baners of Seynt Kateryn*c*	j
Baners of the armes of England*d*	v
Baners of the armes of England and Castell*e*	iiij
Baners of the Rede lyon in metall	j
Baners of Seynt Edward in metall	ij

[p. 68]

Yet the Petyr Pome Granett

Yet stuff and tacle delyverd to John Hopton by indenture as aforeseid that is to sey:

Baners of Seynt Petyr in metall	j
Baners of the rose and pome granettes*a*	iiij
Baners of the Castell in metall	ij
Stremours of Seynt George in colors	j
Stremers of the Rede lyon in colours	j
Stremours of the Castelles in colours	j
Baner staves	xviij
Coper ketilles sett in furnos*b*	ij
Brasen ketilles for sethyng of fysh	ij
Terre ketilles*c*	j
Spittes	j
Cobberdes	j

---

*a*SP adds 'of the maynsaill'.
*b*SP adds 'sett in lyme and breke closed above with lede'.
*c–e*SP adds 'in metall'.

1. The use of these is obscure, rather than the meaning. They probably formed a reserve supply of leather for various purposes.

*a*SP adds 'in metall'.
*b*SP adds 'In the cokis rome' [heading to this and following entries].
*c*SP adds 'worne'.

[p. 69]

Yet the Petyr Pome Granett

Ordynaunce artillarie and habillamentes for the warre left in the seid ship in the charge and custodie of William Forde master and David Boner purser of the same by indenture as aforeseid that is to sey:

In the wast of the seid ship:

Doble serpentynes of yron	xviij
Chambers to the same with ther apparell	l

In the upper lop of the seid ship:

Grete murderers of yron	vj
Chambers to the same with all their apparell	xij

In the forecastell of the seid ship:

Stonne gonnes of yron	vj
Chambers to the same with all their apparell	xij
Spare chambers	viij
Single serpentynes of yron	iiij
Chambres to the same and their apparell	ix

In the upper forecastell of the seid ship:

Smale serpentynes of yron	x
Chambers to the same with other apparell	xx

In the brest of the somer castell:

Serpentynes of yron	vj
Chambers to the same with all thapparell	xx
Fawcons of brasse apon shod wheles	ij
Grete peces of yron	v
Chambres to the same and other apparell	ix
Peces of brasse with a chamber	j
Slynges of yron	j
Chambers to the same and other apparell	ij

In the sterne of the somer castell:

Serpentynes of yron doble	iiij
Chambers to the same and other apparell	viij

In the deck of the seid shipp:

Smale serpentynes of yron	xv
Chambers to the same	xxx

In the brest of the smale deck: [blank]

[p. 70]

Yet the Petyr Pome Granett

Yet ordynaunce artillarie and habillamentes for the warre delyverd to the master and purser by indenture as aforeseid that is to sey:

Pott gonnes	iiij
Chambres to them belongyng with all other apparell	viij
[S]lynges of yron grete	ij
Chambres and other apparell to the[m] belongyng	iiij
Hakbusshes stocked	vij
Belles of brasse	j
Doble serpentynes of yron	iiij
Chambers to the same	viij
Broken chambers of brasse	j
Chargynges for hacbusshes of plate^a	c
Capsteyn gonnes of yron	ij
Chambers to the same	vj
Smale top gonnes	j
Chambers to the same	ij^b
Crowes of yron	xj
Dartes of wyldfyre	viij
Caltrappes	ix^c _{iiij}^{xx}vj
Chestes with quarelles arrowes and trompes of wyldfyre	ij
Balles of wyld fyre smale (xx) and grete (xij)	xxxij
Pykes of yron	xx
Mouldes of brasse	ij
Gonnehamers	xx
Spare forelockes	xvij
Spare boltes	xliij
Spare miches	xlij
Salthides	x
Bromestone	di barell

^aTwo words inserted
^bCorrected from, or to, 'iiij'

[p. 71]

Yet the Petyr Granett Pome*a*

Artillarie and habillamentes for the warre delyverd to John Millet and Thomas Elderton by indenture and bill signed with the hand of the seid commissioners that is to sey:

Arrowes	dccxx sheff
Chestes to the same	xiiij
Bowes of ewe	lxiiij
Billes	cccvij
Bowes of wychehasill	${}^{xx}_{iiij}$ix
Shott of yron of dyverse sortes	c${}^{xx}_{iiij}$iiij
Stakes for the feld	cclxxj
Dartes	cclx
Shott of lede for pot*b* gonnes	${}^{xx}_{iiij}$x
Shot of lede for serpentynes	ix*c*
Pellettes of lede for hacbusshes	cc
Dyce of yron	m^{l}cccl
Brestes	clxvj
Backes	clxv
Splentes	cxx payer
Salettes	cxxx
Standardes of mayle	xlv
Morys pykes	ccccxij

[p. 72]

The Kynges Ship called the *Grete Elizabeth*

Stuff tacle and apparell delyverd to John Hopton by indenture as aforeseid that is to sey:

The mayne mast	j
The mayne yerd	j
The parell to the same	j
Trusses	ij
Shrowdes with dedemens hies	xxiiij
Cheynes of yron to the same	xxiiij
Bowsyng tacle on ladbordsyde	v
Poleis to the same with colkes of brasse	v
Single poleis with shevers of brasse	iiij
Single poleis apon the breteyn tacles	ij
Shevers of brasse to the same	ij
Doble poleis on sterbordsyde with x colkes of brasse	v
Single poleis with shevers of brasse	iiij
Trusses	ij
Drynges	ij
Doble poleis to the same with viij colkes of brasse	iiij
Single poleis with shevers of brasse	iiij
Doble stayes	j
Geres with ij shevers of brasse	j
Tyes	ij
Lyftes	ij
Braces	ij
Mayne tackes	ij
Shutes	ij
Bowlyns	ij
Garnettes	ij
Mayne*a* sayle a corse and ij bonettes	j
The mayne top	j
The top mast	j
Topsayle	j
Yerdes to the same	j
Shrowdes	xij

*a*Sic.
*b*MS 'pot pott'.

*a*MS 'mayle'. SP adds 'old'.

[p. 73]

Yet the Grete Elizabeth

Yet stuff and tacle delyverd to John Hopton by indenture as aforeseid that is to sey:

Bowlyns	ij
Braces	ij
Tyes	j
Halyers with ii shevers and colkes of brasse	j
The foremast	j
The yerd	j
Shrowdes with dedemens hies	xvj
Cheynes to the same	xvj
The bote tacle on the foremast with iij shevers of brasse	j
Tacles with viij poleis belongyng to the same	iiij
Colkes of brasse to the same	viij
Devettes with ij shevers of brasse	j
Shetes	ij
Shyvers of brasse to the same	ij
Drynges	ij
Trusses with acolk of brasse	ij
Tyes	j
Shyvers of brasse to the same	vij
Braces	ij
Lyftes	ij
Bowlyns	ij
Shevers of tree iiij poleis to the lyftes	iiij
Tackes to the foreseyle	ij
The foresayle acorse and ij bonettes	j
The foretop	j
The top seyle with thapparell therto belongyng	j
Stayes with dedemens hies	j
The bowspret with iiij poleis ij of them with colkes of brasse and other ij with shevers of brasse	j
The meson mast	j
The yerd to the same	j

[p. 74]

Yet the Grete Elizabeth

Yet stuff and tacle delyverd to John Hopton by indenture as aforeseid that is to sey:

Shrowdes with dedemens hies	xij
Cheynes of yron to the same	xij
Tackes with doble poleis and colkes of brasse	ij
Lyftes with iij smale poleis and shevers of tre	j
Single poleis with colkes of brasse	ij
Trusse with adoble pole and asingle with colkes of brasse	j
Brace with ij single poleis and shevers of tree	j
Tyes	j
Shevers of brasse to the same	vi
The corse to the meson sayle	j
Owtlygger	j

Ankers called	bowers	ij	
	caggers	j	
	shete ankers	j	v
	destrelles	j	

The bote	j
Devettes	j
Mastes	j
Sayles	j
Shevers of brasse in the botehede	j
Ores	xx
Sculles to the same	j
The cocke	j
Ores	x
Sculles to the same	j
The jolywat	j
Ores	iiij

Cables of	xvij ynch compas	vj	vij
	caggyng cables	j	

Hawsers of vj ynch compas	j
Junckes of ynch compas xiij	ij
New hawsers of v ynch compas	j

[p. 75]

Yet the Grete Elizabeth

Yet stuff and tacle delyverd to John Hopton by indenture as aforeseid that is to sey:

New hawsers of vij ynch compas	j
Fysh hokes	j
Canhokes	ij
Boyes	ij
Boy Ropes	ij
Crawdrons of brasse sett in furnos	ij
A grete ketill of xx galons*a*	j
Pottes of brasse of iiij galons*b*	j
Grete trevettes of yron	j
Pothokes	ij

[p. 76]

Yet the Grete Elizabeth

Ordynaunce artillarie and habillamentes for the warre left in the seid ship in the charge and custodie of John Clogge master and William Felow purser of the same by indenture as aforeseid that is to sey:

In the forecastell in the neder deck:

Smale serpentynes of yron	xij
Stone gonnes of yron	viij
Chambers with their apparell	lix

In the myddell deck:

Smale serpentynes of yron	xvj
Chambers with their apparell	xl

On the upper lopp:

Grete murderers of brasse	ij
Chambers to the same and other apparell	iiij

In the sterne:

Half slynges of brasse	ij
Chambers to the same	iiij

In the neder deck:

Grete stone gonnes	xvj
Half slynges of yron	ij
Chambers with other apparell	xliiij
Grete murderers of yron wherof oone broken	vj
Chambers to the same	xj
Single serpentynes of yron in the sterne	iiij
Chambers to the same	ix

In the medill deck:

Single serpentynes of yron	xlj
Chambers to the same	cxv

In the upper deck:

Half slynges of yron	ij
Chambers to the same	iiij
Single serpentynes	vj
Chambers and other apparell	xix
Single serpentynes of yron	vj
Stone gonnes	j

*a*SP adds 'or more'.
*b*SP reads 'iij or iiij'.

[p. 77]

Yet the Grete Elizabeth

Yet ordynaunce artillarie and habillamentes for warre delyverd to the seid master & purser by indenture as aforeseid that is to sey:

Chambers with other apparell	xxxv
Stone gonnes in the foretop	j
Stone gonnes in the meson top	j
Shott of stone of dyverse sortes	cccclx
Shott of yron	cclx
Pellettes of lede	dcccc
Cast of wyldfyre	xl
Stone pykes	vij
Stone hamers	vj
Bowes	xx
Arrowes	xxiiij sheff
Billes	xx

Artillarie and habillamentes for the warre delyverd to John Millet and Thomas Elderton by bill signed with thandes of the foreseid commissioners that is to sey:

Billes	cclxxvij
Stakes for the feld	xix doss'
Mores pykes	c$_{iiij}^{xx}$xj
Bowes of ewe	cliiij
Bowstrynges	cc
Arrowes	dccclxvi sheff
Chestes for the same	xviij
Standardes of mayle	c
Salettes	cxiij
Splenttes	$_{iiij}^{xx}$iiij payer
Brestes	cxxx
Backes	cxiiij
Gonnepowder	di barell
Hackbusshes hole and broken	xv

[p. 78]

The Kynges Ship called the *Crist of Grenewich*

Stuff tacle and apparell delyverd to John Hopton by indenture as aforeseid that is to sey:

The bowsprett	j
Bowlyne polies	ij
Sayles	j
Yerd	j
Halyers to the same	ij
Polies of wode	ij
Lyftes	ij
Smale poleis of wode	iiij
Old spret seales	j
The foremast	j
Shrowdes	xiiij
Stayes	j
Tacles	iiij
Powles with iij shevers of brasse	ix
Tyes	j
Halyers to the same	ij
Poleis with iij brasen shevers	j
The fore seyleyerd	j
Parelles to the same	j
Trusses	ij
Poleis of wode to the same	iiij
Braces with ij poleis	ij
Bowlynnes	ij
Foresayles acorse old and anew corse ij half worne bonettes	j
Shutes	ij
Tackes	ij
Poleis to the same	ij
The foretop	j
The top mast	j
Shrowdes	viij
The yerd	j
The tye	j
Halyers to the same	ij

[p. 79]

Yet the Crist of Grenewich

Yet stuff and tacle delyverd to John Hopton by indenture as aforeseid that is to sey:

Poleis to the same	ij
Lyftes	ij
Poleis to the same	iiij
Braces with ij single poleis	ij
The parell	j
Trusses with ij poleis	j
The foretop sayle	j
Shutes with ij poleis	ij
Cattes with ij shevers of brasse*a*	ij
Shevers of brasse in the forecastell	ij
The mayne mast	j
The mayne yerd	j
The parell	j
Shrowdes with dedemens hies	xxvj
Cheynes of yron	xxvj
Stayes made of iij cablettes	j
Poleankers with vj poles and v shevers of brasse	ij
Breteyn tacles	j
Poleis to the same with ij shevers of brasse	ij
Garnettes with ij poleis	j
Swyftyng tacles with iiij poleis	ij
Poleankers of sterbord with ix poleis and ij shevers of brasse	iiij
Swyftyng tacles with iiij poleis*b*	ij
Garnettes on sterbord with ij poleis	j
Tyes	ij
Halyers	ij
Shevers of brasse in the rame hede	j
Shevers of brasse in the knyghtes	ij
Trusses with iiij poleis	ij
Drynges*c* with iiij poleis	ij

[p. 80]

Yet the Crist of Grenewich

Yet stuff and tacle delyverd to John Hopton by indenture that is to sey:

[Sp]lentes with iiij poleis and vj shevers of brasse	ij
Braces with ij poleis of wode	ij
The mayne sayle a new corse and one old corse with ij bonettes worne	j
Shutes	ij
Tackes	ij
Mayne bowlyns	ij
Loffhokes of yron	ij
The mayne top	j
The top mast	j
The yerd	j
Shrowdes	x
Stayes	j
Top sayles	j
New top sayles	j
Halyers with ij poleis to the same	j
Shutes to the topsayle	ij
Poleis to the same	ij
Lyftes	ij
Smale poleis to the same	iiij
Braces with ij smale poleis	ij
Bowlyns	ij
A cranelyne with ij canvas bagges	j
The meson mast	j
The yerd	j
The parell	j
Shrowdes	vj
Poleis of wode to the meson yerd	vj
Tyes	j
Halyers	ij
Poleis to the same	ij

*a*SP adds 'the one broken'.
*b*SP adds 'this stuff ys littill worth'.
*c*SP reads 'thrynges'.

[p. 81]

Yet the Crist of Grenewich

Yet stuff and tacle delyverd to John Hopton by indenture as aforeseid that is to sey:

Shutes*a*	j
Poleis to the same	ij
The owtlygger	j
New cables	iiij
Jonkes	iiij

Ankers called	bowers	ij	
	destrelles	j	iiij
	shut ankers	j	

Ollerons canvas	iiij boltes di
Warpyng hawsers	iiij
New hawsers	j
Half a new hawser	di
Hawsers for the lyftes new*b*	ij
Smale ropes for braces	j
Cables for boyes*c*	j
Smale lyne spare	j
Smale ropes new*d*	j
Hawsers new	j
Snach poleis with ashever of brasse	j
Spare poleis with iiij brasen shevers	iij
Spare shevers of brasse	iiij
Smale ropes	ij coyle
Old worne ropes	j
Agrapill of yron for the bote	j
Fysh hokes	j
Cranehokes of yron	ij

The bote	j

The cocke	j
Ores	xvj

Pech keptilles	j
Terr ketilles old	ij
Ketilles of coper sett in furnos	iij

[p. 82]

Yet the Crist of Grenewich

Ordynaunce artillarie and habillamentes for the warre left in the seid ship in the charge and custodie of Philip Tyes master and John Bayly purser of the same by indenture as aforeseid that is to sey:

In the forecastell of the seid ship:

Serpentynes of yron	viij
Stone gonnes	vij
Chambers to the same and other apparell	xxxij
Half fawcons of yron	j
Chambers to the same and other apparell	iij*a*

In the barbycan:

Stone gonnes of yron	viij
Serpentynes of yron	xv
Chambers to the same and other apparell	lxviij
Murderers of yron	iiij
Chambers to the same and other apparell	vj
Slynges of yron	j
Chambers to the same	ij

In the sterne:

Murderers of yron	j
Chambers to the same and other apparell	ij

In the highest deck:

Slynges of yron	j
Chambers to the same	j
Single serpentynes of yron	iij
Chambers to the same	vj
Top gonnes	j
Chambers to the same	j
Slynges of yron with astoke	j
Chambers to the same	ij

In the upper lopp of the ship:

Murderers of yron with viij chambers	iiij
Spare miches	xj
Spare boltes	iiij

Pykes for stone	j
Gonnehamers	j
Crowes of yron	j
Bowes of ewe	x
Arrowes	vj sheff
Billes	xij

*a*SP adds 'The mysen sayle' [heading to this and following entries].
*b*SP gives 'a new warpe for lyftes of the sayle'.
*c*SP gives 'a half'.
*d*SP gives 'halfe'.

*a*Corrected from 'viij'.

[p. 83]

Yet the Crist of Grenewich

Artillarie and habillamentes for the warre delyverd to John Millet and Thomas Elderton by bill signed with thandes of the seid commissioners that is to sey:

Shott of yron grete and smale	cxliij
Billes	cxxxvj
Pellettes of lede grete and smale	cxl
Dyce of yron	lxvij
Stakes for the feld	clxiiij
Morys pykes	c$\overset{xx}{iiij}$
Hacbusshes broken (j) and hole (xvj)	xvij
Bowes of wych hasell	$\overset{xx}{iiij}$
Brestes	$\overset{xx}{iiij}$vj
Backes	$\overset{xx}{iij}$viij
Salettes	$\overset{xx}{iiij}$vij
Splentes	$\overset{xx}{iiij}$vij payer
Standardes of mayle[a]	$\overset{xx}{ij}$xix
Bowes of ewe	lxvj
Arrowes	cccc sheff
Chestes to the same	viij
Bowstrynges	ccc
Old arrowes	xiij sheff
Gonnepowder	v di barelles

[p. 84]

The Kynges Ship called the *Kateryn Galie*

Stuff tacle and apparell delyverd to John Hopton by indenture as aforeseid that is to sey:

The mayne mast	j
Shrowdes with dedemens hies	xvj
Cheynes of yron to the same	xvj
Swyftyng tacles	iiij
Poleis to the same with iiij shevers of brasse	xij
Mayne stay	j
Tyes	j
Halyers	j
Blok poleis with ashever of brasse	j
Shevers of brasse in astock	ij
Mayne lyftes	ij
Poleis with shevers of wode	iiij
Shutes for the top sayle	ij
Poleis of wode to the same	ij
Brases	ij
Shutes to the mayne sayle	ij
Tackes	ij
Mayne trusses	ij
Poleis of wode to the same	iiij
Bowlyns	ij
Mayne yerdes	j
Parelles	j
Sayles the corse and ij bonettes old	j
The top	j
The top sayle	j
Yerdes to the same	j
Mastes with the apparell[a]	j
The foremast	j
Shrowdes	vj
Stayes	j
Tacles with vj poles of wode	ij
Tyes	j
Halyers to the same with ij poleis and ashever of brasse	j

[a] MS 'smayle'.

[a] Three words inserted.

[p. 85]

Yet the Kateryn Galie

Yet stuff and tacle delyverd to John Hopton by indenture
as aforeseid that is to sey:

Lyftes with iiij poleis of wode	ij
Brases and ij poleis of wode	ij
Bowlyns	ij
Doble poleis with shevers of wode	j
Tackes	ij
Shutes	ij
The foreyerd	j
Parelles to the same	j
Sayles a corse and ij bonettes old	j
The foretop sayle	j
The bowsprett with all the apparell to the same	j
Trusse	j
The meson mast	j
Shrowdes	vj
Poleis	xij
Tyes	j
Halyers	j
Poleis to the same	ij
Trusses	j
The meson sayle yerd	j
The parell	j
Sayles acorse	j
Cables of vij ynch compas	j

Hawsers	of iij ynch di compas j iiij ynch compas j of vj ynch compas j	iij

Ankers called	bowers ij caggyng ankers j iij	iij

Botes	j
Ores	viij
Sayles	j
Ketilles	j
Gyrdyorons	j
Axes	j
Crowes of yron	j
Ores for the galie	xxviij

[p. 86]

Yet the Kateryn Galie

Ordynaunce artillarie and habillamentes for the warre
delyverd to John Millet and Thomas Elderton by bill
signed with thandes of the commissioners aforeseid that is
to sey:

Hacbusshes hole (xx) and broken (iij)	xxiij
Doble serpentynes of yron	vj
Chambers to the same hole (viij) and broken (ij)	x
Miches boltes and forelockes to the same	†
Slynges of yron	j
Chambers to the same*a*	j
Culveryns of brasse apon shodd wheles*b*	j
Slynges of yron grete	j
Chambers to the same broken*c*	ij
Grete gonne shott of yron	xxx
Smale shott of yron	cxxiij
Pellettes of lede	lviij
Shott of stone	xiiij
Chestes with arrowes	ij
Grete*d* dyce of yron	xxiiijxxxviij
Smale dyce of yron	ccxl
Morys pykes	lxxvj
Brestes	lvj
Backes*e*	lvj
Shodd stakes for the feld	xxj
Splentes broken and hole	lvj payer
Standardes of mayle	xlv
Salettes good and badd	lxj
Bowes of ewe in a chest	xlj
Bowstrynges	iij doss'
Gonnepowder	iij di barelles
Billes *f*	iiijxxxj
Dartes	cccxx

*a*SP adds 'stokked'.
*b*Five words inserted.
*c*Word inserted.
*d*MS 'Grege'. SP reads 'grete'.
*e*SP adds 'some of them lackynge peces'.
*f*SP adds 'helved good and badd'.

[p. 87]

The Kynges Ship called the *Roose Galie*

Stuff tacle and apparell delyverd to John Hopton by indenture as aforeseid that is to sey:

The bowsprete	j
Doble poleis to the same	ij
The foremast	j
The foreyerd	j
The foresayle acorse and ij bonettes	j
Shutes	ij
Tackes	ij
Trusses	j
Tacles with halyers to the same	j
Poleis of wode	ij
Shrowdes	viij
Cheynes of yron to the same	viij
Lyftes	ij
Bowlyns	ij
Braces	ij
The mayne mast	j
The mayne yerd	j
Sayles acorse and iij bonettes old	j
Shutes	ij
Tackes	ij
Waretackes	ij
Bowlyns	ij
Lyftes	ij
Braces	ij
Trusses	ij
Tackes	ij
Garnettes	j
Poles with vj shevers of brasse	v
Poleis with v shevers of brasse	iiij
The mayne halyer	j
Poleis to the same with vj shevers of brasse	iiij
Shrowdes with poleis and halyers to the same	xiiij
Cheynes of yron to the same	xiiij

[p. 88]

Yet the Roose Galie

Yet stuff and tacle delyverd to John Hopton by indenture as aforeseid that ys to sey:

The mayne top	j
The top mast	j
Garlandes of yron	j
Top sayles	j
Shutes	ij
Tyes	j
Halyers	j
Bowlyns	j
Lyftes	ij
Braces	ij
Shrowdes	vj
The meson mast	j
The meson yerd	j
The meson sayle	j
Halyers	j
Tyes	j
Shutes	j
Trusses	j
Shrowdes	vj
Ores*a*	xxx
Bote	j
Ores to the same bote	vj
Ankers for the seid galie	iij
Cables new (j) and old (ij)	iij
Hawsers	iij

*a*E gives 'xxxj longe ores bellongynge to the galley'.

[p. 89]

Yet the Roose galie

Ordynanunce artillarie and habillamentes for the warre delyverd to John Millet and Thomas Elderton by bill signed with the handes of the seid commissioners that is to sey:

Murderers of yron	ij
Chambers to the same*a*	iiij
Murderers of yron	ij
Chambers to the same and other apparell	iij
Slynges of yron	iij
Chambers to the same hole and broken and all other apparell to them belongyng*b*	iiij
Doble serpentynes of yron	ij
Chambers to the same hole (iij) and broken (iij)	vj
Miches boltes and forlockes to the same of yron	iij
Stone gonnes	j
Chambers to the same with miches boltes and forelockes	iij
Doble serpentynes without stok or chamber	j
Shott of yron of dyverse sortes	xxix
Shott of stone	cix
Shott of lede for serpentynes	xxiiijij
Shott of lede for hacbusshes	ccl
Hackbusshe shott smale	j bagge full
Gonne powder	v di barelles*c*
Gonnehamers	vj
Stone pykes	vij
Ladilles for meltyng of lede	ij
Spare miches	iij
Spare forelockes	ix
Spare boltes of yron	iij
Crowes of yron	j
Bowes of ewe	lv
Chestes of arrowes	v
Elmyn bowes	xl
Morispykes	cxxviij
Stakes*d*	c
Dartes	iiij doss'
Billes	l
New harnes	xxxviij payer
Old Backes	xx
Old Brestes	xx
Salettes	xx
Dyce of yron	cc

*a*SP adds 'stokked'.
*b*SP gives 'iiij chambers hole and one broken'.
*c*SP adds 'and one that is broken half owt'.
*d*SP adds 'for the feld'.

[p. 90]

The Kynges Storehouse at Erith[1]

Stuff and tacle delyverd to John Hopton by indenture as aforeseid that is to sey:

Ollerons canvas*a*	l boltes
Poldaveis*b*	xxxviij boltes
Grete shevers of brasse without stokkes	xxij
Smale shevers of brasse in astokk	j
Doble blockes of tymber with shevers of brasse	j
Blokes of tymber with single shevers of wode	xv
Blockes of tymber with doble shevers of wode	xiiij
Blockes of tymber with single shevers of brasse	ij
Doble blockes of tymber without shevers	j
Single blockes of tymber without shevers	ij

which blockes of tymber and shevers of brasse serwith*c* for settyng up of mastes hallyng into the dock and owt of the dock the grete shippes

Hawsers of	v ynch iij quarter compas	vj
	v ynch di compas	iiij
	v ynch compas	xxij
	vj ynch quarter compas	j
	iiij ynch iij quarter compas	xiiij
	v ynch j quarter compas	viij
	iiij ynch di compas	xiiij
	iiij ynch j quarter compas	x
	iiij ynch compas	vij
	iij ynch iij quarter compas	vij
	iij ynch di compas	vj
	vj ynch compas	vij
	vij ynch j quarter compas	j
	viij ynch compas	ij
	vij ynch di compas	j
	viij ynch iij quarter compas	j
	iij ynch compas	j
	ix ynch compas	ij
	vij ynch iij quarter compas	j

lcxv

*a*E adds 'brought in by Ric' Nele' [Richard Nele was factor of Richard Gresham and William Coplande of London, merchants, and appears elsewhere in the accounts: *LP*, I, ii, nos 3133, 3608 (p. 1498)].
*b*E adds 'brought in by the vice admyrall of the remayne [that is the unused material] of the Mary Rose' [Sir Thomas Wyndham was the vice-admiral].
*c*Or 'servith'. Corrected from illegible form.

1. Built in 1512–13, as a part of the provision then being made to keep a fleet in being. Hopton was the first keeper (1514–24).

[p. 91]

Yet the Storehouse at Erith

Yet stuff and tacle delyverd to John Hopton by indenture
as aforeseid that is to sey:

Cables new not tarred of

v ynch iij quarter compas	j	
vij ynch compas	iij	
vj ynch compas	j	
vij ynch iij quarter compas	iij	
viij ynch di compas	vj	
xj ynch quarter compas	iij	
xij ynch compas	iij	
viij ynch compas	iij	
xij ynch di compas	iiij	
vij ynch di compas	ix	
x ynch j quarter compas	ij	
x ynch compas	iiij	lxij
x ynch di compas	iij	
ix ynch compas	iij	
ix ynch di compas	iiij	
xj ynch di compas	j	
viij ynch j quarter compas	ij	
ix ynch j quarter compas	j	
ix ynch iij quarter compas	j	
xv ynch compas	j	
xiiij ynch di compas	j	
xiiij ynch quarter compas	j	
Grete cable	ij	

Cables redy tarred of

xxj ynch compas	iiij	
xx ynch compas	ij	
xvij ynch di compas	ij	xij
xvij ynch compas	ij	
xvj ynch compas	ij	

[p. 92]

Yet the Storehouse at Erith

Yet stuff and tacle delyverd to John Hopton by indenture
as aforeseid that is to sey:

Yet cables redy tarred of

xv ynch compas	iij	
xiiij ynch compas	ij	xj
xiij ynch di compas	j	
vij ynch di compas	v	

Hawsers redy tarred of

viij ynch compas	ix	xix
iiij ynch compas	x	

Gonnepowder weyt	iij barelles
Weying bemes of yron	j
Scoles to the same	j payer
Leede weight amountyng to	cccij quarter
Grete mastes	xiiij
Smale mastes	xiij

[p. 93]

Yet the Storehouse at Erith

Ordynaunce artillarie and habillamentes for the warre delyverd to John Millet and Thomas Elderton by bill signed with thandes of the foreseid commissioners that is to sey:

Morys pykes	cccxv
Grete gonnes of yron	iij
Chambres to the same	iij
Hole slynges of yron cast without chamber	j
Caste peces of yron called slynges*a*	j
Serpentynes of yron	xvij
Chambres to the same	vj
Hacbusshes broken and hole	viij
Cartewhelys shod with yron	ij payer
Pott gonnes broken and hole*b*	ij
Bowes*c*	lx
Billes*d*	xiiij
Stakes for the feld	xxvj
Slynges of yron	ij
Chambers to the same and other apparell*e*	iiij
Grete playne peces of yron cont' xxij fote*f*	j
[S]lynges of yron ryngyd containing xx fote besides the chambers*g*	i
Chambers to the same broken & hole	ij
Stone gonnes of yron with stockes	iiij
Serpentynes of brasse with stockes	ij
Serpentynes of yron with abroken stock	j
Shodd wheles for gonnes	v payer
Unshodd wheles for gonnes	vij payer
Empty barelles for gonnepowder*h*	v
Serpentynes of brasse without chamber	j

[pp. 94–100 blank]

---

*a*E adds 'without chamber'.
*b*E adds 'with oute chambres'.
*c*SP adds 'of ewe and wytch hasill'.
*d*SP adds 'broken and holle'.
*e*SP adds 'out of David Milners ground'.
*f*SP adds 'with stoke and wheles unshodde'.
*g*E adds 'wherof one is broken and a holle stocke'.
*h*SP adds 'from Edmund Smythes durre' [door, i.e. premises].

Appendix I
Lord Admiral Lisle's Instructions of 1545

Thorder for the saied flete taken by the Lord Admirall the xth day of August 1545.

1. First, yt is to be consithered, that every of the capitaignes with the saied shippes appointed by this order to the vanwarde, battail and wyng shall ryde at ancker according as they be appoynted to saile by this saied order, and that no shipp of any of the saied wardes or wyng shall presume to comme to an ancker before thadmirall of the saied ward.

2. Item that every capitaign of the saied wardes and wyng shalbe in every thyng ordered by thadmirall of the same.

3. Item when we shall se a convenient tyme to fight with thenimies, our vanward shall make with ther vanward if they have any, and if they be in one compenye, our vanward (takyng thadvauntaige of the wynde) shall set uppon ther foremost ranck, bryngyng them oute of order, and our viceadmirall shall seake to bourd ther viceadmirall, and every capitaign shall chose his equall as nere as he maye.

4. Item thadmirall of the wyng shalbe allwayes in the wynde with his hole compenye, and when we shall joyne with thenimies he shall kepe still thadvauntaige of the wynde, to thentent he with his compenye maye the better beate of the gallies from the greate shippes.

5. Item the lord admirall shall beare one banner of the Kinges majesties armes in his mayne topp and one flag of Saint George crosse in his fore topp, and every shipp appoynted to the battaill shall beare one flag of Saint Georges crosse in his mayne toppe.

6. Item thadmirall^a of the vanwarde ys appoynted to beare too flagges of Saint Georges crosse, thone in his mayne topp and thother in his fore topp. And every shipp appoynted to the vanward shall beare one flag of Sainte Georges crosse in his fore toppe.

7. Item thadmirall of the wyng shall beare a flag of Saint Georg crosse in either of his mesyn^b toppes, and every shipp, galliasse, pynnesse and shalupe appoynted to the wyng shall have in ther mesyn toppe^c one flag of Saint George crosse.

8. Item the lord admirall shall beare iij lightes in the night,^d one great light in the poupe behynde, and too smaller lightes in the myddes of the bonaventure mesyn shrowdes.

9. Item thadmirall of the vanwarde shall beare too lightes in the night to be a knowledge to all that warde, and those too lightes to be borne in the saied bonaventure shrowdes withoute any other light in the poupe.

10. Item thadmirall of the wyng shall beare one light in his saied bonaventure shrowdes withoute any other light, for a token to all that warde.

11. The watch wourde in the night shalbe thus: God save King Henrye; thother shall answer: And long to raign over us.

[PRO, SP 1/205, ff. 163–4 (new ff. 168–9) (*LP*, XX, ii, no. 88). A previous transcription printed in *State Papers ... Henry the Eighth*, I, ii, pp. 813–14. Articles 1–4 (modern spelling) are in J.S. Corbett, ed., *Fighting Instructions, 1530–1816* (NRS XXIX, 1905), pp. 23–4; articles 5-7 in Perrin, *British Flags*, p. 87.]

^aReplacing 'every' deleted.
^bAltered from 'mesyns'.
^cTwo words inserted replacing 'poupe' deleted.
^dThree words inserted replacing 'and' deleted.

Appendix II
List of Ships

Only ships featured in the Anthony Roll and E 36/13 inventory are included here; for other ships mentioned in the volume see the index. Ships are identified here by the standard modern form of the name where possible; variant spellings of the names are recorded in the index. After each name is, as appropriate, the number of entry in the Anthony Roll (an editorial numeration), and the page number of the Pepys Library volume or the membrane of the British Library roll; for ships in E 36/13, the page numbers of that MS (at the head of each column in this edition). Service histories are restricted to dates of building or acquisition by the crown, rebuilds, loss, disposal or last known occurrence. Tonnages (by burthen) were never more than approximate measurements, in some cases complicated by rebuilding or by conflicting estimates.

The most frequently cited sources are here abbreviated:

Glasgow   T. Glasgow, 'List of ships ... 1539 to 1558', *MM* (1970), citing the numerical sequences there assigned to ships by reign

Loades   D.M. Loades, *The Tudor Navy* (1992)

Rodger   N.A.M. Rodger, *The Safeguard of the Sea* (1997)

For the full titles of these works see the general List of Abbreviations on pp. xv–xvi.

Anne Gallant   [Roll, no. 22 (BL, m. 1)]
built 1545   450 tons
last occ. March 1559
[Glasgow, p. 302 (Henry VIII, no. 30). Rodger, p. 478]

Antelope   [Roll, no. 24 (BL, m. 2)]
built 1546, rebuilt 1581, 1618   300 tons
defected to royalist fleet 1648; blown up by parliamentary forces 1649, Helvoetsluis
[Glasgow, pp. 302, 306 (Henry VIII, no. 43, Eliz. I, no. 33). Rodger, pp. 478, 479, 481. B.S. Capp, *Cromwell's Navy* (Oxford, 1989), pp. 23, 28, 66]

Brigandine   [Roll, no. 43 (Pepys, pp. 66–7)]
built 1545   40 tons
lost to French Oct. 1562, Caudebec
[Glasgow, p. 302 (Henry VIII, no. 38). T. Glasgow jr, 'English royal ships lost at Caudebec, 1562', *MM*, LI (1965), p. 356]

Bull   [Roll, no. 26 (BL, m. 3)]
built 1546, rebuilt 1570   200 tons
last occ. 1594
[Glasgow, pp. 302, 305 (Henry VIII, no. 40, Eliz. I, no. 22). Rodger, pp. 478, 479]

Christ of Greenwich   [E 36/13, pp. 79–83]
bought 1512   300 tons
taken by Barbary pirates 1515
[Rodger, p. 476]

Christopher of Bremen   [Roll, no. 11 (Pepys, pp. 22–3)]
hired 1544   400/500 tons
bought from Hanse 1545

sold 1555
[Glasgow, p. 302 (Henry VIII, no. 28). Rodger, p. 478]

Cloud in the Sun rowbarge
  built 1546
  sold 1548
  [Glasgow, p. 303 (Henry VIII, no. 55)]

      [Roll, no. 50 (Pepys, pp. 82–3)]
      20 tons

Double Rose rowbarge
  built 1546
  sold Apr. 1548
  [Glasgow, p. 303 (Henry VIII, no. 47)]

      [Roll, no. 46 (Pepys, pp. 74–5)]
      20 tons

Dragon
  built 1542
  dropped late 1553
  [Glasgow, p. 301 (Henry VIII, no. 12). Rodger, p. 477]

      [Roll, no. 35 (BL, m. 6)]
      120/140 tons

Falcon
  built 1545, rebuilt 1558
  sold Jan. 1575
  [Glasgow, pp. 302, 304 (Henry VIII, no. 33, Eliz. I, no. 7). Rodger, p. 478]

      [Roll, no. 36 (Pepys, pp. 54–5)]
      80 tons, rebuilt as 100 tons

Falcon in the Fetterlock rowbarge
  built 1546
  dropped *c.* 1550
  [Glasgow, p. 303 (Henry VIII, no. 59)]

      [Roll, no. 54 (Pepys, pp. 90–1)]
      20 tons

Flower de Luce rowbarge
  built 1546
  sold Apr. 1548
  [Glasgow, p. 303 (Henry VIII, no. 48, misnumbered 47)]

      [Roll, no. 47 (Pepys, pp. 78–9)]
      20 tons

Gabriel Royal
  Genoese, probably carrack
  bought 1512
  last occ. 1526
  [Rodger, p. 476. Spont, *War with France*, p. 80]

      [E 36/13, pp. 24–30]
      c. 800 tons

Galley Subtle
  alias *Red Galley, English Galley*
  built 1544
  last occ. March 1559
  [Glasgow, p. 301 (Henry VIII, no. 19). Rodger, p. 477. Adair, 'English galleys', pp. 498–504]

      [Roll, no. 30 (BL, m. 4)]

      200/300 tons

George
  built 1546
  hoy 1560 x 1588
  [Glasgow, p. 303 (Henry VIII, no. 45)]

      [Roll, no. 19 (Pepys, pp. 38–9)]
      100 tons as hoy

Gillyflower rowbarge
  built 1546
  dropped *c.* 1553
  [Glasgow, p. 303 (Henry VIII, no. 57)]

      [Roll, no. 57 (Pepys, pp. 98–9)]
      20 tons

Grand Mistress   [Roll, no. 21 (BL, m. 1)]
   built 1545   420 tons
   sold 1555
   [Glasgow, p. 302 (Henry VIII, no. 29). Rodger, p. 478]

Great Barbara   [E 36/13, pp. 38–42]
   formerly *Magdalene*   400 tons
   bought 1513
   last occ. 1524
   [Rodger, p. 476]

Great Bark   [Roll, no. 5 (Pepys, pp. 10–11)]
   alias *Great Galley*   500/600 tons, rebuilt as 900/910 tons
   built 1515, rebuilt *c.* 1538
   rebuilt to larger ship as *White Bear* 1564, rebuilt 1599
   sold 1629
   [Glasgow, pp. 301, 305 (Henry VIII, no. 9, Eliz. I, no. 19). Rodger, pp. 477, 479 *bis*, 480. R.C. Anderson, 'Henry VIII's Great Galley', *MM*, VI (1920), pp. 274–81]

Great Elizabeth   [E 36/13, pp. 72–7]
   hulk, formerly *Salvator of Lübeck*   *c.* 900 tons
   bought 1514
   lost same year
   [Rodger, p. 476]

Great Nicholas   [E 36/13, pp. 43–7]
   bought 1512   400 tons
   declared unserviceable 1526
   [Rodger, p. 476. Loades, p. 112]

Greyhound   [Roll, no. 32 (BL, m. 5)]
   built 1545   160/200 tons
   wrecked Apr. 1563, Rye
   [Glasgow, p. 302 (Henry VIII, no. 32). Rodger, p. 478. T. Glasgow jr, 'The wreck of the *Greyhound*, 1563', *MM*, LI (1966), p. 78]

Hare   [Roll, no. 44 (Pepys, pp. 70–1)]
   built 1545   15 tons
   rebuilt to larger ship 1558
   sold Jan. 1573
   [Glasgow, pp. 302, 304 (Henry VIII, no. 39, Eliz. I, no. 1)]

Harp rowbarge   [Roll, no. 49 (Pepys, pp. 82–3)]
   built 1546   20 tons
   dropped *c.* 1548
   [Glasgow, p. 303 (Henry VIII, no. 58)]

Hart   [Roll, no. 23 (BL, m. 2)]
   built 1546   300 tons
   lost *c.* May 1563, Portsmouth
   [Glasgow, p. 302 (Henry VIII, no. 42). Rodger, p. 478. J.S. Corbett, ed., *Papers relating to the Spanish War, 1585–1587* (NRS XI, 1898), p. 311]

Hawthorn
    built 1546
    sold Apr. 1548
    [Glasgow, p. 303 (Henry VIII, no. 49)]

[Roll, no. 52 (Pepys, pp. 86–7)]
20 tons

Henry Grace à Dieu alias *Great Harry*
    built 1514, rebuilt 1539 or 1540
    renamed *Edward* 1547
    accidentally burned at moorings, 25 Aug. 1553, Woolwich
    [Glasgow, p. 301 (Henry VIII, no. 11). Rodger, pp. 476, 477. Loades, p. 158. J.A. Williamson, 'The two ships named *Great Harry*', *Blackwood's Magazine*, CXCV, no. 1180 (Feb. 1914), pp. 205–15]

[E 36/13, pp. 3–16; Roll, no. 1 (Pepys, pp. 2–3)]
1,500 tons, rebuilt as 1,000 tons

Hind
    built 1545
    sold 1555
    [Glasgow, p. 302 (Henry VIII, no. 37)]

[Roll, no. 38 (Pepys, pp. 58–9)]
80 tons

Hoy Bark

[Roll, no. 18 (Pepys, pp. 38–9)]

Jennet
    built *c.* 1538
    rebuilt to larger ship 1559
    made a lighter 1580
    dropped *c.* 1589
    [Glasgow, pp. 301, 304 (Henry VIII, no. 8. Eliz. I, no. 2). Rodger, pp. 477, 478]

[Roll, no. 33 (BL, m. 5)]
160/180 tons, rebuilt as 300 tons

Jesus of Lübeck
    hired 1544
    bought from Hanse *c.* 1545
    lent to Hawkins
    abandoned to Spanish 23 Sept. 1568, San Juan d'Ulloa
    [Glasgow, p. 302 (Henry VIII, no. 25. Rodger, p. 478. M. Lewis, 'The guns of the *Jesus of Lubeck*', *MM*, XXII (1936), pp. 324–45. J.A. Williamson, *Hawkins of Plymouth* (1969), pp. 68–70, 111–12 and *passim*]

[Roll, no. 6 (Pepys, pp. 14–15)]
600/700 tons

John Baptist
    bought 1512
    lost *c.* 1534
    [Rodger, p. 476]

[E 36/13, pp. 48–54]
400 tons

Katherine Fortileza
    Genoese, probably carrack
    bought 1512
    last occ. 1526
    [Rodger, p. 476. Loades, p. 112]

[E 36/13, pp. 31–7]
700 tons

Katherine galley or bark
    first occ. 1512
    [Oppenheim, *History*, pp. 49, 58]

[E 36/13, pp. 84–6]
80 tons

Lartique
    prize 1543 (ex *Ferronière*)
    sold Apr. 1547
    [Glasgow, p. 301 (Henry VIII, no. 15). Rodger, p. 477]

[Roll, no. 16 (Pepys, pp. 34–5)]
140 tons

Less Pinnace   [Roll, no. 42 (Pepys, pp. 66–7)]
  built 1544   40 tons
  last occ. 1549
  [Glasgow, p. 302 (Henry VIII, no. 23)]

Lion   [Roll, no. 34 (BL, m. 5)]
  built 1536   140 tons
  dropped 1559
  [Glasgow, p. 301 (Henry VIII, no. 3). Rodger, p. 477]

Maiden Head rowbarge   [Roll, no. 55 (Pepys, pp. 94–5)]
  built 1546   20 tons
  sold Apr. 1548
  [Glasgow, p. 303 (Henry VIII, no. 50)]

Mary [of] Hamburg   [Roll, no. 10 (Pepys, pp. 22–3)]
  hired 1544   400 tons
  bought from Hanse 1545
  sold 1555
  [Glasgow, p. 302 (Henry VIII, no. 27). Rodger, p. 478]

Mary James   [Roll, no. 20 (Pepys, pp. 42–3)]
  French prize 1543   60 tons
  dropped 1546
  [Glasgow, p. 301 (Henry VIII, no. 17). Rodger, p. 477]

Mary Rose   [E 36/13, pp. 55–62; Roll, no. 2 (Pepys, pp. 6–7)]
  built 1510, rebuilt 1536   500/600 tons, rebuilt as 700 tons
  lost in action 19 July 1545, Portsmouth
  raised 11 Oct. 1982
  [Glasgow, p. 301 (Henry VIII, no. 6). Rodger, pp. 476, 477. Rule, *Mary Rose*]

Mary Thomas   [Roll, no. 17 (Pepys, pp. 34–5)]
  French prize 1543   90 tons
  dropped *c.* 1546
  [Glasgow, p. 301 (Henry VIII, no. 18). Rodger, p. 477]

Matthew   [Roll, no. 4 (Pepys, pp. 10–11)]
  bought/acquired 1545   600 tons
  dropped *c.* 1554
  [Glasgow, p. 302 (Henry VIII, no. 24). Rodger, p. 478]

Merlin   [Roll, no. 41 (Pepys, pp. 62–3)]
  prize 1545   40 tons
  sold 1550
  [Glasgow, p. 302 (Henry VIII, no. 35)]

Minion   [Roll, no. 15 (Pepys, pp. 30–1)]
  built 1523, rebuilt same year   180 tons, rebuilt as 300 tons
  merchantman 1550 x 1556
  dropped 1570
  [Glasgow, p. 301 (Henry VIII, no. 5). Rodger, p. 477 *bis*]

Morian [of Danzig]
  bought from Hanse 1545
  sold Dec. 1551
  [Glasgow, p. 302 (Henry VIII, no. 31). Rodger, p. 478]

[Roll, no. 8 (Pepys, pp. 18–19)]
500 tons

New Bark
  built 1543
  dropped late 1566
  [Glasgow, p. 301 (Henry VIII, no. 14). Rodger, p. 477]

[Roll, no. 31 (BL, m. 4)]
200 tons

Pauncy [Pansy]
  built 1543
  dropped late 1557
  [Glasgow, p. 301 (Henry VIII, no. 13). Rodger, p. 477]

[Roll, no. 7 (Pepys, pp. 14–15)]
450 tons

Peter alias *Peter Pomegranate*
  built 1510, rebuilt *c.* 1536
  dropped 1558
  [Glasgow, p. 301 (Henry VIII, no. 7). Rodger, pp. 476, 477]

[E 36/13, pp. 63–71; Roll, no. 3 (Pepys, pp. 6–7)]
450 tons, rebuilt as 600 tons

Phoenix
  built 1546
  sold Jan. 1573
  [Glasgow, p. 303 (Henry VIII, no. 44)]

[Roll, no. 40 (Pepys, pp. 62–3)]
70 tons

Portcullis rowbarge
  built 1546
  sold 1548
  [Glasgow, p. 303 (Henry VIII, no. 51)]

[Roll, no. 48 (Pepys, pp. 78–9)]
20 tons

Roo
  built 1545
  captured by French 1547
  [Glasgow, p. 302 (Henry VIII, no. 34)]

[Roll, no. 39 (Pepys, pp. 57–8)]
80 tons

Rose Galley or bark
  built 1512
  [Oppenheim, *History*, p. 49]

[E 36/13, pp. 87–9]
80 tons

Rose in the Sun rowbarge
  built 1546
  sold 1548
  [Glasgow, p. 303 (Henry VIII, no. 54)]

[Roll, no. 51 (Pepys, pp. 86–7)]
20 tons

Rose Slip rowbarge
  built 1546
  sold 1555
  [Glasgow, p. 303 (Henry VIII, no. 56)]

[Roll, no. 56 (Pepys, pp. 94–5)]
20 tons

Saker
  built 1545
  last occ. Nov. 1568
  [Glasgow, p. 302 (Henry VIII, no. 36)]

[Roll, no. 56 (Pepys, pp. 54–5)]
80 tons

Salamander   [Roll, no. 27 (BL, m. 3)]
    Scotch prize (previously French) 1544, Leith   300 tons
    last occ. March 1559
    [Glasgow, p. 301 (Henry VIII, no. 20). Rodger, p. 477]

Small Bark alias *Less Bark, Less Galley*   [Roll, no. 13 (Pepys, pp. 26–7)]
    built *c.* 1512, rebuilt 1536   160/240 tons, rebuilt as 400 tons
    dropped 1553
    [Glasgow, p. 301 (Henry VIII, no. 4). Rodger, pp. 476, 477]

Struse [of Danzig]   [Roll, no. 9 (Pepys, pp. 18–19)]
    hired 1544   400 tons
    bought from Hanse
    sold Dec. 1553
    [Glasgow, p. 302 (Henry VIII, no. 26). Rodger, p. 478]

Sun rowbarge   [Roll, no. 48 (Pepys, pp. 98–9)]
    built 1546   20 tons
    sold 1548
    [Glasgow, p. 303 (Henry VIII, no. 53)]

Swallow   [Roll, no. 29 (BL, m. 4)]
    built 1544   300 tons
    rebuilt 1559, 1580
    last occ. 1603
    [Glasgow, pp. 302, 305, 306 (Henry VIII, no. 22, Eliz. I, nos 4, 31). Rodger, pp. 478 *bis*, 479]

Sweepstake   [Roll, no. 14 (Pepys, pp. 30–1)]
    built 1535   300 tons
    dropped early 1559
    [Glasgow, p. 301 (Henry VIII, no. 2). Rodger, p. 477]

Three Ostrich Feathers rowbarge   [Roll, no. 53 (Pepys, pp. 90–1)]
    built 1546   20 tons
    sold 1548
    [Glasgow, p. 303 (Henry VIII, no. 52)]

Tiger   [Roll, no. 25 (BL, m. 2)]
    built 1546, rebuilt 1570   200 tons
    exchanged 1584
    [Glasgow, pp. 302, 305 (Henry VIII, no. 41, Eliz. I, no. 23). Rodger, pp. 478, 479]

Trego Renneger alias *Spanish shallop*   [Roll, no. 45 (Pepys, pp. 70–1)]
    built 1546   20 tons
    dropped *c.* 1550
    [Glasgow, p. 303 (Henry VIII, no. 46)]

Trinity Harry   [Roll, no. 12 (Pepys, pp. 26–7)]
    built *c.* 1530   250 tons
    sold June 1566
    [Glasgow, p. 301 (Henry VIII, no. 1). Rodger, p. 477]

Trinity Sovereign   [E 36/13, pp. 17–23]
   not originally known by this name, but almost certainly the *Sovereign* carrack
   built 1487, rebuilt 1509   650/1,000 tons
   declared unserviceable 1526, Woolwich. Perhaps the remains unearthed there 1912
   [Loades, pp. 39, 112. W. Salisbury, 'The Woolwich ship', *MM*, XLVII (1961), pp. 81–90]

Unicorn   [Roll, no. 28 (BL, m. 3)]
   Scotch prize 1544, Leith   240 tons
   sold 1555
   [Glasgow, p. 301 (Henry VIII, no. 21). Rodger, p. 478]

Note on Ships' Names

In some cases ships are deemed to have continuing existence through one or more rebuilds, often with very little of the original structures remaining. Conversely some ships changed their names (most commonly on becoming prize, but occasionally for other reasons). An individual ship might at any one time be called by a variety of names. Some of these, such as 'Great galley' or 'Less pinnace' were descriptions rather than fixed titles. Modern typography, in the use of capital letters and italics, imposes a significance which has no contemporary authority. None of the ships of Henry VIII's fleet would have carried a name painted on the side. Some were identified by figureheads, of which examples may be seen in Anthony's illustrations of the *Salamander* and *Unicorn*, together with the badge of the *Mary Rose*. On the other hand the *Galley Subtle* sports a dragon which has no relevance to its name. Many of the names, such as *Antelope* and *Pansy* may seem unadventurous, even frivolous, to those accustomed to naval vessels with heroic styles. Henry VIII's warships were, though, in many cases close cousins to the merchant vessels from which they had developed. Not a few were acquired from private owners. The nomenclature reflects this kinship, particularly in the many ships with saints' or other religious names. Ships acquired from foreigners often retained the name of provenance, generally in a corrupt form (*Katherine Fortileza, Trego Renneger*). Animal names are generally allusions to the arms or other heraldic emblems of the Tudors and their predecessors.

   Among the ship names of the Roll the following may be noted:

   Anne Gallant. Not a reference to Henry VIII's second wife Anne Boleyn; a ship of this name had been in the navy from at least 1513.

   Antelope. Used as a supporter for the arms of the Lancastrian kings.

   Brigandine. General name for a small vessel (now commonly 'brigantine' or 'brig').

   Bull. A badge of the house of Clare, adopted *jure uxoris* by Lionel, duke of Clarence, through whom the Yorkist claim to the throne descended; therefore adopted by Edward IV as a royal emblem.

   Cloud in the Sun. A badge of Edward III.

   Double Rose. The Tudor badge symbolising the uniting of the rival houses of York and Lancaster, the white rose and the red.

   Dragon. The Welsh emblem, much promoted by the Tudors.

   Falcon. A white falcon had been a favourite badge of Anne Boleyn; but the bird was so generally associated with royal sport that no embarrassment was presented by continued use of the name.

   Falcon in the Fetterlock. A badge of Richard, duke of York. Much favoured by his son Edward IV, apparently because of its erotic overtones. Subsequently employed by Edward's bastard son Arthur Plantagenet, Viscount Lisle.

   Flower de Luce. The fleur-de-lis, emblem of the French monarchy, used by English monarchs from Edward III to George III to express their claim to the French throne.

Galley Subtle. In the sense of 'thin' not the modern use of the word.

Gillyflower. Wallflower.

Greyhound. A silver greyhound was a badge of the earldom of Richmond, Henry VII's title before becoming king; the greyhound was used as a supporter for the Tudor royal arms.

Harp. The Irish emblem. Henry VIII was the first to assume the title of king of Ireland (1542).

Hart. The badge of Richard II was the white hart.

Hawthorn. Common in Tudor imagery, alluding to the hawthorn bush from which Richard III's crown was supposedly retrieved after the battle of Bosworth, to be placed on the head of Henry VII.

Henry Grace à Dieu. The king's formal style: 'By the Grace of God'.

Hind. The emblem of Philippa, queen of Edward III.

Jennet. A small Spanish horse.

Lartique. From the French captain Pierre de Bidoux, sieur de l'Artigue. Cf. 'Artigo's bark in *LP*, XVII, ii, no. 348 and John Bennell above, pp. 34, 37. Oppenheim's suggestion of 'artichaut' (*History*, p. 51) should be disregarded.

Mary Rose. Named after the king's sister Mary, later queen of France and duchess of Suffolk, who launched her.

Minion. The gun (see Glossary).

Morion. Probably a variant of 'Marian'.

Peter Pomegranate. The pomegranate featured in the heraldry of the city of Granada, whose capture from the Moors (1492) was celebrated throughout Christendom. Following Catherine of Aragon's coming to England to marry Prince Arthur, the pomegranate was widely used in royal imagery; a reminder that in the first half of the 16th century the Spaniards were generally allies not enemies of the English.

Portcullis. Badge of the Beaufort family, through whom the Tudors descended from Edward III.

Rose in the Sun. A badge of Edward IV.

Saker. The gun (see Glossary).

Salamander. A badge of the French kings, especially François I, in whose chateaux it proliferates. The creature's legendary invulnerability to fire would have seemed a good omen for the ship, and may explain the prominent figurehead.

Three Ostrich Feathers. Badge of the prince of Wales (Henry VIII's son, the future Edward VI, was never formally created prince, but was commonly referred to by the title).

Unicorn. A supporter of the royal arms of Scotland (introduced into the arms of the United Kingdom in 1603).

Appendix III
Glossary

Headwords in **bold** are established modern forms. Variant spellings found in the MSS here printed are given in *italic*, which is also used in headwords where no certain modern form can be identified. In many cases in E 36/13 the definite or indefinite article is contiguous with the succeeding word, giving forms as 'ashyver' and 'thapparel'. These usages are ignored in the Glossary, which treats only the substantial parts of such compounds. Words are normally defined in the singular, but plural variants are often given where occurring. In the definitions **bold** indicates terms which are separately defined within the alphabetical sequence. The Glossary also serves to identify certain spellings by modern terms which are considered to require no further explanation. The Glossary includes some technical terms used in the editorial matter.

almain rivets (*almen revettes, almyne ryvettes*)
Sets of body armour for heavy infantry, comprising breast and back plates. So called from their German origin

axle-tree (*extrys*)
Axle of gun carriage, commonly ash.

badge
A personal or family armorial device, not normally part of the coat-of-arms.

banner
A square or rectangular flag, usually charged with arms.

barbican (*barbycan*)
Wooden superstructure; castle.

base (*baesses, baessys*)
Small gun, usually of wrought iron and breech-loading; bore of 1"–6", firing round cast lead shot, or **dice** of iron inside a cast lead shot. Usually mounted on a **miche** with a drop-in **chamber**. Elevated and traversed by means of a tail at the rear of the chamber-holder. For anti-personnel use.

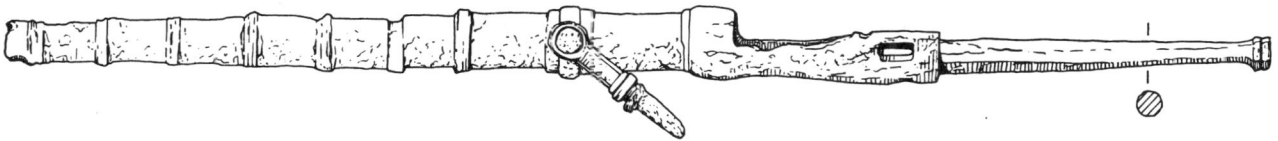

Wrought iron breech-loading swivel gun recovered from the *Mary Rose*; one of the 'bases' listed in the Anthony Roll. (Archaeological drawing reproduced by courtesy of the Mary Rose Trust)

bend (*bendes*)
Band or clamp.

bill (*byllys*)
Staff weapon for heavy infantry, having wooden handle (commonly ash) approx. 6', with iron head approx. 19" having recurved cutting edge, top spike and triangular fluke on the back edge; weighing about 5 lb.

bolt (*boltes*)
Cylindrical pin of iron or copper to hold a movable object in place.

bolt rope
Rope sewn around the edge of a sail to prevent the canvas from tearing.

bombard (*bumberds*)
Large gun, usually of wrought iron and muzzle-loading; the barrel 5 or 6 times longer than the bore, with integral powder chambers of smaller bore than the barrel; bore greater than 12".

bonaventure (*boneaventure*)

   The outer mizzen.

bonnet (*bonet, bonettes*)

   An additional part laced to the bottom of a sail, commonly ⅓ of its depth.

bowelynnes see **bowline**

bower

   One of two anchors at the bow.

bowline (*bowelynnes, bowlynnes, bowlyns*)

   A rope leading forward which is fastened to a space connected by bridles to cringles on the perpendicular edge of the sail. Used to keep the weather edge of the sail tight.

bowser *(bowsyng tacle)*

   Any arrangement of **tackle.**

braces

   Ropes belonging to all the yards of a ship, rove through blocks fastened to the yards. Used to square or traverse the yards horizonally.

brail ropes (*brayle ropes*)

   Ropes passing through leading blocks for furling lateen sails on the mizzen and bonaventure masts.

breadth

   The unit of width (measured along the **hoist**) in which British naval flags were traditionally measured. Pepys recorded a breadth in his day as about 11".

breast rope *(brest rope)*

   A rope securing the yard-parrels

breeching (*brechyng*)

   Ropes to secure a gun to the side of a ship; might be attached to either the gun or the carriage.

bretayn, breten, breteyn tacles **burton tackle**

bridles (*brydelles*)

   The upper part of the moorings.

brigandine (*brygandynes*)

   Body armour comprised of rings or small plates.

bumberds see **bombard**

burton tackle (*bretayn, breten, breteyn tacles*)

   Small tackle of 2 or 3 blocks used to tighten rigging, or for moving bulky objects about the ship.

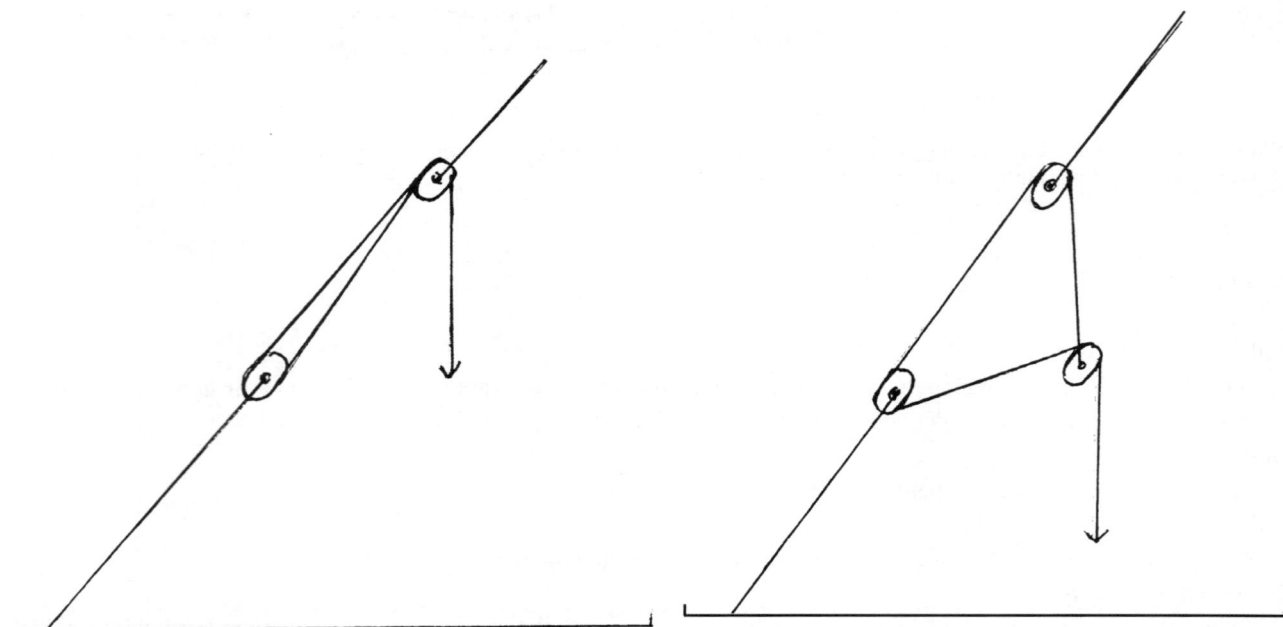

The variant forms of burton tackle. (Drawing by D.M. Loades, based on Howard, *Sailing Ships of War*, p. 33)

cablet (*cablettes*)

Small cable.

cagers, caggers see **kedge anchor**

caggyng cables see **kedging cable**

calbens, calbyns

A type of sail cloth. Cf. 'kelyn' (Rose, *Navy of the Lancastrian Kings*, 257)

caltrop (*caltrappes*)

Iron ball with 4 spikes. Used principally to disable cavalry horses.

can hook (*can hokes, cannehokes*)

Formed by reeving the two ends of a rope through the eyes of two flat hooks, which is then hooked to the middle of the bight. Used to sling a cask by the end of its staves.

cannon

Largest type of cast mounted gun, usually of bronze and muzzle-loading; smooth bore of 7" or more, weighing 7,000 lb. Firing mostly cast iron shot of 45 lb or more. Subdivided by bore size, length and thickness of metal, as double, royal, first, Venetian and (the commonest), **demi-cannon**.

cannon petro (*cannon perer*)

Wrought or cast iron or bronze piece, breech- or muzzle-loading; bore of 6"–8" or more, often chambered. Firing stone shot, nails, iron **dice** or cracked flint flakes. Of similar dimensions to smooth-bore muzzle-loading cannon.

capsteyn gonnes

Probably a gun on a **miche.**

cartouche (*cartowces, cartowche, cartowchys, cart tuches*)

Fold of paper, parchment or cloth in which a charge of gunpowder is held. Comes to mean the same as 'cartridge'.

cat hook (*cathokes*)

Strong hook used to retain the ring of the anchor when it is raised.

cats (*cattes*)

Cat ropes, used for hauling the cat hooks.

chamber

Wrought-iron compartment for gunpowder in breech-loading gun.

coak (*colk, colkes*)

Small brass plate inserted into the wooden **sheave** of a block to make a stronger socket for the pin.

cobbard (*cobbe herdes, cobberdes*)

Kitchen rack, similar to but as a word distinguished from next.

cob-iron (*cobyrons, gobyrons*)

One of the irons upon which a spit turns.

cock boat (*cocke bote, cokkbotes*)

Small boat for inshore use.

colk see **coak**

colour (*colors*)

Heraldic term for the background to devices used on flags (except for yellow and white, termed **metals**). Hence 'colour' for a flag.

commander (*comaunders*)

Large wooden mallet. For removing or placing wedges, quoins or forelocks.

corn powder

Gunpowder which has been hydrated, ground and pressed through sieves to make granules of a certain size ('coarse grained' or 'fine'); this made the mixture more reliable (as it was thoroughly mixed and could not segregate like **serpentine powder**) and stronger. The larger grained powder was used for heavy ordnance, the finer for priming and handguns.

course (*corse*)

Sail attached to the lower yards. Generally, the main portion of a sail.

crane hooks (*cranehokes*)

Hooks for lifting heavy objects.

crane lines (*cranelynes, cranelynnes*)

Small lines for keeping lee shrouds from chafing against the yards.

crapnolles see **grapnel**

crawdrons

Cauldrons.

cresset (*cressetes*)

Basket or vessel containing fuel for illumination.

cross bar shot (*crosse barre shott*)

Cast iron shot transfixed by two diagonally opposed wrought iron bars emerging as spikes.

crow (*crowes*)

Iron crowbar. Used for moving gun carriages and locating breech chambers into large guns.

culverin (*culveryn*)

Cast iron or bronze muzzle-loading gun, long in relation to its bore (average length 14', bore typically 5"–5½" but ranging 4"–6") weighing approx. 4,770 lbs; firing cast iron shot of 7 lb 5 oz to 26 lbs 6 oz.

curtal (*curtalles, curtowes*)

Large gun, short in relation to bore; firing shot of 40 lb, suggesting bore of over 6". Possibly replaced in general terminology by **cannon**.

dart (*daertes for toppys*)

Arrow, spear or similar weapon thrown down from the tops.

davit (*davettes, devettes*)

Piece of timber or iron with sheaves or blocks at its end, projecting over a vessel's quarter or stern to hoist up or suspend one end of a boat.

dead-eye, deadman's eye (*dede manes hies, dedemens hies, hies, hyes*)

Round flat wooden block fixed to the channels by the chain plate; pierced with 3 or more holes in order to receive a rope called the laniard, which, corresponding with holes in another dead-eye on the shroud end, creates a purchase to set up and extend the shrouds and stays.

demi-cannon (*demy cannons*)

Cast bronze or iron, muzzle-loading gun, 12' long with bore of approx. 6¼"–6½", weighing 5,800 lb; firing cast-iron shot of 33–34 lb.

demi-culverin (*demy culveryn*)

Cast bronze or iron, muzzle-loading gun, long in relation to bore; length approx. 13', bore approx. 4¼"–4½", weighing 4,760 lb; firing cast iron shot of 10 lb 10 oz to 14 lb 14 oz.

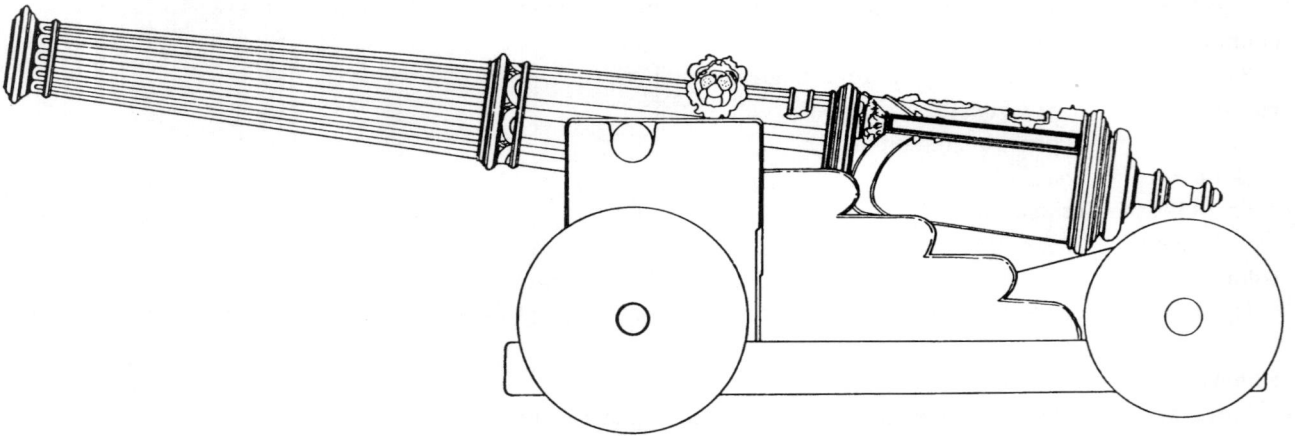

Bronze demi-culverin on elm carriage. (Drawing by Debbie Fulford of one of the two recovered from the *Mary Rose*. Reproduced by courtesy of the Mary Rose Trust)

demi-curtal (*demi curtowe*)

A type of **demi-cannon**.

demi-sling (*demy, half slynges*)

A form of **sling**; but uncertain if prefix means half bore size or weight of shot.

destrelle

Type of anchor. Oppenheim (*History*, p. 378) suggests from Catalan 'destre', to bridle.

devettes see **davit**

di

Half (abbreviation for 'dimidium').

dice (*dyce of yron*)

Cast or wrought iron cubes, either to be placed loose in a barrel as a projectile, or within lanthorn shot. Often cast into a cast lead shot for a **base**.

dryng, drynges see *thrynges*

dyce see **dice**

ell (elles)

Measure of length (45").

elmyn

Of elm.

extrys see **axle-tree**

falcon (*fawcon*)

Cast bronze or iron, muzzle-loading gun, long in relation to bore; length approx. 7', bore approx. $2^3/_4$", weighing 700 lb; firing cast iron shot of about 2 lb 2 oz.

falconnet (*fawconettes*)

Cast bronze or iron, muzzle-loading gun, long in relation to bore; length approx. 6', bore approx. $2^1/_4$", weighing approx. 500 lb; firing cast iron shot of about 1 lb 1 oz.

field (*feld*)

1. (heraldry) The background **colour** or **metal** to a shield.
2. (general) The field of battle.

firkin (*fyrkyns with pursys*)

Barrel, of perhaps 8 or 9 gallon capacity, with tied material or leather drawstring top.

fish hook (*fyshe hokes, fyshokes*)

For recovering anchors. Later called a 'fish davit'.

fly

The part of a flag furthest from the pole.

forelock (*forelokes*)

1. Of wood: large block (usually elm) fashioned to fit into the back of the carriage of a large breech-loading gun to secure the chamber into the hall of the gun.
2. Of iron: Wedge used to secure the chamber of a **base** or swivel-gun into position within the chamber-holder.

form (*fourmes for cartowches*)

Wooden former around which paper or cloth is moulded in making a **cartouche**.

fowler

Sometimes cast brass but usually wrought iron, breech-loading gun, carriage mounted; of uncertain size and length at this period, but bore larger than 2"; fired stone shot.

garland (*garlantes*)

Collar or rope wound around the head of a mast to keep the shrouds from chafing.

garnet (*garnettes*)

A purchase fixed to the main stay, used for hoisting cargo in and out.

geers, geres see **jeer**

gobyrons see **cob-iron**

gorget (*gorgettes, gorgeyttes*)

Armour for throat and neck.

grapnel (*crapnolles, grape yrons, grappers, grapilles, grapulles, grapyrons, gravulles*)

1. Iron hooked or clawed instrument for grappling with an enemy ship. In some cases perhaps a specific device lowered from the yard-arm to clear the enemy's anti-boarding nets.
2. A small anchor for a boat.

ground tackle (*growntacle*)

General term for the furniture attached to the anchors.

gyrde yrons, gyrdyorons

Gridirons.

hackbut (*hacbusshes, hackbusshes, hakbushes, hakebushes*)

Portable matchlock firearm with large hook beneath the barrel to attach to a rail as a recoil mechanism; heavier than a **handgun** and requiring support (and perhaps two individuals) in firing. Also called 'arquebus' or 'harquebus'.

hail shot (*heyle shott*)

Another name for **dice**.

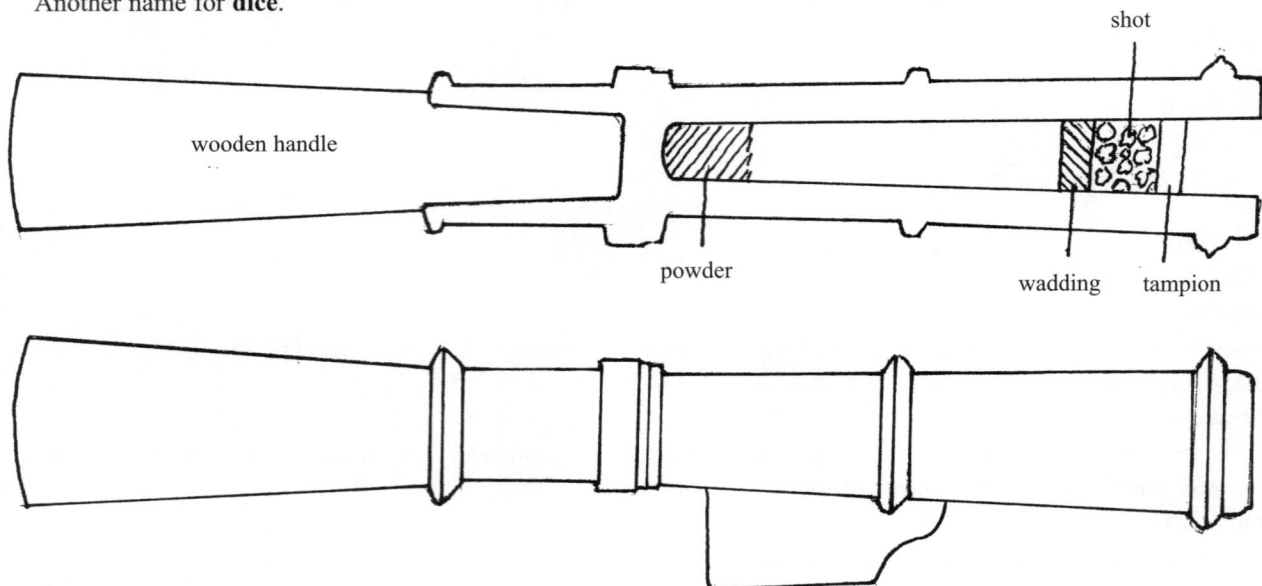

Cast iron hailshot piece. (Drawing by D.M. Loades, based on archaeological drawing provided by the Mary Rose Trust).

hailshot piece (*hayle shott pecys*)

Cast or wrought iron gun, breech- or muzzle-loading, with rectangular bore causing spread of the iron **dice** which formed the charge; weighing about 30 lb. Supported over a rail by a hook or lug beneath the gun.

half hake (*halfe hoke*)

A small **hackbut**.

hall

The tube of a wrought-iron gun which forms the bore, into which the breech chamber is located.

halyard (*halyers*)

Rope or tackles used to hoist or lower any sail upon its respective yards.

handgun (*handgonnes*)

Portable firearm, mostly smooth-bore muzzle-loaders with matchlock ignition. Usually fitted with a wooden stock. All but the largest operable, unsupported, by one man.

harness

Body armour.

helm (*helme*)

Tiller.

hempen

Made of hemp.

heyle shott see **hail shot**

hoist

The part of a flag nearest the pole.

jeers (*geers, geres, jeres*)

Two-fold or three-fold blocks used to hoist, suspend or lower the main and fore yards.

jolywat (*jolyvatt*)

The captain's boat.

junk (*jonkes, junckes*)

Remnants or pieces of old cable.

kedge anchor (*cagers, caggers*)

Small anchor used for mooring and warping.

kedging cable (*caggyng cables*)

For use in association with the above.

keptilles
Kettles.

knights (*knyghtes*)
Strong pieces of timber, bolted to beams, having a number of sheaves. They are the lower, fixed ends of the foreyard or mainyard halyard **tackle**, the **ramshead** being the upper half.

koynnys, koyns, koynys see **quoin**

lantrons
Lanterns.

lanyers
Lanyards.

last (*lastes*)
Measure of weight (variable according to commodity).
Of gunpowder: 656 gallons (dry measure).

latten (*laten*)
Alloy, commonly zinc ore and copper.

lech, leche hokes see **leech hook**

ledden, leder
Leather.

leech hook (*lech, leche, lyche, lynch hokes*)
Leeches were the borders or edges of sails. These hooks were possibly devices for attaching **bowlines**.

lifts (*lyftes*)
Ropes which reach from each mast head to their respective yard arms.

livery (*lyvere*)
Standard issue.

livery colours
Used by noble families to distinguish their retainers and property. The Tudor livery colours were green and white.

luff hook (*loff, love, luff hokes*)
A luff **tackle** was composed of a double and single block, the fall coming from the double. The function of the hook was to secure the tackle to a strong point.

lyche hokes see **leech hook**

lyftes see **lifts**

lynch hokes see **leech hook**

lynch pin (*lynch hokes, pynnes*)
The iron pin which keeps the trucks of a gun carriage confined to the **axle-trees**.

lytill crankett
The winding mechanism for a crossbow.

lyvere see **livery**

meson
Mizzen.

metal
Gold and silver used in heraldic devices to represent yellow and white.

miche (*myches*)
Yoke and peg forming the mounting of a **base**. Linstock.

minion (*mynnyon, mynyon*)
Cast iron, or more usually bronze, smooth-bore muzzle-loading gun; length approx. 8', bore approx. $3\frac{1}{4}$", weighing 1300 lb. Firing cast iron shot of 3" diameter, weighing $3\frac{3}{4}$ lbs.

morris pike (*mores, moris, morys / pyckes, pykes*)
Staff weapon with long haft and small leaf-shaped steel head; length 16'–20', head length 8", weighing about 1 lb 2 oz. Supposedly Moorish in origin.

murderer
Any size of anti-personnel gun, firing **dice**, or small pieces of iron or flakes of stone loose in a cannister. Mounted on a pintle.

myches see **miche**

mynnyon, mynyon see **minion**

myson, mysson
   Mizzen.

nave
   The hub of an axle (the primary meaning of the word).

oleron (*olleron, olrons*)
   Type of sail canvas, named from the island of Oléron on the Atlantic coast of France.

organ (*orgons*)
   Artillery piece consisting of a number of barrels laid side by side within one carriage, linked together, each barrel firing lead shot of 1$\frac{1}{2}$ lbs or cast iron shot of 1 lb.

orlop (*upper lop, lopp*)
   Lowest of the main decks.

outligger (*owtlygger*)
   Strong beam which was passed through the ports of a ship and firmly lashed at the gunwale to secure the masts in the act of careening. Also any boom rigged out from a vessel to hand boats from, and a fixed boom to help trim a sail extending over the hull end or side, as in a **bonaventure** sail.

panlankers
   Ropes or chains retaining the anchor when raised. Equivalent to the modern 'painter'.

paper, royal (*paper ryall*)
   Paper of 24" x 19". Used to make **cartouches**.

parrel (*parell*)
   A loose collar of rope or iron fitted around the mast, retaining the yard to the mast, but able to slide up and down with the yard.

pavis (*paveses*)
   Shield or buckler. Then, an arrangement of these along the side of a ship as a defensive screen. By Henry VIII's time becoming a decorative blindage of heraldic display.

pawes, power
   A claw, or anything that holds.

pech, peche
   Pitch.

pendant pulley (*pendant polies*)
   A pendant was a short piece of rope fixed on each side, under the shrouds, upon the heads of the main and fore masts, to link with the **tackles**.

pennant or **pennon**
   A long tapering flag, especially one flown from the masthead of a naval vessel.

piche
   Pitch.

pickhammer (*pyckhamers*)
   Small pick to finish stone shot.

polancre pulleys (*poleanker poleis, pollankers*)
   Combination of pulleys connected by a rope. Probably to help with catting the anchor. From the French 'palanquer', to hoist or haul.

poldavis (*poldaves, poldaveis*)
   A sail canvas, originally made in Poldavide (now Pouldavid), Brittany.

poleis, poleys, polies
   Pulleys.

pollankers see **polancre pulleys**

polles, pollies
   Pulleys.

pomegarnade, pomegarnet, pomegarnettes
   Pomegranate.

portcoles, portcules
   Portcullis.

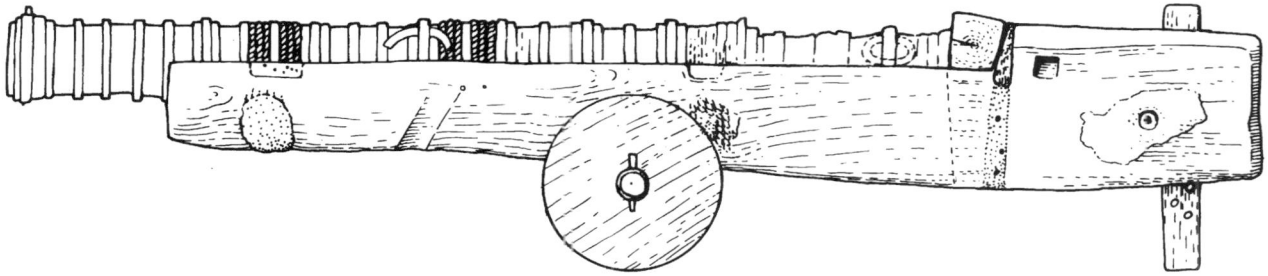

Wrought iron breech-loading port piece on carriage, recovered from the *Mary Rose*. (Archaeological drawing by courtesy of the Mary Rose Trust)

port piece (*porte pecys*)

Large breech-loading gun, usually wrought iron, of up to 10" bore. The largest carriage-mounted iron gun, consisting of breech chamber (two with each gun) and **hall**, each chamber weighing about 200 lb, the hall 900 lb to 1,000 lb. Mounted on a large sledge with single axle and a pair of spoked wheels or solid trucks.

pot gun (*pott gonnes*)

Small, short-barrelled, short-range mortar, usually cast bronze or iron. For lobbing large projectiles; mainly anti-personnel.

pot hook (*pothokes*)

Hook to hang cooking pots for storage.

potokes see **puttock**

power see *pawes*

powles

Pulleys.

puttock (*potokes*)

Small **shroud** connecting the lower shrouds to the top.

pych, pyche

Pitch.

pyckhamers see **pickhammer**

pyke

1. (**Morris**) pike.
2. **Pickhammer**.
3. (pl.) Spikes protruding from **cross-bar shot**.

quarrel (*quarelles*)

Short arrow fired from crossbow.

quarter-sling

A form of **sling**; but uncertain if prefix means quarter bore size or weight of shot.

quire (*qwayer*)

A quantity of paper or parchment (normally 4 sheets, sometimes 24).

quoin (*koynnys, koyns, koynys*)

Wooden wedge with short handle, placed under a muzzle-loading gun on its carriage to level or elevate during firing.

ramshead (*ramehede*) see **knights**

revett see **almain rivets**

roders

Rudders.

running glass (*rynnyng glasses*)

Hour glasses used to mark the passage of time (commonly in $\frac{1}{2}$-hour units).

saker

Cast iron or, more usually bronze, muzzle-loading gun, length 9', bore approx. $3\frac{1}{2}$", weighing 2,000 lb; firing cast iron shot of about 4 lb 12 oz.

sallet (*salettes*)

Type of helmet without visor, with a tail to protect the neck.

scoles
> Scales (for weighing).

scull (*skolles*)
> Oar used to propel boat from stern.

serpentine (*serpentynes*)
> Breech-loading gun, of various sizes, usually long in relation to bore. Often mounted.

serpentine powder
> Manufactured from grinding saltpetre, sulphur and charcoal into a fine mixture.

sheave (*shever, shivers, shyver*)
> Wheel upon which the rope runs in a block.

sheep skin (*shepe skynnys*)
> Used to swab out the bores of guns or chambers.

sheer hook (*sherehokes, sherhokes, shrehokes*)
> Sheers were two or more spars, raised at angles and lashed together at their upper ends. Used for raising or taking in heavy weights.

sheet anchor (*shet, shot, shott, shut, shute ankers*)
> Largest of a ship's anchors. Usually kept in reserve in case an original cable should part.

sheets (*shetes, shotes, shott, shut, shutes*)
> Ropes fastened to one or both the lower corners of a sail to retain the clue down to its place.

shepe skynnys see **sheep skin**

sherehokes, sherhokes see **sheer hook**

shet ankers see **sheet anchor**

shever see **sheave**

shevis, shevys
> Sheaves (of arrows).

shift (*shifters*)
> A means of moving a piece of rigging.

shivers see **sheave**

shod wheels (*shod wheles*)
> gun carriage wheels with iron rings shrunk on to their outer surfaces.

shot, shott ankers see **sheet anchor**

shotes, shott see **sheets**

shrehokes see **sheer hook**

shrouds (*shrowdes*)
> The lower and upper standing rigging. Their use is to support the masts when the ship rolls.

shut, shutes see **sheets**

shut, shute ankers see **sheet anchor**

shyrwyns
> Unidentified.

shyver see **sheave**

skolles see **scull**

sledge (*slegys, sleggys*)
> Sledgehammer.

sling (*slynges*)
> Wrought iron breech-loading gun, long in relation to bore; bore 1"–5". Usually carriage mounted.

snatch pulley (*snach poleis, polleis*)
> A snatch block is a single iron-bound block with an opening in one side, above the shave.

somer castell see **summer-castle**

somer deck see **summer deck**

sow (*sowes*)
> Block of lead (or other metal), on unspecific measure.

Spanish pavis (*Spanyshe paveses*)
> A **pavis** of Spanish leather.

spare wheels (*spaer, spaier, whelis, whelys*)

Large spoked wheels carried as spares for gun carriages.

splints (*splentes*)

Armour for the upper arms.

sponges (*spongys*)

Swabs. Used in connexion with **sheep skins**.

stakes for the field (*feld*)

Anti-cavalry defences.

stamp (*stampes*)

Holder used in the making of cartridges.

standard

A tapering heraldic flag, often with **badges** on a **field** of the **livery colours**.

standard stave (*standard stavers, standart staves*)

Any long pole. Perhaps particularly those on which large flags were displayed.

standards of mail (*standardes of mayle*)

Pieces of chain mail worn above the breast and back plates, to protect the neck.

stays (*steyes*)

Strong ropes extending from the upper end of each mast towards the stem of the ship.

stodynges see **studdings**

stone gun (*stone gonnes*)

Breech-loading gun, usually wrought iron, firing stone shot. Similar to the **cannon petro**.

streamer

A large **pennant** worn on ceremonial occasions

studdings (*stodynges*)

Studding sails were later fair-weather sails. It is uncertain whether the term is used in that sense here.

summer-castle (*somer castell*)

Originally a light wooden structure erected for fighting purposes. By this time the terms seems to have meant the poop, or after-castle.

summer deck (*somer deck*)

By association with the above.

swifters (*swyfters, swyftyers, swyftyng tacle*)

Pairs of shrouds fitted on the port and starboard sides of the lower masts, having **tackles** for adjustment, rather than **dead-eyes**.

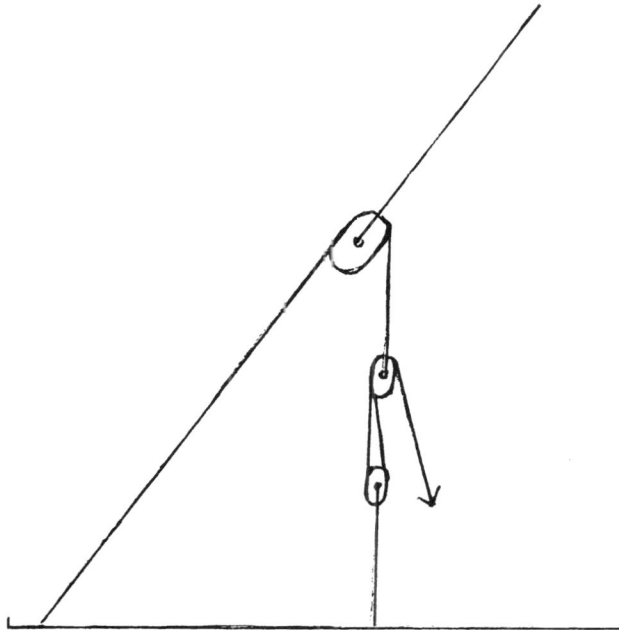

Switfters. (Drawing by D.M. Loades, based on Howard, *Sailing Ships of War*, p. 33)

tackle (*tackelles, tackes, tacle*)

Any arrangement of blocks to increase purchase or lifting power.

tampion

Wooden disk (usually poplar) which seals the mouth of a breech chamber. Also used in smooth-bore muzzle-loaders after the powder, wadding and shot have been placed in the bore. Occasionally also used to seal the mouth of a gun.

target (*targettes*)

Small shield.

terr, terre

Tar.

thrynges (*dryng, drynges*)

Unidentified, but presumably associated with the verb 'thring', to tie. The occurrence in one place of the form 'thrynges' makes it clear that the more common 'd-' forms employ corrupt renderings of the Anglo-Saxon thorn (Þ). Oppenheim (*History*, p. 373) identifies as halyards, perhaps by erroneous association with 'drawing'.

ties (*teyes, tyes*)

Runners of thick rope which form part of the purchase used for hoisting the topsail.

top armour

Cloths tied about the tops of the masts for show.

top gallant (*top galant*)

The third mast above the deck.

top gun (*top gonnes, topp peces, pecys*)

Gun carried in the fighting tops.

tree (*tre*)

Any wooden item.

trivet (*trevettes*)

Three-footed stand for a pot.

trombe (*trompes*)

Tube filled with explosive. Grenade.

trotty wheels (*trotill wheles, trotilles*)

Small solid wheels for gun carriages.

truckles (*truckelles, trustelles*)

As above, or the carriage itself.

truss

A **parrel** used on the lower yards to bind them to their masts.

trustelles see **truckles.**

tuke

Canvas.

tyes see **ties**

upper lop, lopp see **orlop**

vice-pieces

Small or medium-sized guns cast in bronze, usually mounted, of which the barrel and chamber were joined by a screw thread. These were muzzle loaded and not dismembered in the process of loading.

ware, warre tacles

Possibly the **tackle** used in wareing or veering a ship in the process of unmooring.

web (*webbe*)

Sheet of lead, of unspecific measure.

wheel ropes (*whele ropes*)

Ropes attached to winches or windlasses, for the purpose of raising and lowering the sails.

wheels (*whelis, whelys*)

Large spoked wheels used for certain types of gun carriage.

wildfire (*wyldefyre*)

Incendiary mixture of black powder, sulphur and resin (Greek fire), or designed to set fire to an enemy's sails or rigging.

woolding (*woling, wolyng*)

Securing of gun to its carriage.

(i)

tie   tie

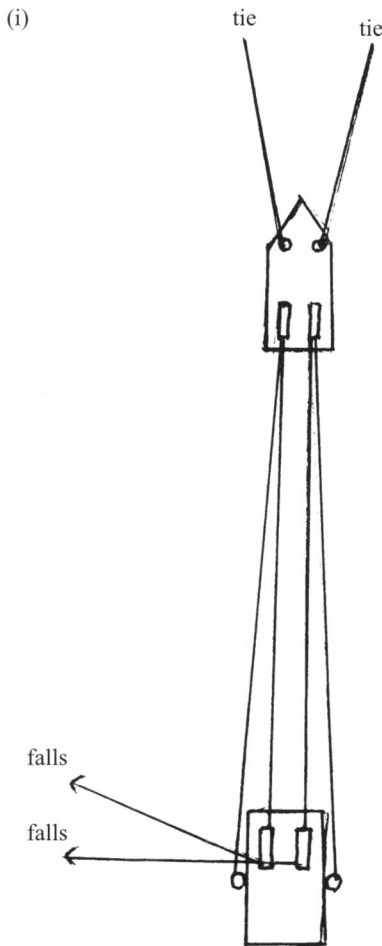

(i)   Hoisting the main yard with a tie
       and a halyard
(ii)   Assembly of 2 ties and 2 halyards
(Drawings by D.M. Loades, based on
Howard, *Sailing Ships of War*, pp. 68–9

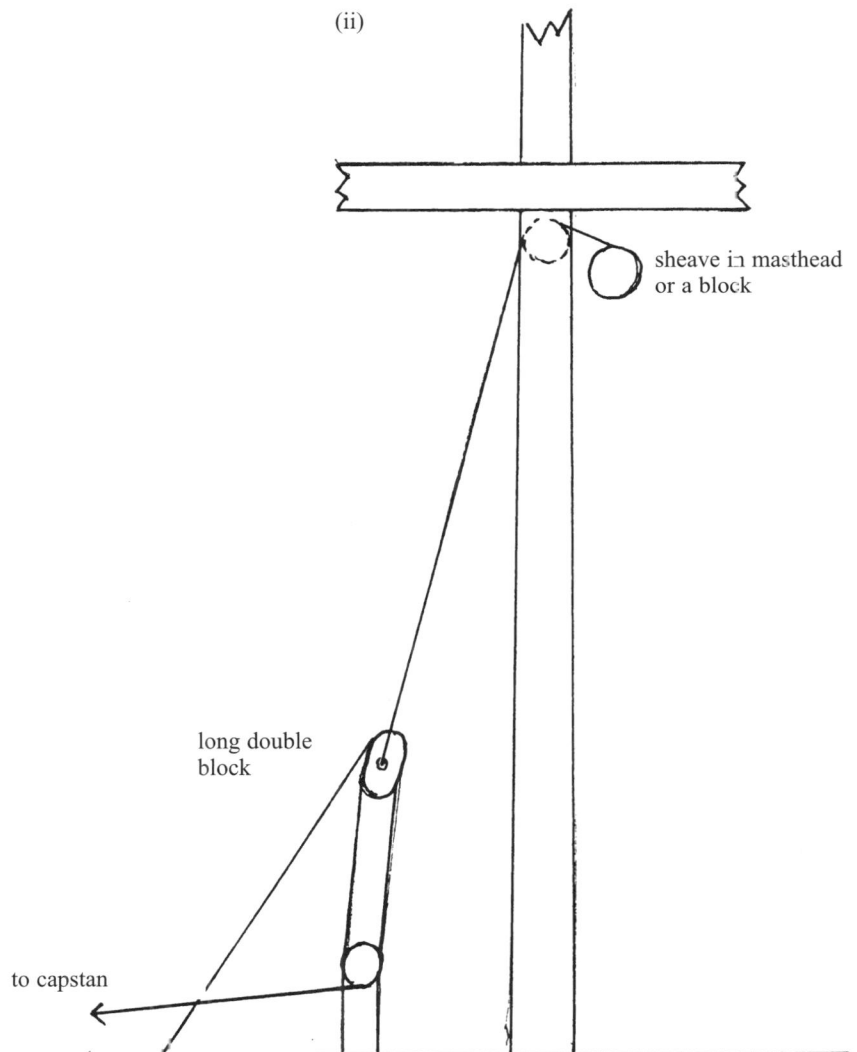

falls

falls

(ii)

sheave in masthead
or a block

long double
block

to capstan

wyskars
  Whiskers (brooms).
yough
  Yew.

Sources

V. Biringuccio, *Pirotechnica* (Venice, 1540, repr. Boston, Mass. 1959)

H.L. Blackmore, *The Armouries of the Tower of London* (1976)

S. Friar, ed., *A New Dictionary of Heraldry* (1987)

D. King, *A Sea of Words* (1995)

Sir H. Mainwaring, 'The seaman's dictionary', in G.E. Manwaring and W.G. Perrin, eds., *The Life and Works of Sir Henry Mainwaring* (NRS LVI, 1922), pp. 67–260

A.V.B. Norman and G.M. Wilson, *Treasures from the Tower of London: Arms and Armour* (1982)

The Oxford English Dictionary

S.P. Rose, ed., *The Navy of the Lancastrian Kings* (NRS CXXIII, 1982), pp. 253–61

J. Smith, *A Sea Grammar* (1627), repr. ed. K. Goell (1970)

W.H. Smyth, *The Sailor's Word-book* (1967)

T. Wilson, *Flags at Sea* (2nd edn., 1999)

Ordnance specifications and much other assistance with the Glossary kindly supplied by Alexzandra Hildred and her colleagues at the Mary Rose Trust. Helpful comments were also made by Mr Bennell. Rigging definitions owe much to the expert advice of Mr Owain Roberts.

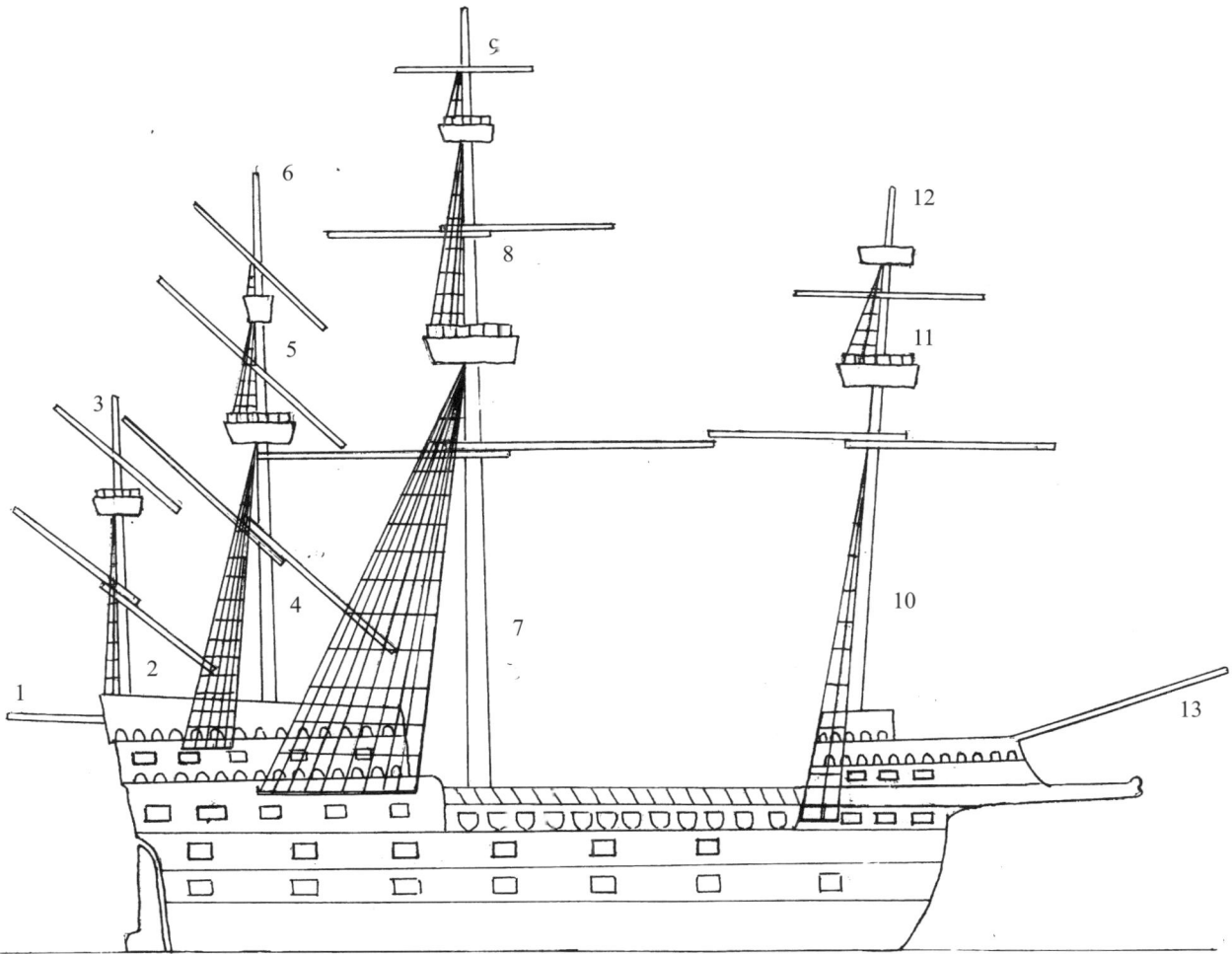

Semi-schematic diagram of the *Henry Grace à Dieu* showing the pattern of masts and spars. The gunport configuration follows that given in the Anthony Roll. (Drawing by D.M. Loades)

1. Outligger
2. Bonaventure/bonaventure mizzen mast
3. Bonaventure topmast
4. Mizzen mast
5. Mizzen topmast
6. Mizzen topgallant
7. Mainmast
8. Maintopmast
9. Maintopgallant
10. Foremast
11. Foretopmast
12. Foretopgallant
13. Bowsprit

Index

Peers are indexed under their family names. **Offices** and **titles** are as held at the period in question; a few later attainments have been added in square brackets.

Subjects are mostly gathered into the following headings:

armour
cloth/fabric/hides
flags
heraldry
metals/minerals
occupations (civilian)
ordnance (i) guns (main classifications)
             (ii) guns (specific types)
             (iii) guns/gun carriages (components)
             (iv) gunpowder/propellants
             (v) shot
             (vi) ancillary equipment
ships (i) general
      (ii) types/function
      (iii) main features
      (iv) masts and spars
      (v) sails
      (vi) cordage
      (vii) rigging/tackle
      (viii) equipment (general)/miscellaneous provisions
      (ix) equipment/kitchen

ships named headword (*italic*) in modern form where possible, followed by variant spellings in MSS here edited (first parenthesis) and other names carried (second parenthesis); ships occurring in the Anthony Roll are identified by the sequence number [**bold**] of the plates and adjacent texts on pp. 40–105. Fuller details of these ships, and those occurring in the Part II text, are given in Appendix II (pp. 160–7). Other ships are briefly identified here (including, where applicable, the entry numbers from Glasgow, 'List of ships').
victuals
weapons
wood

The following additional abbreviations are used:
  * Indicates comment in the Glossary (pp. 169–82)
  I*passim*   References occurring generally in text of Part One (pp. 41–106)
  II*passim*   References occurring generally in text of Part Two (pp. 113–58)
  n.   References occurring in one of the alphabetically-flagged textual notes on the page stated

Navy Records Society
Works in Print

The Navy Records Society was established for the purpose of printing unpublished manuscripts and rare works of naval interest. Membership of the Society is open to all who are interested in naval history, and any person wishing to become a member should apply to the Hon. Secretary, Professor A. D. Lambert, Department of War Studies, King's College London, Strand, London WC2R 2LS, United Kingdom. The annual subscription is £30, which entitles the member to receive one free copy of each work issued by the Society in that year, and to buy earlier issues at reduced prices.

A list of works, available to members only, is shown below; very few copies are left of those marked with an asterisk. Volumes out of print are indicated by **OP**. Prices for works in print are available on application to Mrs Annette Gould, 5 Goodwood Close, Midhurst, West Sussex GU29 9JG, United Kingdom, to whom all enquiries concerning works in print should be sent. Those marked 'TS', 'SP' and 'A' are published for the Society by Temple Smith, Scolar Press and Ashgate, and are available to non-members from the Ashgate Publishing Group, Gower House, Croft Road, Aldershot, Hampshire GU11 3HR. Those marked 'A & U' are published by George Allen & Unwin, and are available to non-members only through bookshops.

Vol. 1. *State papers relating to the Defeat of the Spanish Armada, Anno 1588*, Vol. I, ed. Professor J. K. Laughton. TS.

Vol. 2. *State papers relating to the Defeat of the Spanish Armada, Anno 1588*, Vol. II, ed. Professor J. K. Laughton. TS.

Vol. 3. *Letters of Lord Hood, 1781–1783*, ed. D. Hannay. **OP**.

Vol. 4. *Index to James's Naval History*, by C. G. Toogood, ed. by the Hon. T. A. Brassey. **OP**.

Vol. 5. *Life of Captain Stephen Martin, 1666–1740*, ed. Sir Clements R. Markham. **OP**.

Vol. 6. *Journal of Rear Admiral Bartholomew James, 1752–1828*, ed. Professor J. K. Laughton & Cdr. J. Y. F. Sullivan. **OP**.

Vol. 7. *Holland's Discourses of the Navy, 1638 and 1659*, ed. J. R. Tanner. **OP**.

Vol. 8. *Naval Accounts and Inventories in the Reign of Henry VII*, ed. M. Oppenheim. **OP**.

Vol. 9. *Journal of Sir George Rooke*, ed. O. Browning. **OP**.

Vol. 10. *Letters and Papers relating to the War with France 1512–1513*, ed. M. Alfred Spont. **OP**.

Vol. 11. *Papers relating to the Spanish War, 1585–1587*, ed. Julian S. Corbett. TS.

Vol. 12. *Journals and Letters of Admiral of the Fleet Sir Thomas Byam Martin, 1773–1854*, Vol. II (see No. 24), ed. Admiral Sir R. Vesey Hamilton. **OP**.

Vol. 13. *Papers relating to the First Dutch War, 1652–1654*, Vol. I, ed. Dr S. R. Gardiner. **OP**.

Vol. 14. *Papers relating to the Blockade of Brest, 1803–1805*, Vol. I, ed. J. Leyland. **OP**.

Vol. 15. *History of the Russian Fleet during the Reign of Peter the Great, by a Contemporary Englishman*, ed. Admiral Sir Cyprian Bridge. **OP**.

*Vol. 16. *Logs of the Great Sea Fights, 1794–1805*, Vol. I, ed. Vice Admiral Sir T. Sturges Jackson.

Vol. 17. *Papers relating to the First Dutch War, 1652–1654*, ed. Dr S. R. Gardiner. **OP**.

*Vol. 18. *Logs of the Great Sea Fights*, Vol. II, ed. Vice Admiral Sir T. Sturges Jackson.

Vol. 19. *Journals and Letters of Admiral of the Fleet Sir Thomas Byam Martin*, Vol. II (see No. 24), ed. Admiral Sir R. Vesey Hamilton. **OP**.

Vol. 20. *The Naval Miscellany*, Vol. I, ed. Professor J. K. Laughton.

Vol. 21. *Papers relating to the Blockade of Brest, 1803–1805*, Vol. II, ed. J. Leyland. **OP**.

Vol. 22. *The Naval Tracts of Sir William Monson*, Vol. I, ed. M. Oppenheim. **OP**.

Vol. 23. *The Naval Tracts of Sir William Monson, Vol. II*, ed. M. Oppenheim. **OP**.

Vol. 24. *The Journals and Letters of Admiral of the Fleet Sir Thomas Byam Martin*, Vol. I, ed. Admiral Sir R. Vesey Hamilton. **OP**.

Vol. 25. *Nelson and the Neapolitan Jacobins*, ed. H. C. Gutteridge. **OP**.

Vol. 26. *A Descriptive Catalogue of the Naval MSS in the Pepysian Library*, Vol. I, ed. J. R. Tanner. **OP**.

Vol. 27. *A Descriptive Catalogue of the Naval MSS in the Pepysian Library*, Vol. II, ed. J. R. Tanner. **OP**.

Vol. 28. *The Correspondence of Admiral John Markham, 1801–1807*, ed. Sir Clements R. Markham. **OP**.

Vol. 29. *Fighting Instructions, 1530–1816*, ed. Julian S. Corbett. **OP**.

Vol. 30. *Papers relating to the First Dutch War, 1652–1654*, Vol. III, ed. Dr S. R. Gardiner & C. T. Atkinson. **OP**.

Vol. 31. *The Recollections of Commander James Anthony Gardner, 1775–1814*, ed. Admiral Sir R. Vesey Hamilton & Professor J. K. Laughton.

Vol. 32. *Letters and Papers of Charles, Lord Barham, 1758–1813*, ed. Professor Sir John Laughton.

Vol. 33. *Naval Songs and Ballads*, ed. Professor C. H. Firth. **OP**.

Vol. 34. *Views of the Battles of the Third Dutch War*, ed. by Julian S. Corbett. **OP**.

Vol. 35. *Signals and Instructions, 1776–1794*, ed. Julian S. Corbett **OP**.

Vol. 36. *A Descriptive Catalogue of the Naval MSS in the Pepysian Library*, Vol III, ed. J. R. Tanner. **OP**.

Vol. 37. *Papers relating to the First Dutch War, 1652–1654*, Vol. IV, ed. C. T. Atkinson. **OP**.

Vol. 38. *Letters and Papers of Charles, Lord Barham, 1758–1813*, Vol. II, ed. Professor Sir John Laughton.

Vol. 39. *Letters and Papers of Charles, Lord Barham, 1758–1813*, Vol. III, ed. Professor Sir John Laughton.

Vol. 40. *The Naval Miscellany*, Vol. II, ed. Professor Sir John Laughton.

*Vol. 41. *Papers relating to the First Dutch War, 1652–1654*, Vol. V, ed. C. T. Atkinson.

*Vol. 42. *Papers relating to the Loss of Minorca in 1756*, ed. Captain H. W. Richmond, R.N.

*Vol. 43. *The Naval Tracts of Sir William Monson*, Vol. III, ed. M. Oppenheim.

Vol. 44. *The Old Scots Navy, 1689–1710*, ed. James Grant. **OP**.

Vol. 45. *The Naval Tracts of Sir William Monson*, Vol. IV, ed. M. Oppenheim.

*Vol. 46. *The Private Papers of George, 2nd Earl Spencer*, Vol. I, ed. Julian S. Corbett.

Vol. 47. *The Naval Tracts of Sir William Monson*, Vol. V, ed. M. Oppenheim.

Vol. 48. *The Private Papers of George, 2nd Earl Spencer*, Vol. II, ed. Julian S. Corbett. **OP**.

*Vol. 49. *Documents relating to Law and Custom of the Sea*, Vol. II, ed. R. G. Marsden.

*Vol. 50. *Documents relating to Law and Custom of the Sea*, Vol. II, ed. R. G. Marsden.

Vol. 51. *Autobiography of Phineas Pett*, ed. W. G. Perrin. **OP**.

Vol. 52. *The Life of Admiral Sir John Leake*, Vol. I, ed. Geoffrey Callender.

Vol. 53. *The Life of Admiral Sir John Leake*, Vol. II, ed. Geoffrey Callender.

Vol. 54. *The Life and Works of Sir Henry Mainwaring*, Vol. I, ed. G. E. Manwaring.

Vol. 55. *The Letters of Lord St Vincent, 1801–1804*, Vol. I, ed. D. B. Smith. **OP**.

Vol. 56. *The Life and Works of Sir Henry Mainwaring*, Vol. II, ed. G. E. Manwaring & W. G. Perrin. **OP**.

Vol. 57. *A Descriptive Catalogue of the Naval MSS in the Pepysian Library*, Vol. IV, ed. Dr J. R. Tanner. **OP**.

Vol. 58. *The Private Papers of George, 2nd Earl Spencer*, Vol. III, ed. Rear Admiral H. W. Richmond. **OP**.

Vol. 59. *The Private Papers of George, 2nd Earl Spencer*, Vol. IV, ed. Rear Admiral H. W. Richmond. **OP**.

Vol. 60. *Samuel Pepys's Naval Minutes*, ed. Dr J. R. Tanner.

Vol. 61. *The Letters of Lord St Vincent, 1801–1804*, Vol. II, ed. D. B. Smith. **OP**.

Vol. 62. *Letters and Papers of Admiral Viscount Keith*, Vol. I, ed. W. G. Perrin. **OP**.

Vol. 63. *The Naval Miscellany*, Vol. III, ed. W. G. Perrin. **OP**.

Vol. 64. *The Journal of the 1st Earl of Sandwich*, ed. R. C. Anderson. **OP**.

*Vol. 65. *Boteler's Dialogues*, ed. W. G. Perrin.

Vol. 66. *Papers relating to the First Dutch War, 1652–1654*, Vol. VI (with index), ed. C. T. Atkinson.

*Vol. 67. *The Byng Papers*, Vol. I, ed. W. C. B. Tunstall.

*Vol. 68. *The Byng Papers*, Vol. II, ed. W. C. B. Tunstall.

Vol. 69. *The Private Papers of John, Earl of Sandwich*, Vol. I, ed. G. R. Barnes & Lt. Cdr. J. H. Owen, R.N. **OP**.

Corrigenda to *Papers relating to the First Dutch War, 1652–1654, Vols I-VI*, ed. Captain A. C. Dewar, R.N.

Vol. 70. *The Byng Papers*, Vol. III, ed. W. C. B. Tunstall.

Vol. 71. *The Private Papers of John, Earl of Sandwich*, Vol. II, ed. G. R. Barnes & Lt. Cdr. J. H. Owen, R.N. **OP**.

Vol. 72. *Piracy in the Levant, 1827–1828*, ed. Lt. Cdr. C. G. Pitcairn Jones, R.N. **OP**.

Vol. 73. *The Tangier Papers of Samuel Pepys*, ed. Edwin Chappell.

Vol. 74. *The Tomlinson Papers*, ed. J. G. Bullocke.

Vol. 75. *The Private Papers of John, Earl of Sandwich*, Vol. III, ed. G. R. Barnes & Lt. Cdr. J. H. Owen, R.N. **OP**.

Vol. 76. *The Letters of Robert Blake*, ed. the Rev. J. R. Powell. **OP**.

*Vol. 77. *Letters and Papers of Admiral the Hon. Samuel Barrington*, Vol. I, ed. D. Bonner-Smith.

Vol. 78. *The Private Papers of John, Earl of Sandwich*, Vol. IV, ed. G. R. Barnes & Lt. Cdr. J. H. Owen, R.N. **OP**.

*Vol. 79. *The Journals of Sir Thomas Allin, 1660–1678*, Vol. I (1660–1666), ed. R. C. Anderson.

Vol. 80. *The Journals of Sir Thomas Allin, 1660–1678*, Vol. II (1667–1678), ed. R. C. Anderson.

Vol. 81. *Letters and Papers of Admiral the Hon. Samuel Barrington*, Vol. II, ed. D. Bonner-Smith. **OP**.

Vol. 82. *Captain Boteler's Recollections, 1808–1830*, ed. D. Bonner-Smith. **OP**.

Vol. 83. *Russian War, 1854. Baltic and Black Sea: Official Correspondence*, ed. D. Bonner-Smith & Captain A. C. Dewar, R.N. **OP**.

Vol. 84. *Russian War, 1855. Baltic: Official Correspondence*, ed. D. Bonner-Smith. **OP**.

Vol. 85. *Russian War, 1855. Black Sea: Official Correspondence*, ed. Captain A.C. Dewar, R.N. **OP**.

Vol. 86. *Journals and Narratives of the Third Dutch War*, ed. R. C. Anderson. **OP**.

Vol. 87. *The Naval Brigades in the Indian Mutiny, 1857–1858*, ed. Cdr. W. B. Rowbotham, R.N. **OP**.

Vol. 88. *Patee Byng's Journal*, ed. J. L. Cranmer-Byng. **OP**.

*Vol. 89. *The Sergison Papers, 1688–1702*, ed. Cdr. R. D. Merriman, R.I.N.

Vol. 90. *The Keith Papers*, Vol. II, ed. Christopher Lloyd. **OP**.

Vol. 91. *Five Naval Journals, 1789–1817*, ed. Rear Admiral H. G. Thursfield. **OP**.

Vol. 92. *The Naval Miscellany*, Vol. IV, ed. Christopher Lloyd. **OP**.

Vol. 93. *Sir William Dillon's Narrative of Professional Adventures, 1790–1839*, Vol. I (1790–1802), ed. Professor Michael Lewis. **OP**.

Vol. 94. *The Walker Expedition to Quebec, 1711*, ed. Professor Gerald S. Graham. **OP**.

Vol. 95. *The Second China War, 1856–1860*, ed. D. Bonner-Smith & E. W. R. Lumby. **OP**.

Vol. 96. *The Keith Papers*, 1803–1815, Vol. III, ed. Professor Christopher Lloyd.

Vol. 97. *Sir William Dillon's Narrative of Professional Adventures, 1790–1839*, Vol. II (1802–1839), ed. Professor Michael Lewis. **OP**.

Vol. 98. *The Private Correspondence of Admiral Lord Collingwood*, ed. Professor Edward Hughes. **OP**.

Vol. 99. *The Vernon Papers*, 1739–1745, ed. B. McL. Ranft. **OP**.

Vol. 100. *Nelson's Letters to his Wife and Other Documents*, ed. Lt. Cdr. G. P. B. Naish, R.N.V.R. **OP**.

Vol. 101. *A Memoir of James Trevenen, 1760–1790*, ed. Professor Christopher Lloyd & R. C. Anderson. **OP**.

Vol. 102. *The Papers of Admiral Sir John Fisher*, Vol. I, ed. Lt. Cdr. P. K. Kemp, R.N. **OP**.

Vol. 103. *Queen Anne's Navy*, ed. Cdr. R. D. Merriman, R.I.N. **OP**.

Vol. 104. *The Navy and South America, 1807–1823*, ed. Professor Gerald S. Graham & Professor R. A. Humphreys.

Vol. 105. *Documents relating to the Civil War, 1642–1648*, ed. The Rev. J. R. Powell & E. K. Timings. **OP**.

Vol. 106. *The Papers of Admiral Sir John Fisher*, Vol. II, ed. Lt. Cdr. P. K. Kemp, R.N. **OP**.

Vol. 107. *The Health of Seamen*, ed. Professor Christopher Lloyd.

Vol. 108. *The Jellicoe Papers*, Vol. I (1893–1916), ed. A. Temple Patterson.

✓ Vol. 109. *Documents relating to Anson's Voyage round the World, 1740–1744*, ed. Dr Glyndwr Williams. **OP**.

Vol. 110. *The Saumarez Papers: The Baltic, 1808–1812*, ed. A. N. Ryan. **OP**.

Vol. 111. *The Jellicoe Papers*, Vol. II (1916–1935), ed. Professor A. Temple Patterson.

Vol. 112. *The Rupert and Monck Letterbook, 1666*, ed. The Rev. J. R. Powell & E. K. Timings.

Vol. 113. *Documents relating to the Royal Naval Air Service*, Vol. I (1908–1918), ed. Captain S. W. Roskill, R.N.

*Vol. 114. *The Siege and Capture of Havana, 1762*, ed. Professor David Syrett.

✓ Vol. 115. *Policy and Operations in the Mediterranean, 1912–1914*, ed. E. W. R. Lumby. **OP**.

✓ Vol. 116. *The Jacobean Commissions of Enquiry, 1608 and 1618*, ed. Dr A. P. McGowan.

✓ Vol. 117. *The Keyes Papers*, Vol. I (1914–1918), ed. Professor Paul Halpern.

Vol. 118. *The Royal Navy and North America: The Warren Papers, 1736–1752*, ed. Dr Julian Gwyn. **OP**.

✓ Vol. 119. *The Manning of the Royal Navy: Selected Public Pamphlets, 1693–1873*, ed. Professor John Bromley.

✓ Vol. 120. *Naval Administration, 1715–1750*, ed. Professor D. A. Baugh.

✓ Vol. 121. *The Keyes Papers*, Vol. II (1919–1938), ed. Professor Paul Halpern.

✓ Vol. 122. *The Keyes Papers*, Vol. III (1939–1945), ed. Professor Paul Halpern.

✓ Vol. 123. *The Navy of the Lancastrian Kings: Accounts and Inventories of William Soper, Keeper of the King's Ships, 1422–1427*, ed. Dr Susan Rose.

✓ Vol. 124. *The Pollen Papers: the Privately Circulated Printed Works of Arthur Hungerford Pollen, 1901–1916*, ed. Professor Jon T. Sumida. A & U.

✓ Vol. 125. *The Naval Miscellany*, Vol. V. ed. Dr N. A. M. Rodger. A & U.

✓ Vol. 126. *The Royal Navy in the Mediterranean, 1915–1918*, ed. Professor Paul Halpern. TS.

Vol. 127. *The Expedition of Sir John Norris and Sir Francis Drake to Spain and Portugal, 1589*, ed. Professor R. B. Wernham. TS.

Vol. 128. *The Beatty Papers*, Vol. I (1902–1918), ed. Professor B. McL. Ranft. SP.

Vol. 129. *The Hawke Papers: A Selection, 1743–1771*, ed. Dr R. F. Mackay. SP.

Vol. 130. *Anglo-American Naval Relations, 1917–1919*, ed. Michael Simpson. SP.

Vol. 131. *British Naval Documents, 1204–1960*, ed. Professor John B. Hattendorf, Dr Roger Knight, Alan Pearsall, Dr Nicholas Rodger & Professor Geoffrey Till. SP.

Vol. 132. *The Beatty Papers*, Vol. II (1916–1927), ed. Professor B. McL. Ranft. SP.

Vol. 133. *Samuel Pepys and the Second Dutch War*, transcribed by Professor William Matthews & Dr Charles Knighton; ed. Robert Latham. SP.

Vol. 134. *The Somerville Papers*, ed. Michael Simpson, with the assistance of John Somerville. SP.

Vol. 135. *The Royal Navy in the River Plate, 1806–1807*, ed. John D. Grainger. SP.

Vol. 136. *The Collective Naval Defence of the Empire, 1900–1940*, ed. Nicholas Tracy. A.

Vol. 137. *The Defeat of the Enemy Attack on Shipping, 1939–1945*, ed. Eric Grove. A.

Vol. 138. *Shipboard Life and Organisation, 1731–1815*, ed. Dr Brian Lavery. A.

Vol. 139. *The Battle of the Atlantic and Signals Intelligence: U-boat Situations and Trends*, 1941–1945, ed. Professor David Syrett. A.

Vol. 140. *The Cunningham Papers*, Vol. I, *The Mediterranean Fleet, 1939–1942*, ed. Michael Simpson. A.

OCCASIONAL PUBLICATIONS

Vol. 1. *The Commissioned Sea Officers of the Royal Navy, 1660–1815*, ed. Professor David Syrett & Professor R. L. DiNardo. SP.